A BRIEF HISTORY
OF THE CARIBBEAN

D. H. FIGUEREDO

Director, Library and Media Center at
Bloomfield College

FRANK ARGOTE-FREYRE

Kean University

Facts On File
An imprint of Infobase Publishing

D. H. F: To my wife and inspiration, Yvonne, and to my joyful children, Daniel and Gabriela, the Caribbean sun shines in them.

F. A. F: For Popi—George Freyre (1924–2000).

A Brief History of the Caribbean

Facts On File, Inc.
An imprint of Infobase Publishing
132 West 31st Street
New York NY 10001

Library of Congress Cataloging-in-Publication Data

Figueredo, D. H., 1951–
    A brief history of the Caribbean / D. H. Figueredo, Frank Argote-Freyre.
        p. cm.—(Brief history)
    Includes bibliographical references and index.
    ISBN-13: 978-0-8160-7021-3
    ISBN-10: 0-8160-7021-0
    1. Caribbean Area—History. I. Argote-Freyre, Frank. II. Title.
    F2175.F54 2007
    972.9—dc22   2007008202

Maps by Melissa Ericksen

Printed in the United States of America

MP Hermitage 10 9 8 7 6 5 4 3 2

This book is printed on acid-free paper.

CONTENTS

Appendixes

LIST OF ILLUSTRATIONS

LIST OF MAPS

LIST OF TABLES

FOREWORD

The customs and traditions of the Caribbean are visible on the streets of many cities of the United States. The bodegas of Upper Manhattan or the Jamaica Plain neighborhood of Boston conduct business with salsa and merengue playing in the background. Warm Cuban bread and espresso coffee, sometimes with a *pastelito*, or pastry, are consumed at little coffee stands across South Florida every morning. Botanicas in Union City, New Jersey, sell the ingredients required for Vodun or Santeria ceremonies that promise a better life. Voices speaking in Haitian Kreyol (or Creole) reverberate in the Brooklyn neighborhood of East Flatbush or on Chicago's North Side. The *cuatro*, a musical instrument native to Puerto Rico, can be heard not only in New York, the second home for many islanders, but in locations as far afield as Hawaii and San Gabriel, California, where there is a festival dedicated to the instrument. Jamaican jerked chicken, beef patties, ackee, and salt fish are part of the local cuisine in New York City, Miami, and Windsor, Ontario. As of the 2000 Census, approximately 7 million people in the United States identified their nationality, at least in part, as originating in the Caribbean. The authors of this book count themselves among that 7 million, and it is that heritage that makes us passionate about spreading the history.

There is a hunger for knowledge about these Caribbean communities, not only among immigrants seeking to stay in touch with their original homelands, but within the larger community seeking to understand the history, customs, and traditions of these vibrant ethnic enclaves. The central goal of *A Brief History of the Caribbean* is to provide this information in a way that is free of academic jargon and yet conveys the complexities of the Caribbean for the educated reader. At its core, the book is a primer on the last 500 years of Caribbean history. We see ourselves as tour guides on an amazing journey to destinations both glorious and disturbing. We seek to whet the appetites of readers for the themes that have dominated the history of the Caribbean, including the conquest, genocide, race construction, slavery, colonialism, immigration, economic dependency, revolution, and struggle to create viable democracies.

The book should be seen as a gentle entry to deeper study. To further that aim, an extensive bibliography is included so that readers can follow up with additional research in areas of specific interest. Sidebars sprinkled throughout the work add information on subjects both serious and curious, from the ideology of racism that justified slavery to the lovable transparent *coquí* of Puerto Rico. The sidebars are intended to explore some subjects that are part of popular culture, yet are seldom addressed. Here again, we seek to make serious subjects accessible. For example, the sidebar on female pirates will be viewed by some as a curiosity, but it raises important questions about the role of women in this most "manly" of colonial occupations. It is, likewise, an indication of the growing importance of gender studies and how, over the last two decades, they have contributed nuance to our understanding of gender roles. The importance of Evangelina Cisneros as the consummate "damsel in distress" and the role she played in propelling the United States to intervene in the Cuban Independence War of 1895 is another indication of the importance of gender studies to our analysis.

In writing the book, we tried to play to our specific strengths. Figueredo, an expert on the literature of the Caribbean, used this knowledge to enrich the analysis throughout the book. History created the themes for much Caribbean literature, while the literature influenced the historical path. The section on the slave narrative of Olaudah Equiano is a good example for this interaction between history and literature. Equiano's slave narrative was a "must read" in abolitionist circles of the 18th century and was important in establishing an ideological and humanitarian argument against slavery, which ultimately contributed to its demise. Other examples are the early Cuban revolutionary literature and the reaction of Haitian writers to U.S. occupation in the early part of the 20th century. Argote-Freyre's extensive experience teaching Caribbean history in the classroom has allowed him to shape the book with this specific audience in mind. His interpretations on slave resistance, prerevolutionary Cuba, the Cuban Revolution of 1959, and Caribbean immigrant communities in the United States have been dissected by students in years of classroom discussions. Beginning college students and advanced high school students are an ideal audience for our book, given that emphasis. With regard to prerevolutionary Cuba, Argote-Freyre drew greatly on the research done for his two-volume biography on Cuban dictator Fulgencio Batista.

A few points are in order about some of the content decisions. This work concentrates on the Caribbean islands rather than the Caribbean Basin, a larger region including parts of Mexico, Central America,

Venezuela, and Colombia. The task was daunting enough without adding in this larger region, although we acknowledge that there are strong arguments for including those areas in a history of the Caribbean. We examined regional trends among the islands, such as the impact of black nationalism in Jamaica and Trinidad and Tobago, and the relationship of all the islands to the United States. The struggle for political and economic sovereignty by the island-nations of the Caribbean is a central theme of the work. Independence and the establishment of an identity apart from the European colonial powers was a key goal of the 18th and 19th centuries. Independence from the United States was a central theme of the 20th century and remains an aspiration in the 21st. Emphasis is given to key individuals whose strong personalities shaped the culture, politics, and legacy of the Caribbean.

Some events in North America, specifically in Florida, are dealt with in the book because they affected, or were affected by, events in the Caribbean. We specifically look at Florida in terms of the War of Jenkins' Ear and the U.S. Revolutionary War. During the first conflict, Spanish and Spanish-Cuban soldiers defended the Castillo de San Marcos in Saint Augustine, Florida, against a British attack in 1740. During the Revolutionary War, Spain declared war on Britain, and the Spanish governor of Louisiana, Bernardo de Gálvez, led troops from Spain, Cuba, Hispaniola, and Puerto Rico against British forces in Florida.

One final point is in order: How to be balanced about the Caribbean, a region we love, a region that is the birthplace of most of our parents and grandparents? Marxist writers try to mold history to fit their ideology, though still making a major contribution to the study of history. Writers who claim objectivity are often the products of systems that tend to favor European and North American perspectives, maybe even elite interpretations. Knowing this, we have tried to examine issues from different viewpoints and have tried to be as balanced in our interpretations as possible. Yet we know that our Caribbean roots—Cuban, to be precise—might not allow us to see that part of the world through the same eyes as someone who is not from the Caribbean. That might be good. That might be bad. It might encourage readers to debate our conclusions. And that, we welcome.

—Frank Argote-Freyre and D. H. Figueredo

ACKNOWLEDGMENTS

First, foremost, and forever: thanks to our families—Yvonne, Daniel, and Gabriela Figueredo and Caridad, Amanda, and Andrew of the Argote-Freyre clan. *Abrazos* to our agent, Ed Claffin, for his guidance through the project and to Claudia Schaab, executive editor at Facts On File, who was patient and willing to take risks; she is a woman of vision.

Although the actual writing of this volume took less than a year, many years were dedicated to researching, tracking down information, and consulting with experts. Dozens of libraries were visited, and dozens of librarians and scholars helped us in those libraries: Lesbia Orta Varona, Cuban Heritage Collection, the Otto C. Richter Collection, University of Miami; Nelida Pérez, Center for Puerto Rican Studies, Hunter College; Daisy Cocco de Filippis, Hostos Community College; the staff at St. Martin Public Library, St. Martin/Sint Maarten; Fernando Acosta-Rodríguez, Firestone Library, Princeton University; Emilio Jorge Rodríguez, Centro de Investigación y Desarollo de la Cultura Cubana Juan Marinello, Havana, Cuba; Jay B. Haviser, archaeologist for the Netherlands Antilles government. The collective recollections of numerous individuals shaped some of the information presented in this volume: Dr. Kamau Brathwaite, New York University and recipient of Canada's Griffin Poetry Prize International of 2006; Shujah Reiph, president of Conscious Lyrics Foundation; Nicole Cage-Florentiny, University of the Antilles; Marguerite Laurent, poet and legal adviser to the former president of Haiti, Jean-Bertrand Aristide; Linton Kwesi Johnson, poet and founder of LKJ Records; Carrol F. Coates, Binghamton University-SUNY; Alfredo Massip, Luis Martínez Fernández, University of Central Florida; Alfonso Roman, Congreso Boricua.

Research and writing on the part of Argote-Freyre was made possible by a reduction in teaching time granted by Kean University through the Office of Research and Sponsored Programs. Special thanks also go to the members of the Kean history department who contributed to an intellectually stimulating environment for research, particularly Chairman Mark Lender, Sue Gronewold, Christopher Bellitto, Brid Nicholson, Larry Zimmer, Robert Mayer, Jay Spaulding, Dennis Klein,

Frank Esposito, Thomas Banit, Edward Blum, Joe Czachowski, and the person who makes it all run smoothly, Mary Woubneh. Special thanks go to Maria Perez, an inspiration to the Kean community, and Kean University president Dawood Farahi for encouraging an atmosphere of dialogue and discourse.

INTRODUCTION

When students think of the Caribbean, they think of the region as a whole, unless, that is, they happen to have an affinity for a particular island, say Jamaicans for Jamaica and Haitians for Hispaniola. But the overall tendency is to conjure up an image defined by generalities: palm trees, beaches, lively music, peoples of diverse and mixed ethnicity. This generalization invites the danger of stereotyping, but nevertheless there are sufficient geographic similarities and common historical and political developments—essentially being conquered by European powers and serving as servants of those powers for several centuries—to offer historians the opportunity to write of the Caribbean islands as one body. Of course, as in the human anatomy, the parts can look different from each other—say an arm from a nose—but the finished product is one entity, one body where one part affects the others. Thus, in the Caribbean, the wars of independence of the 19th century that started in one location spread to other islands, for example from Cuba to Puerto Rico. And the revolution that shook the island of Cuba in 1959 inspired the political struggles of such neighbors as Grenada and Jamaica in the late 1970s.

The history of the islands binds them as one: first encounter with Europeans, conquest and colonization, imposed European monopoly, slavery, the era of piracy, stirrings of a national identity, slave rebellions, abolition, wars of independence, economic dependence on outside sources, local political fragmentation, strong rulers, and dependence on tourism. But after acknowledging the similarities, the individual traits of individual islands, or of a group of islands, must be accepted: For example, the political experience of the anglophone Caribbean in the 20th century tends to be different from the political experience of the Hispanic and francophone islands.

It is all suggestive of a duality, of two competing and different perspectives: the uniqueness of each island and the likeness of all the islands taken as a whole. It is the whole that is usually projected onto the world, and it is the whole that students, travelers, and investors tend to conjure up in their heads when thinking of the Caribbean. Therefore, it makes sense to write of the region as one large body while also devoting attention to its parts.

Geography

Geography binds the islands together as an entity—a community of nations worth studying as a whole. At the risk of oversimplification, geography is history, or at the very least is critical in understanding the history of a region. A quick glance at a map of the Caribbean reveals how it lies to the east of Mexico and Central America, forming an oddly shaped Y, with the larger islands of Cuba, Hispaniola, Jamaica, and Puerto Rico forming one arm, the Bahamian Archipelago another, and the smaller islands of the Lesser Antilles the base of the Y.

The location of the islands and their proximity to each other is critical to understanding their history. In the pre-Columbian era, the closeness of the islands made it possible for Amerindians to island-hop from one to the other and avoid the more powerful currents of the Atlantic. Long before the arrival of the Europeans, there was a community of islands trading, learning, and sometimes fighting with each other. Once the Spaniards arrived, the location of the islands made them key jumping-off points for exploration of the North and South American mainlands. Shortly thereafter, their position made them ideal as defensive outposts for the gold and silver trade from Mexico (known as the viceroyalty of New Spain) and other parts of the Spanish Empire. The fact that they form a natural defensive barrier for Mexico and Central America was not lost on the United States, and these same islands became crucial for the defense of the Panama Canal in the 20th century. The proximity of the Caribbean to the United States and the relatively small size of the island-nations make the region vulnerable to exploitation and undue influence by its powerful neighbor to the north. The position of the islands near the equator is key to their current economic development as tourist havens, making the sun and surf important commodities.

The Caribbean, also called the West Indies and the Antilles, stretches over 2,500 miles, descending from the north toward the south like a string of pearls. Formed by volcanic eruptions, the Caribbean islands consist of over 700 isles, islets, cays, and atolls—islands are large bodies of land, such as Cuba, surrounded on all sides by water; islets are smaller islands, Vieques in Puerto Rico, for example; cays are much smaller, made up of corals and sands, and usually roundish in shape though not always so; atolls are small and surrounded by algae and corals with a depression in the center of its mass. The Caribbean islands are part of a submerged mountain range that at its highest is 10,417 feet above sea level (on Hispaniola) and at its lowest (on the Cayman Islands) is less than 100 feet above sea level. On the highest peaks of

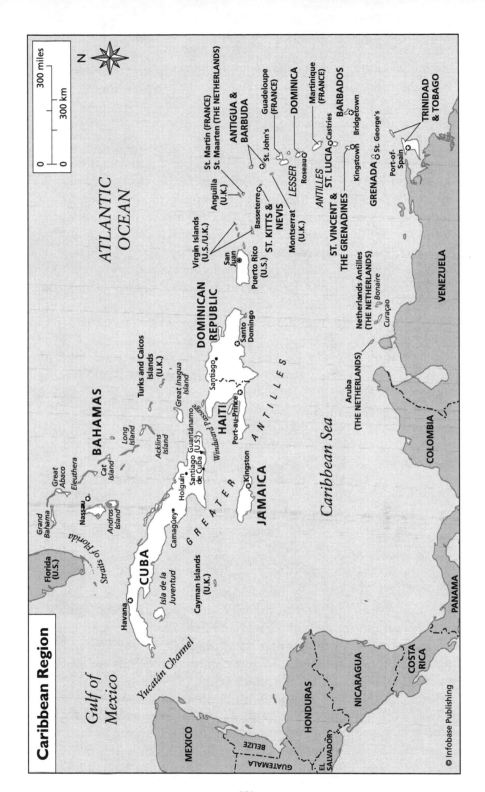

Caribbean Region

300 miles
300 km

N

ATLANTIC OCEAN

Gulf of Mexico

Yucatán Channel

Straits of Florida

Florida (U.S.)

BAHAMAS

Grand Bahama
Great Abaco
Eleuthera
Nassau
Andros Island
Cat Island
Long Island
Acklins Island
Great Inagua Island

Turks and Caicos Islands (U.K.)

CUBA
Isla de la Juventud
Havana
Cayman Islands (U.K.)
Camagüey
Holguín
Santiago de Cuba
Guantánamo (U.S.)

GREATER ANTILLES

JAMAICA
Kingston

HAITI
Port-au-Prince
Santiago
Windward Passage

DOMINICAN REPUBLIC
Santo Domingo

Puerto Rico (U.S.)
San Juan

Virgin Islands (U.S./U.K.)

Anguilla (U.K.)

St. Martin (FRANCE)
St. Maarten (THE NETHERLANDS)

ANTIGUA & BARBUDA
St. John's

Guadeloupe (FRANCE)

DOMINICA
Roseau

Martinique (FRANCE)

Basseterre
ST. KITTS & NEVIS
Montserrat (U.K.)

LESSER ANTILLES

ST. LUCIA
Castries

BARBADOS
Bridgetown

ST. VINCENT & THE GRENADINES
Kingstown

GRENADA
St. George's

Port-of-Spain

TRINIDAD & TOBAGO

Netherlands Antilles (THE NETHERLANDS)
Bonaire
Curaçao

Aruba (THE NETHERLANDS)

Caribbean Sea

COLOMBIA

VENEZUELA

PANAMA

COSTA RICA

NICARAGUA

HONDURAS

EL SALVADOR

GUATEMALA

BELIZE

MEXICO

© Infobase Publishing

xv

Hispaniola, along the Cordillera Central, the temperature occasionally drops below freezing and frost forms.

Bodies of Water

The islands are located in the Caribbean Sea, a stretch of water that is actually part of the Atlantic Ocean and occupies more than 1 million square miles. To the north of the Caribbean Sea are the islands of Cuba, Hispaniola, Jamaica, and Puerto Rico. To the south are the countries of Colombia, Panama, and Venezuela. Central America and the Yucatán Peninsula rest on the west of the Caribbean Sea, and to the east are the smaller islands of Grenada, Trinidad, and Martinique. The Cayman Trench, between Cuba and Jamaica, is the deepest area of the Caribbean Sea, with a depth of over 24,000 feet. The well-known Gulf Stream, which warms parts of the Atlantic Ocean, originates in the Caribbean.

The Gulf of Mexico is to the north and west of the Caribbean Sea and the islands, extending over 600,000 square miles from the tip of Florida to the coasts of Texas and Mexico and the tip of the Yucatán Peninsula. The waters of the Gulf of Mexico connect with the Caribbean Sea through the Yucatán Channel and with the Atlantic Ocean through the Florida Straits, located between Florida and Cuba.

The Atlantic Ocean flanks the Caribbean on the east. This ocean, the second largest in the world (the Pacific Ocean is the first, with 70 million square miles), covers more than 32 million square miles and is located between the continents of North America and South America on the west and Europe and Africa on the east. Today, most of the world's shipping occurs on this ocean.

Main Islands

Cuba is the largest island in the Caribbean. Shaped like an alligator, the island is 775 miles long and 118 miles at its widest. It is long and essentially flat but for several mountain ranges, the largest being the Sierra Maestra in southeastern Cuba, the head of the alligator. There is a second smaller mountain range in south-central Cuba known as the Escambray. The island is located to the south of the Florida Straits and to the east of the Yucatán Peninsula.

Hispaniola, which consists of Haiti on the western side and the Dominican Republic in the eastern section, is the second-largest island in the Caribbean, having a length of 400 miles; at its widest point, Hispaniola is 150 miles. The island is located between Cuba, to the west, and Puerto Rico, to the east. Hispaniola is mountainous, especially on the one third of the island that is occupied by Haiti; the Dominican Republic covers the remaining two thirds.

The third-largest island is Jamaica, less than 500 miles south of Florida, 146 miles long and 51 miles wide. Hills rise on the center plateau, and on the easternmost part are the famous Blue Mountains, over 7,000 feet tall and home to the legendary Jamaican Maroons, runaway slaves who built villages in the mountains. On a map, Cuba appears to sit atop this island, 95 miles to the northeast.

To the southeast of Florida is Puerto Rico. The island is 111 miles long and 39 miles wide. While beaches flank its coast, the island is mountainous with terrains that appear to be poised on the edge of a blue precipice. From a plane, Puerto Rico seems to jut out into the air from the ocean floor.

These four islands are known as the Greater Antilles. The appellation refers to Antilia, a mythical island located somewhere in the Atlantic Ocean, near the Canary Islands, off Spain. Antilia, also Antillia, called the phantom island, might have been the basis for the legend of Atlantis. Spanish and Portuguese traditions maintained that Catholic bishops visited the island during the 700s. In the early 1400s, it was rumored that Portuguese and Spanish sailors had sighted the island.

Island Groups

The Bahamas Group, also known as the Bahamian Archipelago, consists of the Bahamas and Turks and Caicos Islands, forming a chain that lies to the southeast of Florida and to the north of Cuba. These islands, which are actually coral reefs, are flat with miles of white and pinkish sandy beaches. There are no rivers in the Bahamas, and 5 percent of the world's corals are found on this island group. The corals produce calcium that in turn clears the coastal waters, affording the sea near the island a visibility of 200 feet.

The group that includes the U.S. and British Virgin Islands, Barbados, Grenada, Guadeloupe, Martinique, Saint Lucia, Saint Martin, and Trinidad-Tobago is known as the Lesser Antilles. These islands form an arc that extends from Puerto Rico to the northeast of South America and the north of Venezuela. There are numerous mountains and hills spread out on these islands, with some, such as Saint Lucia and St. Martin, having very little land mass.

Some of these islands are part of a group known as the Leeward Islands, referring to their location facing downwind, or leeward, from the winds that blow from the east to the west in the Caribbean. The Leeward Islands include these islands that are in the Lesser Antilles:

Anguilla, Antigua, Barbuda, Dominica, Guadeloupe, Montserrat, Netherlands Antilles, Nevis, Saint Kitts, St. Martin, and the Virgin Islands. Those known as the Windward Islands—referring to the islands facing the winds blowing from the east to the west, thus facilitating the arrival of ships whose sails were propelled by the wind—are the Grenadines, Grenada, Martinique, Saint Lucia, and Saint Vincent. Three small islands—Grand Cayman, 76 square miles; Little Cayman, 20 square miles; and Cayman Brac, 22 square miles—form the Cayman Islands group. This group is south-southwest of Cuba and northwest of Jamaica.

Geology and Topography

The geology and topography of the Caribbean can be similar within an island group but can vary from group to group, making it possible to see both similarities and diversity within the region. While the beaches might offer long strands of fine sands and crystalline water, a trek into the countryside can expose the traveler to swamps and quicksand, such as in Cuba, or desertlike terrain in Curaçao in the Netherlands Antilles. A long savannah, or flat valley, in the Dominican Republic might not suggest the hint of a forest nearby, but a half-hour drive from San Juan, in Puerto Rico, can transport the driver to the primeval world of a rain forest.

There are three types of rain forests in the Caribbean. There is the dry forest, also called tropical deciduous, areas where there is rain accumulation of 30 to 50 inches a year and seven months or so of humid weather. The trees in this forest grow together and reach a height of about 30 feet. Since little sunlight reaches the forest floor, there is an absence of lush vegetation.

Seasonal rain forests are characterized by pine trees, cedar trees, and logwood. The seasonal rain forest receives about 50 to 80 inches of rain during seven to nine months a year. Seasonal rain forests can also have extensive grasslands.

The tropical rain forests are the best known and most dramatic. A rain forest consists of tall trees and thick vegetation. The recipient of nearly 80 to 250 inches of rain a year, the water accumulation in the forest allows for the growth of plants. Even when there is no rain, the water that accumulates on the leaves of plants nurtures them. Most rain forests are located near the equator, and the temperature within the habitat ranges between 64 and 95°F. The rain forests of the world are important to the development of new drug treatments because many of

The lush rain forest and mountains of El Yunque, Puerto Rico, where the dense vegetation forms a natural canopy (Photos by D. H. Figueredo)

the plants are unique and may have medicinal applications. Some of the plants and animals dwelling in the rain forests are yet to be identified and cataloged, so preserving the rain forests of the world has emerged in recent decades as an important ecological issue.

Hills of Saint Martin/Sint Maarten hugging the bay and beaches (Photo by D. H. Figueredo)

El Yunque, in Puerto Rico, is the best-known rain forest in the Caribbean. Within sight of San Juan, the island's capital, El Yunque receives over 80 inches of rain a year. As the mountain ascends, the temperature drops and the trees, reaching heights of 120 feet, grow closer together, blocking sunlight and creating a veritable green wall and roof that can prevent onlookers from peeking inside the forest and those inside from catching a glimpse of the outside world. In fact, in a similar rain forest in Guadeloupe, some of Columbus's men were lost for days in 1502 because they could not catch a glimpse of the sky above them and were therefore unable to see the stars and the Sun for direction. Eventually, they stumbled back to the beach.

There are mountains that seem to stretch out into infinity. So vast is the mountainous expanse in Haiti, for example, that Haitians are fond of saying of their country, *deyè mon, gin mon* (beyond mountains are more mountains) (Bellegard-Smith, 1). There are ranges of striking beauty, such as the famous Blue Mountains of Jamaica, composed of different rocks that in combination form the blue stone that gives the range its name. There are picturesque hills that seem to embrace harbors, such as in St. Martin, and in Trinidad there are formations that rise from the bottom of the ocean like a closed fist, forming inhospitable islets.

HOW CORAL ISLANDS ARE MADE

Coral islands are constantly forming and re-forming themselves. This is how an expert describes it: "The coral polyp is a tiny sea creature that lives in a shell in fairly shallow waters that are warm and clear. When the polyp dies, the softer parts of the body are washed away, but the skeleton is left behind. New polyps grow on shells of dead ones, eventually forming a great mass of coral. An atoll is a coral reef that forms an almost complete circle around a lagoon. The circular coral reefs of most atolls reach deep down into water where no coral can grow. . . . As the island sinks, or the sea level changes, the coral continues to grow. The original . . . island disappears far below the lagoon, and the reef forms an atoll."

David, Kenneth C. *Don't Know Much about Geography: Everything You Need to Know about the World but Never Learned.* New York: William Morrow and Co., 1992, p. 184.

But not all the terrain is mountainous. Cuba and Hispaniola, for example, have large areas of savannahs, which are flat dry grasslands with scattered scrub trees, mangrove swamps in coastal areas (some containing salt), and rolling hills encircling valleys. The Curaçao islands are home to thorny woodlands and cactus scrub, with large areas resembling deserts. The Bahamian Archipelago consists of many small coral islands. (Coral is a substance secreted by certain marine animals that accumulates over long periods of time into reefs or small islands.) As a result, the Bahamian islands are rich in marine life but lack the sediment to support diverse agriculture.

Flora and Fauna

At the time of Columbus's arrival in 1492, most animals found in the Greater Antilles were small because the natural environment did not favor the evolution of larger beasts, and the animals of South America were unable to migrate across to the islands. Some animals that did evolve in the Caribbean included a small dog that did not bark, bats, crocodiles (*caimanes*), iguanas, snakes, turtles, and parrots. On the islands closer to the continent, such as Trinidad, some larger animals were found, such as sloths, anteaters, tiger cats, raccoons, and small deer. In the sea and rivers there were groupers, red snappers, tuna, clams, crabs, lobsters, squid, and manatees, the slow-moving sea cow that lives comfortably in fresh and salt water. The flora included palm trees, orchids, oleanders, begonias, pineapples, guava trees, mamey trees, peanuts, corn, beans, squash, peppers, tobacco, yams, and yucca. The latter was well suited to the climate and the soil and could survive drought, rain, and strong winds, since hurricanes, for example, could uproot trees, while the gusts of winds could bend but not tear the yucca's leaves.

There were and still are some spectacularly unique animals and plants in the region. Cuba is home to the smallest bird in the world, the *zunzuito,* or the bee hummingbird—the *Calypte heleane*—which is the size of a thumbnail. Cuba's royal palm tree grows very thin and tall, over 75 feet, with a white bark that appears to the eye to be hand painted. The *coquí* of Puerto Rico is a frog that sings a beautiful song—co-quí, co-quí, co-quí—thus the name. The watapana, or divi-divi tree, flourishes on the sandy beaches of Aruba. It is a shrub with a trunk that seems to be permanently bent by the wind, topped by a green canopy that resembles a bristly crown.

The imperial and jaco parrots, from the island of Dominica, pair for life and can live up to 70 years; they are emerald green with red stripes. The chuchubi, a gray mockingbird, lives in the islands of the Curaçao group. It announces the arrival and departure of strangers with harmonious chirps. There are also luminous lagoons where the thickness of the plankton makes the water glow as if lit by an underwater lamp.

Climate

Located south of the tropic of Cancer and with an average temperature ranging from 78 to 88°F, the Caribbean offers temperate weather throughout the year. The climate is pleasantly affected by the northeast trade winds, which blow at about 15 to 25 knots. The trade winds originate in the Azores, off the Iberian Peninsula, and then in the Bermudas shift to the south, always warmed by the Sun. The ocean current benefits from the trade winds. It was the trade winds and the current that helped Columbus reach the Caribbean in 1492.

The size and height of an island can affect the trade winds, cooling it off and thus creating rain as the moisture in the wind condenses. Low islands receive less rain than high islands, especially mountainous islands such as Hispaniola. Clouds hover over the mountains, the result of the wind becoming hotter during the day and thrusting an upward draft that forms the clouds. The clouds cool off the land, ending the rise

THE COQUÍ, A FROG FROM PUERTO RICO

In the evenings in Puerto Rico, especially in the countryside, the air is enriched by the melodic pattern of a natural lullaby: co-quí, co-quí, co-quí. It is the song of a tiny amphibian warning other males to get away from its territory and inviting female frogs to mate. Local tradition maintains that the sound "co" means "go away" and "qui" means "come over."

This miniature frog is between 15 and 80 millimeters long and is colored brown, green, yellow, or gray. The coquí has only three toes and no swimming membrane between the toes. Instead, the coquí's toes end in pads or discs that allow the amphibian to cling to any vertical surface. Coquís do not give birth over water but lay their eggs on a leaf. The male guards the tiny eggs from which the young emerge as exact replicas of the parents, bypassing the tadpole stage.

There are 16 coquí species, 13 of them endemic to Puerto Rico. The tiny frog has been taken to other countries, such as Panama and the United States, but according to tradition, once removed from Puerto Rico, the coquí no longer sings. Some question this assertion, but islanders take it as a point of pride and believe it to be true.

For Puerto Ricans, the coquí is symbolic of the purity of the land and of the love of the island. Paintings or small sculptures of the coquí are found throughout Puerto Rico.

Silva Lee, Alfonsoe. *Coquí y sus amigos: Los animales de Puerto Rico* (Coquí and his friends: The animals of Puerto Rico). St. Paul, Minn.: Pangaea, 2000.

of hot air and bringing sudden heavy rains. (Most islands experience three seasons: a dry season from February to April and a wet season in the fall; summer extends from May to September, the time when islanders prefer to swim in the sea [tourists flock to the beaches and swim all year long, much to the surprise of locals].)

Natural Phenomena

The region is subject to earthquakes, floods, volcanic eruptions, and hurricanes. In 1527, explorer and chronicler Álvar Núñez Cabeza de Vaca (1490?–1556?) described how the winds of a hurricane snatched a boat from a ship on the bay and tossed it several miles inland: "We went into the woods, and a quarter of a league into them we found one of the ship's boats in some trees. Ten leagues from there we found the bodies of two persons from my ship . . . were so disfigured from having struck the rocks that they could not be recognized" (Cabeza de Vaca, 32). In 1692, an earthquake destroyed much of Kingston, Jamaica, and a subsequent tidal wave swallowed up the section known as Port Royal, which was once a haven for pirates. In 1902, the eruption of Mont Pelée, in Martinique, wiped out the town of Saint-Pierre. More recently, in 1995, a series of volcanic eruptions from the Soufrière Hills Volcano devastated the island of Montserrat, forcing two-thirds of the 9,500 residents to flee the island. Volcanic activity there remains a danger, with the most recent eruptions occurring in 2003. It is difficult to know whether, or if, the island population will ever return to pre-1995 levels. Of these catastrophes, hurricanes are the most common, with an average of 18 per year sweeping through the Caribbean.

Natural Resources

Sugar is identified with the Caribbean. It is a crop cultivated on all the islands for domestic consumption and export, although different islands have dominated production in different periods. In the 18th century Haiti and Jamaica were the best-known sugar producers, while in the mid 19th and early 20th centuries, Cuba became the primary producer of sugar in the region. At the turn of the 21st century, Cuba was still producing over 3 million tons per year, although its importance as the dominant export was in decline. Sugar remains an important export for the Dominican Republic, Barbados, Jamaica, Martinique, and Guadeloupe.

Coffee and tobacco are cultivated in Cuba, the Dominican Republic, and Puerto Rico, with the Dominican Republic exporting an average of 36,000 kilograms of coffee per year. Cuba and Puerto Rico produce coffee primarily for local use. The cigar industry is associated with Cuba and the Dominican Republic. The exportation of bananas provides half the income for the smaller islands of Dominica, the Grenadines, Saint Lucia, and Saint Vincent, and in Jamaica the banana industry is second to sugar. Other important products are cocoa, coconuts, and citrus.

Some of the islands are blessed with oil, gas, and mineral wealth, most notably Trinidad–Tobago, which exports substantial quantities of oil and natural gas. A recent estimate by the U.S. Central Intelligence Agency noted that Trinidad–Tobago produces 150,000 barrels of oil per day and has reserves of 990 million barrels. The same estimate found substantial natural gas reserves as well. Nickel and cobalt deposits are ample in Cuba, and alumina/bauxite mining is an important industry in Jamaica. Other resources include fishing, which provides $3 to 4 billion a year to the nations of the Caribbean.

Economy

The predominant industry is tourism. In the last 20 years of the 20th century, nearly 2 billion tourists visited the Caribbean, providing half the national budget of many of the smaller islands. The Caribbean tourist industry depends on the prosperity of other nations, mainly the United States, as the average family that vacations on the islands spends about $3,000 for a one-week stay. There are negative by-products of the tourism industry as well, including prostitution and child exploitation. In addition, many of the resorts are too expensive for the islanders to patronize, creating what some have called "tourism apartheid" in the Caribbean.

1

PRE-COLUMBIAN INHABITANTS

Guanahatabey

Before Europeans arrived, three major groups of people were indigenous to the Caribbean: the Guanahatabey, the Tainos, and the Caribs. The Guanahatabey (sometimes mistakenly referred to as the Ciboneyes) were the least populous of the three communities, and their civilization was the least sophisticated. Not much is known about them; historians believe that they were hunters and gatherers: "Their culture was that of the paleolithic or stone age, although they used rough wood, seas shells and fish bones as implements as well as unpolished stones" (Foner 1962: 17). There is no evidence that they practiced military arts, and it is believed that they did not have any form of organized religion, though they seemed to bury their dead in mounds. They tended to live in small, loosely structured groups and were in the process of being culturally assimilated by the Tainos at the times of Columbus's arrival. The Guanahatabey and their civilization vanished before much could be learned about them. Evidence from archaeological expeditions to western Cuba, where they dwelled, suggests that they lived in the open or in caves and relied heavily on shellfish, fish, and game for sustenance. No pottery samples have been found for this community.

It is theorized that the Guanahatabey originated in Florida and sailed to the islands from there, suggesting they were able to build a sailing vessel, probably by hollowing out a tree trunk. Archaeological evidence indicates a cultural link between the Guanahatabey and the indigenous communities of Florida. Columbus made contact with the Guanahatabey with the assistance of Taino guides. The Tainos and Guanahatabey spoke different languages, so communication was difficult; in any case, Columbus lost interest in them because they had few possessions of any kind, and certainly none that he deemed of value.

Tainos

Much more is known about the Tainos and Caribs, beginning with the extensive descriptions left by Columbus. The Tainos probably originated in northeastern South America and reached the Caribbean about 2,500 years ago, sailing on canoes carved out of tree trunks and using paddles for propulsion. Their civilization was quite complex, and scholars generally divide it along geographic boundaries, with the "classic Tainos" living in Hispaniola, Puerto Rico, and a sliver of eastern Cuba. Hispaniola and Puerto Rico were at the center of the Taino world, and trade was most intensive between them. The Tainos living in most of Cuba, Jamaica, and the Bahamas are identified as the western Tainos, and those in the Lesser Antilles are known as the eastern Tainos.

The Europeans referred to all indigenous peoples as "Indians," but the peoples themselves identified each other by region. As an example, the Tainos living in the Bahamian Archipelago were known as Lucayos, while those in Puerto Rico identified themselves as Borinquen. Tainos became another way to identify the indigenous communities of the Caribbean, because it was one of the first words Columbus heard. It means "good" or "noble" in their language and was used by Tainos to differentiate themselves from their rivals, the Caribs. The first Tainos that Columbus saw were those from Cuba and Hispaniola; he described them as good looking, tall, well proportioned, with olive skin.

Taino culture included a complex agricultural system, political divisions based on villages and regions, an appreciation of the arts, and a ritualistic religion. Small sculptures of gods, well-preserved carved stools, carvings of bats on rocks, and the remains of a ball or ceremonial park have been found in the Dominican Republic, near La Romana, and in Tibes, Puerto Rico.

Society

Within Taino society, there was a division of labor, with men responsible for clearing the woods for planting, building canoes, and hunting (usually birds, iguanas, and snakes) and also fishing using nets, spears, and cages. In some areas the men developed fish farms where they bred seafood for consumption.

Women were responsible for harvesting. The main crop was cassava, and so important was it to their diet that their principal deity was Yucahu—the god of cassava. Another powerful deity was Atabey, the goddess of fresh water and fertility. Women wove hammocks and skirts that covered the front of the body and were responsible for preparing meals. Mothers carried their babies on their backs and flattened the infant's head by placing boards on the front and back of the head, since Tainos found a flat forehead an attractive physical attribute. Despite this traditional division of labor among the sexes, many scholars believe that Taino society was quite egalitarian and that women chiefs were not uncommon.

Tainos lived near the coasts or near rivers in settlements that, according to historian Franklin Knight, "ranged from single units of many families to towns of one thousand houses, and probably three to four thousand persons. The village houses were arranged around the ball courts, and the straw-roofed adobe hut of the chief, called a *bohio*" (Knight 1978: 13). They divided their island homes into provinces that were ruled by a cacique, or chief, a position inherited through the

Taino dwelling used throughout the Caribbean in 1492 and even today (Drawing by Carlos Díaz)

3

matrilineal line. The provinces were composed of villages ruled by less powerful chiefs or subchiefs.

A cacique typically had many wives, often from other tribes with the purpose of creating alliances, and oversaw religious events and ceremonial ball games. These chiefs were responsible for settling disputes and were rewarded for their labor with large canoes, special foods such as the giant iguana, and colorful clothes and small ornate statues of *semis* or *zemis,* spirits and gods that the Tainos believed protected individuals and villages. Knight describes the *zemis* statues as resembling "grotesque anthropomorphic figures, often with exaggerated sex organs" (Knight, 12). In addition to a chief, there was a spiritual and natural healer, known as *bohuti,* in every village who tended to the medical and spiritual needs of the community. The *bohuti* were renowned for their knowledge of the desires of the gods and their wisdom regarding the healing benefits of local plants. They were typically paid for their services with cassava.

It appears that the Tainos did not have *zemi* figures that carried weapons or represented warriors, leading some scholars to suggest that the Tainos were not aggressive by nature. Columbus himself served as a witness to the Tainos's kindly disposition. When one of his ships was wrecked off the island of Hispaniola in 1492, the local cacique employed canoes to help rescue the sailors and to transport the goods that were on the ship and then offered Columbus and his men shelter. However, while the Tainos were generally pacific, violence was not unknown to them. Personal disputes were occasionally settled by murder, and villages occasionally went to battle over hunting and fishing rights.

The Tainos did have an enemy: the Caribs. Columbus noticed that some of the Tainos bore scars on their bodies and concluded that another group of inhabitants made war on them. Later on, in Hispaniola, the admiral learned from a cacique that indeed the Caribs not only raided Taino villages but also captured their women and killed and ate their young men.

Columbus turned out to be an enemy of the Tainos as well, though their initial reaction to his arrival did not reveal fear; quite the contrary, the Tainos responded in friendship. The Tainos were willing to share their food with the Europeans and "taught the Spanish about herbs, food crops, and housing" and the cultivation of such crops as tobacco, potatoes, and peanuts (Knight, 1978: 16). However, some were suspicious when Columbus wanted to employ them as translators. The admiral wrote to the Spanish monarch: "I took by force some of them in order that they might learn [Spanish]. . . . I still have them with me" (Morison, 184). It was the beginning of a process whereby Columbus and those who followed took who and what they wanted from the Caribbean, without the permission of those already there.

Traditions, Customs, and Myths

The Tainos saw the world as consisting of good and evil. The deity Yucahu embodied all that was good, such as pleasant weather, good crops, and happiness. Juracán was the opposite: strong winds and storms, flooding, and destruction. There were also evil spirits, called *maboyas,* who hid in the forest and came out at night to hurt people, which is why some Tainos were afraid of the dark. The Tainos believed in life after death, and thus personal objects, such as jewelry, were interred with the deceased. As part of their religious rituals they induced a hallucinogenic state by smoking tobacco.

There were dances and musical activities, called *areyto,* that rendered tribute to the deities. Held on a field or a ceremonial plaza, the *areyto* used a combination of narration, poetry, singing, and dancing to tell events from the past or comment on more recent events such as a birth or a death. *Areytos* were even used to rally the villagers into battle with rival families or other villages.

The Tainos also played a ball game called *batu,* something resembling volleyball. The objective of the game was to keep the ball from falling to the ground; however, hands could not be used to achieve this objective. The team that let the ball fall lost the game. These ball games provided an opportunity for cultural exchange between different villages. Men and women played, although on segregated teams of between 10 and 30 players.

Languages

The language spoken by the Tainos is related to Arawak languages in use today in some regions of the Amazon and Orinoco Rivers in South America. It is a soft, musical-sounding language with a nasal quality, many vowels, and aspirated consonants such as *h;* thus *Hamaca* is pronounced "amaca."

The Caribs seemed to have two types of verbal communication, one used by the men and one used by the women. Scholars who visited the Carib reservation in Dominica noticed that the men and women spoke

CONUCO: AN ENVIRONMENTALLY FRIENDLY AGRICULTURE

The Tainos and the Caribs cultivated cassava, also known as yuca or manioc, using a system know as *conuco,* where a chunk of the root is planted in a position parallel to the surface. There, the seedling is buried just a few inches into the dirt with enough space to allow the root to stretch out sideways. Sometimes, a small pile of soil, shaped into a cone, was used for planting. The *conuco* system did not need much water and much soil, and thus it could be planted near a beach and on the side of a hill or a mountain. The yuca plant sprouted long, thick, angular leaves that could survive the strongest of winds.

The system is still in use today. In Cuba, small farms devoted to genetic planting, protected by the government, are called *conucos;* home gardens in small apartments are also often described as *conucos. Conuco* planting also occurs in the Dominican Republic and Curaçao, where it is called *kunuku.* The term has come to suggest the practice of limited agriculture for a family or small community who are sensitive to the ecosystem and environmentally friendly.

Cassava is still a popular dish in Cuban, Haitian, and Puerto Rican cuisine. Haitians flatten it into a dough, similar to bread, and it is eaten as such. Cubans and Puerto Ricans boil and sometimes fry cassava. The cassava is then served hot with olive oil, garlic sauce, and slivers of either garlic or onion. It accompanies a main meal of beef or pork.

Spector, Amy. "Yuca: Chefs Go Maniac for Manio." *Nation's Restaurant News* 37, 27 (July 2003): 37.

using different words and forms of address, suggesting a language usage determined by gender. This might be a by-product of intermarriage between the Tainos and the Caribs. Taino women who married Caribs, either by choice or abduction, spoke the Taino language, while the men descended from the Caribs on the mainland spoke Cariban. It is also suggested that because the Island Caribs traveled throughout the northern coasts of South America, they picked up the words and sounds of the Cariban language. This language uses vowels, similar in sound to vowels in Spanish, and consonants that sound like their counterparts in English.

TAINO WORDS IN USE TODAY

Hundreds of Taino words are used in Spanish, and a handful have been adopted into English. During the early 20th century, Puerto Rican scholar Cayetano Coll y Toste (1850–1930) identified and collected many Taino expressions. Today an organization called the United Confederation of Taino People, founded in 1998 in New York, is attempting to produce a dictionary of Taino words in Spanish and in English. Here are some Taino words that are used in English today; some of these words were also used by the Caribs, suggesting a linguistic exchange between the Tainos and the Caribs:

Taino	English
barbacoa	barbecue
canoa	canoe
hamaca	hammock
huracán	hurricane
manatí	manatee
yuca	yucca plant

Coll y Toste, Cayetano. *Selección de leyendas puertorriqueñas.* Boston, and Washington, D.C.: Heath, 1932.

Music

Tainos used several instruments to accompany *areyto* performances and religious ceremonies: drums, called *mayohavau,* that were elongated and made of thin wood; the *maracas,* a hollow ball with another ball inside, which musicians shook (a modern variation is still in use); and flutes. A singer or group of singers sang a tune that told of historic events or stories about the gods; the songs were long and could last hours. The musicians were usually prominent leaders of the tribe.

Visual Arts

Taino art represented what Tainos valued in their society and environment. Therefore, gods were often sculpted in wood of various sizes, with large sculptures of the gods given as a gift to caciques, and drawings and carvings depicting such animals as birds, bats, and frogs were made on rocks and shells. Archaeological findings in Puerto Rico have yielded three-peaked stones with human features and animal motifs, stone daggers, stone masks, amulets, and ceramic vases. Vomit spatulas, used during religious rituals, had intricate designs of either humans or animals, and decorated stools, made of wood, revealed sophisticated patterns of animals, people, or geometric shapes. These stools were also used during religious ceremonies. The details found in Taino art indicate a class of workers who could perform such tasks and who took long hours and days to complete the artwork. These craftsmen were probably appreciated in the villages, and some were likely well known throughout a province.

New Research on the Disappearance of the Tainos
It was long thought that there were no Taino descendants in the modern era. The assumption was that either the group was annihilated during the conquest and colonization of the Caribbean or that they intermarried with the Caribs and the Spanish.

In the 1700s a group of Tainos was discovered living on the tiny island of Mona, Puerto Rico. When relocating to central Puerto Rico, these Tainos probably intermarried with Africans and Spanish. The German scientist Alexander von Humboldt (1769–1859) described a surviving indigenous community in 19th-century Cuba in his work *Personal Narrative of a Journey to the Equinoctial Regions of the New Continent* (1800). Early in the 20th century, there were unconfirmed rumors of small Taino communities in the Cuban countryside, which also suggested intermarriage with the locals.

In 2001 Puerto Rican researchers studied the hair and remains of three Tainos found at an archaeological site. The DNA structure in the hair was compared with the DNA of 56 Puerto Rican volunteers from a region on the island where the Tainos once lived. The findings confirmed that nearly 60 percent of the volunteers exactly matched the DNA of the Tainos from the archaeological site. Though historians are waiting for the results of similar studies being conducted in Cuba and the Dominican Republic, it is now believed that while the Tainos were defeated by the Spanish, they were not completely exterminated.

Caribs
Of these three major groups, the Caribs were the last to arrive in the Caribbean. They came from South America, probably over 2,000 years ago. They were culturally and ethnically linked with the Caribs on the

South American mainland; thus, to distinguish them, the ones living in the Caribbean were identified as Island Caribs. They also referred to themselves as the Kalina. At the time of Columbus's arrival, they occupied some of the islands of the Lesser Antilles, including the Windward Islands and Guadeloupe, having conquered these from an earlier civilization known as the Igneri or Eyeri.

They waged periodic warfare on the Tainos. The Caribs were known to be fierce warriors, and the Tainos told Columbus that they were cannibals. Their reputation for cannibalism was probably exaggerated by the Spaniards, who used it as an excuse to conquer them. They likely resorted to cannibalism in some of their religious rituals, but not as a regular source of food.

The Island Caribs built large canoes that carried over 100 men at a time and sailed from island to island, raiding Taino villages. They specifically sought wives on their raiding expeditions because there was a demographic imbalance in their society. The presence of Taino women in Island Carib society influenced it significantly, and evidence of this is seen in the similarity in pottery and home furnishings. In addition to cassava agriculture, the Caribs ate fish, lizards, crabs, and beans, and they brewed beer.

Always ready to move, they did not build large villages or communities the way the Tainos did but favored small gatherings of family members. Research suggests that they lived in sexually segregated housing, with men in a large residence in the center of the village. The women lived in family homes surrounding the main house. The Caribs preferred to settle on hills that afforded them a view of the landscape, a useful strategy in the event of combat. Their weapons included bows, poisoned arrows, spears, and clubs. Unlike the Tainos, who diminished in number a few short years after Columbus's arrival, the Caribs managed to survive, at least in part. This was not solely because of their military abilities but because they lived on islands that were initially too out of the way for the Spanish colonizers. Some aspects of their culture survived the conquest, although they were influenced by the French and the British in the 17th century. The Island Caribs fought numerous wars against the Europeans, and runaway slaves periodically joined their communities, which created a new cultural dynamic. Some of these indigenous communities were labeled the "Black Caribs."

Early in the 20th century, a Carib reservation was established on the east coast of Dominica. The inhabitants were descendants of Caribs who in the 1760s relocated to the north of Dominica and whom a century later the Church of England promised to protect. The result was that in 1903, more than 3,000 acres were declared a Carib reservation. Imperfect as the reservation might have been for the preservation of Carib culture, it did allow scholars something of a glimpse of a pre-Columbian past. Carib influence and culture can still be found on some of the other islands of the Lesser Antilles, including Saint Vincent.

2

TWO WORLDS IN COLLISION: THE SPANISH CONQUEST (1492–1552)

In January 1492, a rider was seen atop a mule heading away from the Spanish court outside Granada. The rider, not a knight but an experienced sailor, had been recently turned away by the rulers of Spain, Queen Isabella (1451–1504) and King Ferdinand (1452–1516). He had offered the monarchs a scheme to bypass the dangerous land crossing needed to reach India and Asia by sailing west across the ocean to the other side of the world.

A middle-aged man, the sailor rode quietly on. What other monarchs could he persuade to fund his trip to India using a new route rather than sailing around Africa? How many other sovereigns could he visit in Europe? From behind him, a man came galloping and calling out his name. The messenger told the sailor that the court, hitherto strapped for cash, had found a way to finance his venture and that the king and queen were now willing to reconsider his proposal (Morison, 136).

As the sailor rode back to Granada, he was setting off on the first leg of a journey that would change the face of the world and that would make the surname Columbus a household word.

The Admiral with Many Names:
Colón, Colombo, Columbus

In the English-speaking world, the "admiral of the ocean-sea" is known as Christopher Columbus. But he was born Cristoforo Colombo Fontanarossa in the republic of Genoa—now in Italy—in 1451. His father was a craftsman who dabbled in real estate and politics. His mother was the daughter of a successful weaver. Genoa was an active port city and a commercial link between Europe and Asia, where tradesmen purchased spices and silk to be sold at higher prices in Europe. Young Colombo felt an attraction for sailing and exploring and as a teenager signed on for several short trips in the Mediterranean. At the age of 20 he embarked on a long voyage to the Aegean Sea in which he augmented his expertise in navigating, the use of ocean currents, and charting the stars. Then in 1476, while on another voyage, his ship was sunk by pirates off the coast of Portugal. Using an oar as a life preserver, Colombo reached the shore.

At the time, the Portuguese ruled the seas. During the 1400s, Portugal colonized Madeira and the Azores in the Atlantic, sailed along Africa's coastline, conquered the city of Ceuta in Africa, and ventured as far inland in Africa as Sierra Leone. The most enthusiastic supporter of these expeditions was a member of the royal family, Prince Henry the Navigator (1394–1460). Prince Henry encouraged his father, King John (1357–1433), and his brother, King Duarte (1391–1438), to expand Portugal's territories and to seek out trade routes through the Sahara. Henry surrounded himself with cartographers and geographers; his legacy was the emergence of Portugal as the center of geographic knowledge in Europe.

In Portugal, Columbus was exposed to new theories of navigation that included observations of the Sun to determine latitude and the use of tides for propulsion, and he associated with learned individuals who did not believe Earth to be flat, as some of the less educated did (scholar Jeffrey Burton Russell, in *Inventing the Flat Earth: Columbus and Modern Historians* [1991], maintains that Europeans familiar with navigation, regardless of educational background, knew that Earth was a globe, and the concept that Columbus had to convince people that Earth was not flat is an erroneous myth). He also began to consider the notion of reaching India and Japan by sailing west. In this he was probably influenced by the theories of Italian geographer and mathematician Paolo dal Pozzo Toscanelli (1397–1482), with whom Columbus corresponded, according to historian

Likeness of Christopher Columbus, though no one knows precisely what he looked like

Queen Isabella and her husband, King Ferdinand, turned their attention to Columbus after their victory over the Muslims in Granada. (From *The Christian Recovery of Spain,* by Henry Edward Watts, New York: G.P. Putnam's Sons, 1894. p. 1,280)

Samuel Eliot Morison (Morison, 13–15). Toscanelli believed that an island, Antilla or Antilia, lay between Europe and Asia and could serve as a way station en route to India and Japan.

In 1479, Columbus married a woman of noble descent with connections to the Portuguese royal court. In 1484, he obtained an audience with King John II, but the king declined to offer Columbus his patronage; he was more interested in reaching India by circumnavigating Africa than in exploring other routes. The royal documents of that period called the sailor by the name Christovao Colom, a Portuguese translation of the Italian original.

When Columbus was widowed in 1485, he and his son Diego moved to Spain. At a monastery, Columbus befriended a Franciscan monk who took an interest in his plans to reach India and introduced him to aristocrats with contacts at the Spanish court. In 1486, the Genoese sailor, now using the name of Cristóbal Colón, was granted an audience with Queen Isabella and King Ferdinand. Queen Isabella, wishing to rival

Portugal's dominance of the sea, displayed an interest in Columbus's plans, but it was not the right time to finance an expedition. The king and queen were dealing with the more pressing matter of finishing the *reconquista,* the reconquest, of Spain and were on the verge of driving the Moors from the Iberian Peninsula.

Finally, in January 1492, the king and queen succeeded in taking back control of Spain from the Muslim rulers. Queen Isabella and King Ferdinand were now ready to consider imperial growth beyond the peninsula. Meeting with Columbus and responding to his promise of gold from India and Japan and untold numbers of new converts to the Catholic faith, Queen Isabella and King Ferdinand provided the sailor with three caravels for the first voyage.

Three Ships Sailing the Ocean Blue

Over a period of eight years, Columbus made four voyages. The first and the third are the most famous. The first voyage began in 1492. On September 6, Columbus and a crew of 100 men left the Canary Islands, a Spanish possession off the west coast of Africa. Legends lend color to the adventure. One story portrays the crew as recently released or

Caravels were lightweight ships, easy to maneuver with two or three masts.

The Four Voyages of Christopher Columbus		
Voyage	Dates	Places Reached
First	1492–1493	San Salvador, the Bahamas, Cuba, Hispaniola
Second	1493–1496	Dominica, Hispaniola, Guadeloupe, Antigua, Puerto Rico, Cuba, Jamaica, Nevis, St. Kitts, St. Croix, Virgin Islands
Third	1498–1500	St. Vincent, Grenada, Trinidad, Margarita, Venezuela, Tobago, Hispaniola
Fourth	1502–1504	St. Lucia, Martinique, Honduras, Nicaragua, Costa Rica, Panama, Jamaica

Bedini, Silvio, ed. *The Christopher Columbus Encyclopedia.* New York: Simon & Schuster, 1992, pp. 693–728.

pardoned convicts terrified of falling off the edge of the world, but a seasoned sailor like Columbus would have been unlikely to accept criminals as crew members. It is probable that he signed on only professionals. Similarly, the sailors most likely did not fear falling into an abyss; rather, they would have been concerned that there would be no east wind to help them return to Spain.

It took Columbus 36 days to travel 2,400 nautical miles and reach the Caribbean, landing on either the island of Samana Cay or Watling's Island on October 12, 1492. On this voyage, he reached the Bahamas, Cuba, and Hispaniola. In Cuba, while venturing inland toward the center of the island, Columbus saw Tainos smoking cigars, the very first time Europeans witnessed the use of tobacco. Toward the end of the journey, Columbus established a fort near Cap-Haïtien in what is Haiti today and left 40 men there to search for gold. On January 16, 1493, the Genoese sailor headed back to Spain.

It was a triumphant return. Welcoming him back as a hero, Queen Isabella and King Ferdinand awarded Columbus the title of Admiral of the Ocean Sea, made him viceroy of the new lands, and permitted him to sit in their presence, a rare boon. After the celebrations, the monarchs ordered Columbus to proceed with preparations for a second voyage.

With a fleet of 17 ships and 1,000 men, the admiral set sail in September 1493. On this voyage, Columbus reached Dominica, Guadeloupe, Antigua, Nevis, St. Kitts, St. Croix, the Virgin Islands, and Puerto Rico and revisited Cuba. Disembarking in Hispaniola, he was met by an unexpected sight: The fort was in ruins, destroyed by the Tainos, and

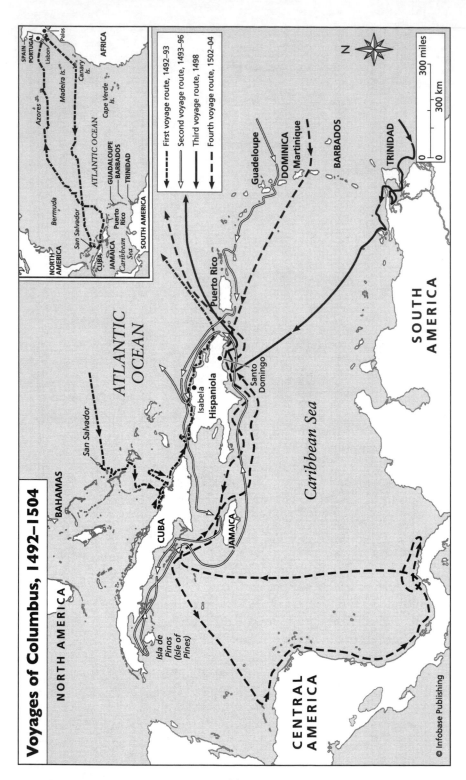

Voyages of Columbus, 1492–1504

NORTH AMERICA

BAHAMAS

San Salvador

ATLANTIC OCEAN

CUBA

Isla de Pinos
(Isle of Pines)

Isabela

Hispaniola

JAMAICA

Santo
Domingo

Puerto Rico

Caribbean Sea

CENTRAL
AMERICA

SOUTH
AMERICA

Guadeloupe

DOMINICA

Martinique

BARBADOS

TRINIDAD

First voyage route, 1492–93
Second voyage route, 1493–96
Third voyage route, 1498
Fourth voyage route, 1502–04

N

300 miles

300 km

SPAIN
PORTUGAL
Lisbon
Palos

AFRICA

Azores

Madeira Is.

Canary Is.

Cape Verde Is.

ATLANTIC OCEAN

Bermuda

San Salvador

NORTH
AMERICA

CUBA

JAMAICA

Puerto
Rico

Caribbean
Sea

GUADALOUPE
BARBADOS
TRINIDAD

SOUTH AMERICA

© Infobase Publishing

the 40 men he had settled there were dead. Leaving Hispaniola and proceeding north, Columbus found an island that he named Isabela. He also reached Jamaica on this voyage. In 1496, he returned to Spain.

Columbus set off on his third voyage on May 30, 1498. He landed on Trinidad, off the coast of mainland South America. He explored part of what is now Venezuela and sighted the islands of Tobago and Grenada. He sailed back to Hispaniola in August. This trip, however, had unfortunate consequences for Columbus.

In Hispaniola, a group of Spanish settlers led by Francisco Roldán rebelled against Columbus's rule, opposing his desire to restrict the mining of gold for personal gain and the exploitation of the Tainos for personal use rather than for the Crown. In addition, these disgruntled aristocrats felt that Columbus had forced them to perform manual labor; they also accused him of keeping some of the gold for himself. Though Columbus yielded to some of the requests made by Roldán and his followers, allowing them to use the Tainos as they wished, the accusations nevertheless reached the Spanish monarchs, who decided to send an official representative to investigate, a request that ironically originated with Columbus, who had asked Queen Isabella to send a judge to help him administer the colony.

In August 1500, the royal representative, Francisco Bobadilla (?–1502), arrived in Hispaniola, where a second rebellion had just been crushed by Columbus. Upon entering the harbor, Bobabilla saw seven Spanish rebels hanging on a gallows, a sight that greatly disturbed him. Since Columbus was in the countryside, tracking down rebels, Bobadilla interviewed only rebels and enemies of the admiral. Bobadilla accepted their grievances as true and in October decided to put Columbus in chains and dispatch him to Spain, not as a hero but as a prisoner. In Spain, the sorry spectacle Columbus made dragging chains about him moved the monarchs to dismiss the charges. The king and queen forgave Columbus for his errors and granted him permission for a fourth voyage, though they did not allow him to resume administrative duties of the islands.

Many Spanish scholars consider that Columbus's treatment was severe and unjust, but for many Caribbean scholars and writers, the admiral's fate was poetic justice. (For instance, in the novel *Annie John*, author Jamaica Kincaid depicts her heroine celebrating Columbus's imprisonment.) To them, Columbus was the destroyer of the Caribbean paradise and the initiator of the capitalist oppression that led to the slavery of Tainos, Caribs, and Africans.

In 1502 Columbus made his fourth and final voyage to the Caribbean. He landed in Martinique, sailed along the coast of Central America and

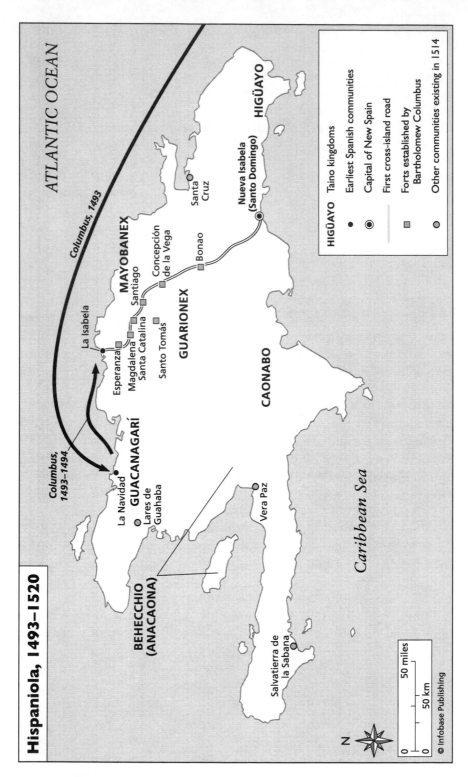

Hispaniola, 1493–1520

ATLANTIC OCEAN

Columbus, 1493

Columbus, 1493–1494

Caribbean Sea

HIGÜAYO

Santa Cruz

Nueva Isabela (Santo Domingo)

MAYOBANEX

Santiago

Concepción de la Vega

Bonao

La Isabela

Esperanza

Magdalena

Santa Catalina

Santo Tomás

GUARIONEX

CAONABO

La Navidad

GUACANAGARÍ

Lares de Guahaba

Vera Paz

BEHECCHIO (ANACAONA)

Salvatierra de la Sabana

HIGÜAYO Taíno kingdoms

● Earliest Spanish communities

◉ Capital of New Spain

— First cross-island road

▪ Forts established by Bartholomew Columbus

● Other communities existing in 1514

50 miles

50 km

N

0

0

© Infobase Publishing

the northern coast of South America, and spent some time in Jamaica before returning to Spain in November 1504. Columbus died two years later in Valladolid, Spain. It is unknown whether Columbus ever realized the significance of his explorations, which led to the opening of the New World rather than a passage to the Far East.

The First Contact between Europeans and Caribbeans

The Europeans were given to pageantry, and their entry into the Caribbean was no exception. How Columbus approached the first island was the pattern followed by other explorers.

In October 1492, the admiral climbed onto a boat, and his officers rowed ashore. Carrying a royal standard, Columbus dropped to his knees when he reached the shore. After thanking God, he proclaimed the island for the Spanish monarchs and then gave the island a name. Cuba became Juana, Quisqueya became Hispaniola, Borinquén became San Juan Bautista, and so on. This ritual of possession was repeated on each new island Columbus approached, and it was always conducted without the participation of the inhabitants.

In giving the islands names in a European language and in assuming that the islands were nameless to begin with, the admiral adopted a position of power—the master over the nameless subject. This became a model used by other Spanish explorers such as Hernán Cortés, and in the next two centuries by explorers from other European powers such as Great Britain and France. The ritual transformed the unwilling Tainos and other indigenous people in the Americas into subjects of the Spanish monarchs. Once in possession of the Caribbean, the Spanish saw themselves as having the right to rule over their newly found subjects as they wished. Though the initial desire might have been to convert the Tainos and Caribs to the Catholic faith, the need to search for gold

Cover of replica of book used by friars to convert indigenous people to Catholicism (An Otomí Catechism, Princeton University Library, 1968)

sidetracked the religious designs, and the original inhabitants of the Caribbean were soon forced into hard labor.

Disease, Slavery, Annihilation

The conquest of the Caribbean began in earnest in 1502, when Queen Isabella dispatched the first Spanish governor to the New World. The first island to be colonized was Hispaniola, between 1502 and 1509. The other large islands were occupied relatively quickly: Puerto Rico in 1508, Jamaica in 1509, and Cuba in 1511. The colonizers were initially sailors and soldiers, but as settlements were established, artisans, farmers, and unskilled laborers were included, with about 3,000 a year migrating to the New World during the first half of the 16th century. These men came primarily from the provinces of Andalucia and Extramadura, either as bachelors or without their wives; they created unions with Taino women—later on with African slaves—whether or not the women consented. Ten years into the colonization, women from Spain began to arrive at a ratio of one for every three men.

There was a pattern to colonization: swift progress through the territories; conversion of the indigenous people to the Catholic faith, as mandated by Queen Isabella; harsh elimination of native insurrection-

Tainos were forced by the Spanish to mine gold from riverbanks in the Caribbean in exchange for religious training. The training, however, was not forthcoming. (North Wind Archives)

ists; and forced labor for the Tainos and Caribs. The aim of the labor was the procurement of gold and silver for the monarchs, an almost fanatic search first encouraged by Columbus, who was convinced that the islands were rich in silver and gold by early findings in Hispaniola of gold nuggets on the Ozama River (at the entrance of present day Santo Domingo). The Spanish supervised the mining, while the work was done by the Tainos. When the Tainos began to fall ill and die in large numbers, the Spanish simply abducted more Tainos from other Caribbean islands. The captured Tainos were taken to Cuba, Hispaniola, Jamaica, and Puerto Rico and put to work there.

By the 1520s, the Tainos were disappearing. Dominican historian Juan de Jesús Domínguez sums up the reasons for their disappearance: "The genocide of defenseless [Taino] women, children, and the elderly. Starvation and disease caused by malnutrition . . . the forced labor in the building of cities and fortresses, agriculture, and digging for gold in rivers and mines. Suicide, voluntary abortions to escape the Spanish, and diseases brought from Spain, the most noticeable small pox [sic]" (Domínguez, 13).

Taino Martyrs and Heroes

Upon realizing Spanish intentions, the Tainos and the Caribs rebelled, beginning with the destruction of Fort Navidad in Hispaniola in 1493. Several leaders emerged: the princess Anacaona, the chief Hatuey, and the rebel leader Enriquillo.

In 1503 a Taino princess named Anacaona reigned in the western region of Hispaniola, where she sought shelter after her husband was kidnapped by Columbus in 1492 and perished en route to Spain. Eager to end Anacaona's rule, Spanish governor Nicolás de Ovando tricked her into meeting him in September 1503. The princess arranged a banquet to welcome her guests, but Ovando ambushed her unarmed warriors and captured the princess. As a display of Spanish power, Ovando sentenced the princess to death by public hanging.

Hatuey, acclaimed by the Dominican Republic, admired in Cuba, and honored by Haitians, became a symbol of liberty in the fight against Spanish oppression. The chief of a region in Hispaniola called Guahabá, Hatuey fought unsuccessfully against the Spanish. Sometime around 1510, he and 400 men, women, and children relocated to the island of Cuba, where they hoped to find peace. In 1511, when Spanish soldiers and settlers under the leadership of Diego Velásquez de Cuéllar (1461–1524) arrived in Cuba, Hatuey and his men attacked the invaders. The cacique employed guerrilla tactics, attacking small numbers of Spanish soldiers and then hiding in the hills. For a few months, Hatuey kept the Spanish at bay; the invaders were unable to leave the fort they had built. In 1512, however, Velásquez captured Hatuey and sentenced him to death by being burned alive.

When Hatuey was tied to the post, a priest offered him Communion and acceptance of Christ so that he might, as the priest believed, go to heaven. Hatuey responded, "Do white men go to heaven as well?" "Yes" the priest replied, "provided they're good." "Then, I do not wish to go to heaven," said Hatuey. Shortly thereafter he was burned at the stake (*Encyclopedia of Cuba*, 87).

More successful was the Taino chief Enriquillo, who fought against the conquistadores for 13 years on the island of Hispaniola. In 1533, he was granted a pardon as part of a truce engineered by Emperor Charles V (King Charles I of Spain; 1500–58). However, although Enriquillo survived and inflicted losses on the Spanish, he could not alter the path to extinction upon which the Spanish led his people and culture.

The 16th Century: Spain Rules

By sailing into the harbors of the New World, Spain was entering into a new arena of global power. Prior to 1492, the empires that emerged in Europe and Asia were ruled from a central authority that was relatively close by. To be sure, there were natural obstacles such as mountains and rivers, but no ocean separated the rulers from the ruled until Spain appropriated the New World.

It was an appropriation achieved with unprecedented speed. In 1513, 11 years after Columbus reached the Caribbean, the Spanish crossed the isthmus of Panama and reached the Pacific Ocean while Juan Ponce de León was claiming Florida for Spain. In the years 1519–21, Cortés subjugated the Aztec Empire in Mexico, and by 1526, Spanish sailors were exploring latter-day South Carolina and Georgia. From 1528 to 1536 Cabeza de Vaca, a survivor of a shipwreck off Tampa, walked from Florida to Texas, traveling naked and barefoot. Between 1532 and 1536, Pizarro conquered the Incas, took over Cuzco, and founded the city of Lima. In 1536, Buenos Aires, Argentina, was founded, followed by the establishment of Bogotá, Colombia, two years later. In 1548, La Paz was founded in what would become Bolivia.

Characteristics of the Occupation of the Caribbean

Francisco Bobadilla, who sent Columbus back to Spain in chains, took over the administration of Hispaniola until he was relieved in 1502 by

Nicolás de Ovando (1540–1618), the first actual governor assigned to the Caribbean. A good administrator who pacified the rebellious Spanish settlers, Ovando efficiently and effectively managed the mining of gold in the new colonies, shipping to Spain the equivalent of $30 million in gold during his seven-year tenure. Though he began the construction of cities and organized food production to make Hispaniola self-sufficient, Ovando was first and foremost a conquistador, a soldier trained to use the sword, display courage in the face of danger, and show no mercy to captives. These were military traits that made the Spanish successful during the reconquest of Iberia in 1492 and were highly esteemed by the Spanish king and queen. For Ovando, pacification of the Tainos did not mean the use of diplomacy, but the elimination of a perceived enemy.

From 1502 to 1504, the 2,500 soldiers and settlers who traveled to Hispaniola with Ovando conducted at least three major campaigns that resulted in the virtual destruction of Taino civilization on that island. The tactics used included outright lying and treachery, as demonstrated in Ovando's treatment of the Taino princess Anacaona.

Ovando's brutal tactics were emulated by other conquistadores. Friar Bartolomé de Las Casas gave this description of the Spanish massacre of a Taino village:

> When the Spaniards arrived at the village and found the Indians at peace in their houses, they did not fail to injure and scandalize them. Not content with that the Indians freely gave, they took their wretched subsistence from them, and some, going further, chased after their wives and daughters, for this and always has been the Spaniards' common custom in these Indies....A Spaniard, in whom the devil is thought to have clothed himself, suddenly drew his sword. Then the whole hundred drew theirs and began to rip open the bellies, to cut and kill those lambs men, women, children, and old folk (de Las Casas, 25).

In Jamaica, Juan de Esquivel employed similar tactics in 1509, and Juan Ponce de León followed suit in Puerto Rico in 1511. In one campaign, Ponce de León led 125 men on a forced march across a mountain range and into a village, which he attacked at night. Of the 6,000 Tainos reportedly sleeping there, more than 200 were slain, while the Spanish suffered no casualties (B. Williams, 24).

The characteristics of the conquistadores were soon clear to the Tainos: audacious, ruthless, and violent. Their professed interest in converting them to Christianity was overshadowed by their gold lust and their need for a labor force. They were capable of virtually any

Spanish conquistador aiming a harquebus, late 1500s (North Wind Archives)

atrocity if it furthered their aims. To deal with the invaders, the Tainos had limited choices: They could fight or avoid the invaders by escaping into the mountains. There was a third choice, death by mass suicide or infanticide, an option that some chose rather than live in the new world that the Spanish were creating.

The Settlement of Cuba, Hispaniola, and Puerto Rico

As the Tainos were conquered and enslaved, the conquistadores proceeded with the settlement of the Caribbean. Some of the cities founded in what would become the island of Puerto Rico included Puerto Rico, Santiago, and San Germán. In 1521, the town of Puerto Rico became known as San Juan, and the island itself became known as Puerto Rico. The Spanish population, however, remained in the low hundreds, and their dwellings were simple wooden structures.

THE CONQUEST OF MEXICO BEGAN IN CUBA

The Caribbean served as a naval base from which to launch expeditions to the Americas. In this passage Bernal Díaz del Castillo, a participant in the conquest of Mexico, recalls preparations in Cuba and departure from that island:

> When the Governor [of Cuba] Diego Velásquez understood how rich were these newly discovered lands, he ordered another fleet, much larger than the former one to be sent off, and he had already collected in the Port of Santiago, where he resided, ten ships.... He had them furnished with provisions, consisting of Cassava bread and salt pork. These provisions were only to last until we arrived at Havana, for it was at that port we were to take in our stores....
>
> ... As soon as Hernando Cortés had been appointed General he began to search for all sorts of arms, guns, powder and crossbows, and every kind of warlike stores which he could get together, and all sort of articles to be used for barter, and other things necessary for the expedition ... whence we set out with the fleet more than three hundred and fifty soldiers in number.... The next day ... after having heard Mass we went to our ships and [Velásquez and Cortés] embraced with many fair speeches one to the other until we set sail.

Díaz del Castillo, Bernal. *The Discovery and Conquest of Mexico*. Translated by A. P. Maudslay. New York: Noonday Press, 1956.

During the same period, however, Spanish conquistadores were also making inroads on the mainland of Mexico and South America. There they found riches greater than anything they had seen in the islands of the Caribbean. In Mexico, Hernán Cortés (1485–1547) saw temples and mansions that dwarfed castles in Spain and canals and bridges that rivaled Venice. In Peru, Francisco Pizarro (1475–1541) described how an Inca prince, bargaining for his survival, filled a large room with gold statues. The gold beckoned the Spanish settlers with the possibility of enormous wealth and a better life than in the Caribbean. A common lament arose: "Dios me lleve a Perú!" (God take me to Peru).

But if the lack of wealth on the islands dissuaded settlers and invited neglect, the very riches from the conquered Aztec and Inca Empires forced the Spanish rulers to keep the islands, if for nothing else than as rest stops for sailors and soldiers. Furthermore, the treasures from South America piqued the desire of European monarchs, who soon began to attack ships transporting the loot to Spain. Therefore, a military presence in the Caribbean was crucial.

Spain passed strict laws prohibiting the emigration of colonists to Mexico, Central America, and South America. Despite this, waves of colonists left the Caribbean. Many of the islands became colonial backwaters, and little attention was paid to developing the economies of the Caribbean. It would be many decades before European powers dedicated themselves seriously to agriculture as a means of economic viability.

In the interim, for most of the 16th and early 17th centuries, the Spanish built military fortifications on the islands to safeguard the lucrative gold and silver trade. The Spanish built a series of *morros,* or forts, in the major Caribbean seaports. The fortified seaports included Havana, San Juan, Santo Domingo, Port of Spain, and even Saint Augustine in northern Florida. These seaports became havens for Spanish merchant ships seeking safety from competing European powers or pirates. For many years, the economies of these cities centered

Colonial city, Santo Domingo, first European city in the Caribbean (Matos Family Archives)

on military investment and the periodic caravans from the American mainland to Spain.

The Establishment of the *Encomiendas*

The decision to maintain the islands meant that the colonies had to be self-supporting and still produce something of an income for the Spanish monarchs. If gold was not available, agricultural products could prove of value to Spain as an export to other European nations. What better way to get workers than through the *encomienda* system? The *encomienda* system was used during the reconquest of Spain from the Muslims. It was introduced in Hispaniola by Columbus in 1499 and institutionalized by Governor Nicolás de Ovando in 1503. Under the *encomienda* system, settlers, known as *encomenderos,* were assigned plots of land and Taino laborers who were forced to mine riverbanks for gold and cultivate the fields to produce food. An *encomendero* could have no more than 300 Tainos, whom he employed as labor gangs assigned to mining, farming, and taking care of cattle. Through the *encomiendas,* "indigenous people were 'entrusted' . . . to each conqueror, who had the responsibility of Christianizing them and the privilege of making them work for him. . . . Conquerors who received *encomiendas* became much like European nobles, able to live from the labor of serflike farmers who delivered part of their crops as regular tribute" (Chasteen, 53). In return for their labor, the indigenous people were meant to be instructed in Catholicism and Spanish culture and to receive military protection. However, very few *encomenderos* kept up their part of the bargain.

The system was not supported by all Spaniards in the colonies. In 1511 a Dominican friar, Antonio de Montesinos (?–1545), protested the system from the pulpit. In 1512 King Ferdinand (1452–1516), who wanted to maintain the *encomiendas* but also wished to help the Tainos, enacted laws to improve the lot of the laborers. The laws stipulated that Tainos were to work only nine months out of the year and that women were excused from work during the ninth month of pregnancy. They also mandated that the sons of chieftains were to be educated.

These laws, however, were essentially ignored, and most *encomenderos* continued to do little for their charges. Instead, they abused the Tainos; when they protested, they were punished. Although there was no claim of ownership, the *encomienda* system was a form of slavery.

The *encomienda* system decimated the Taino and Carib populations; in Hispaniola alone the population dropped from nearly 300,000 Tainos in 1492 to less than 50,000 in 1510. Friar Bartolomé de Las

FRIAR BARTOLOMÉ DE LAS CASAS: TOO LATE THE SAVIOR

A handful of friars in the Caribbean and in Spain protested the harsh treatment received by the natives. Friar Bartolomé de Las Casas became the most vocal and best known, remembered in history as the "defender of the Indians." His best-known work, *Brevísima relación de la destrucción de las Indias* (*Short Account of the Destruction of the Indies*, 1552), was one of the earliest books that attempted to bring about social justice in the Caribbean.

Las Casas (1474–1566) was the first priest ordained in the Americas. The descendant of Jews and the son of a man who took part in Columbus's second journey to the Caribbean in 1494, Las Casas sailed in 1502 for Hispaniola, participating in the suppression of several Taino uprisings. For his effort, he was awarded an *encomienda*.

Ordained a priest in 1510, three years later Las Casas went to Cuba to participate in the conquest of that island, but the abuses he witnessed and the poverty and servitude subjected upon the Tainos made him remorseful of his participation in the conquest. Deciding to dedicate his life to protect the indigenous population, he returned his *encomienda* to Cuba's governor and returned to Hispaniola. From that island, he traveled to Spain, where he pleaded for the Tainos before the royal court.

In 1515 the Spanish king named him "The Protector of the Indians." Las Casas recommended the end of the *encomienda* system, the release of all Tainos from servitude, and the restoration of the lands to the Tainos. He also suggested that, to relieve the natives from hard labor, white and black laborers should be exported to the Caribbean, especially Africans. Thus, inadvertently, Las Casas helped bring about the replacement of one evil with another. Later on, Las Casas's writings were used by other European writers to attack Spanish colonization of the Americas. They used them as a justification to challenge Spanish dominance.

Casas took up the Taino cause and persuaded the Spanish Crown to intercede. In 1542, the New Laws modified the system of *encomiendas*. "Encomiendas were to continue to be inheritable, though only for a limited number of generations; the emphasis now was on Indian tribute rather than labor services; and, in fact, the institution slowly ceased to be of importance" (Collier, 109).

In 1550, the *encomienda* system was officially abolished in the Caribbean, but by that time there were few Tainos left. The world of the Tainos was gone. The Spaniards started to contemplate the importation of a new labor force to make up for their loss—slaves from Africa.

The Keys to the Americas: Havana and Santo Domingo

Despite the disappointment the Spanish felt upon realizing that the hills and rivers of the Caribbean contained very little gold, in the early 1500s cities began to emerge. Santo Domingo, in Hispaniola, was the first. The wooden structures of the town that originally bore this name were destroyed by a hurricane in 1502. Governor Ovando ordered the construction of a new city on the banks of the Ozama River, built of bricks and stones and designed to withstand strong winds. The city was granted a royal charter in 1508, making Santo Domingo the first European-chartered city in the New World. An administrative center, Santo Domingo served as a trading post and was the site of the first cathedral in the Americas, the Basílica Menor de Santa María.

Diego Columbus's house built 1510–11 when Santo Domingo was the main capital of the Caribbean. Diego was Christopher Columbus's son and a colonial administrator. (Matos Family Archives)

By the 1520s the city was a launching pad for colonial expansion, dispatching explorers to Mexico and to Florida and South Carolina in what is now the United States. It was also a hub of development where Spanish planters and merchants planned economic options for Hispaniola, working to keep Santo Domingo a viable option for colonization and trade, despite the greater appeal of the mainland.

In Cuba, the city of Havana was first established in the swamps of southwestern Cuba. In 1519, it was transferred to the north of the island. Its harbor provided protection from such perils as hurricanes and, later, pirates; its taverns and inns welcomed the Spanish soldiers and sailors who arrived twice a year with the Spanish fleet that carried gold to Spain and returned with supplies for the colonies.

The fleets were not the only visitors to Havana. Other Spanish merchants traveling alone in the Caribbean sought the protection of the harbor and eventual union with the fleet for the return to Spain. With these merchants came precious metals and jewelry, leather, spices, dyes, and corn. In return, the merchants traded or purchased water, food, and supplies for the ocean voyage. Ships and boats needed repair, encouraging Cubans to pursue this craft and eventually making shipbuilding a major industry in Cuba.

In 1583, Havana was officially recognized as the capital of Cuba. Its proximity to Mexico helped shift the center of trade and troop movement from Santo Domingo to Havana. This led to a surge in the construction of fortresses and mansions, which in turn attracted artisans, craftsmen, and businesses in the service of the military, such as repair shops for weapons, tailors, and taverns. By the end of the century the Spanish Crown had dubbed Havana the "key of the New World." The population of Havana included 13,000 of the total of 20,000 inhabitants of the island (P. Foner, 34).

The 16th century marked the height of Spanish supremacy in the Americas. Portuguese colonization of Brazil was slow and sporadic. The other European powers gradually formulated strategies to challenge Spanish dominance, first indirectly, then more forcefully and systematically. The Caribbean became a focal point for European competition in the Americas.

3

EUROPEAN CHALLENGES
TO SPANISH RULE
(1500–1850)

When Columbus returned with news of his landfall in the Caribbean in 1492, Spain was transformed from a peninsular nation to a global power, claiming at once ownership of all the new territories. Portugal, until then the reigning sea power and the leader in oceanic exploration, challenged Spanish claims. The dispute was settled by Pope Alexander VI (1431–1503) with the papal bull *Inter caetera* ("Among other [works]") of 1493, formalized in the Treaty of Tordesillas in 1494. This agreement drew an imaginary line 100 leagues west of Cape Verde Island, off the coast of Africa. To the west of this line, any new lands discovered would belong to Spain. To the east, new lands would belong to Portugal. The line was adjusted later on to include portions of Brazil, which Portugal claimed.

The artificial boundary was intended to prevent the rest of Europe from exploring and exploiting the riches of the Caribbean and the Americas. The line created a border between Europe and the New World. When warring European countries agreed to a truce, they often considered that the truce did not apply to the lands "beyond the line," thus leaving them open for conflict and hostilities. That is to say, if Spain and France agreed to a truce in Europe, it was still acceptable to engage in combat beyond the line—in the Americas. The result was that the Caribbean became a war zone for European nations fighting each other, especially fighting against Spain, and for sea robbers—the colorful pirates, corsairs, buccaneers, and privateers of whom legends and novels are made—to prosper and grow rich from their plunder.

Europe's Reaction to Spanish Supremacy

By the 1590s, the islands that attracted Spain's colonial efforts were Cuba, Hispaniola, Jamaica, and Puerto Rico, with a little fewer than 90,000 colonizers spread out unevenly throughout the region. Over time, sea traffic increased dramatically as Spanish ships docked in the Caribbean on the way to and from Mexico and Peru. With the ships, there was always a naval presence that could number anywhere from the hundreds to the thousands.

The British were envious of the activities in the Caribbean, longing to be participants in the colonization and economic exploitation. Thus less than 100 years after Columbus sighted the Caribbean, a British geographer named Richard Hakluyt (1522/3–1616) used his pen to express the sentiments of his countrymen regarding Spanish possession of the New World and to encourage Great Britain to disregard the papal bull of 1493. Hakluyt claimed that the bull reflected the pope's bias, since the pope was of Spanish origin, and that, furthermore, the Spanish "executed most outrageous . . . cruelties in all the West Indies" (Hakluyt, 34). Regardless of Hakluyt's concerns with Spanish abuse of the indigenous populations and his call for Protestant teachings in the New World to combat Catholic indoctrination, the real lure was the wealth of the region and the potential treasure for England.

For most of the 16th century, the European powers were not ready to pose direct challenges to Spanish rule. One deterrent was the knowledge of Spanish might and their proven efficiency and cruelty in the art of conquest. After all, two conquistadores, Hernán Cortés (1485–1547) in Mexico and Francisco Pizarro (1478–1541) in Peru, had annihilated the Aztec and Inca Empires with just several hundred men. And if any doubted Spain's zealousness at keeping its domains untouched by other Europeans, there was a 1564 massacre in Florida in which 200 Frenchmen were executed by the Spanish.

This was a lesson that kept France focused on the exploration of Canada rather than challenging Spanish hegemony farther south. As for Britain, King Henry VIII (1491–1547), despite the establishment of a Protestant state in England, maintained a good relationship with Spain. Henry's first wife, Catherine of Aragon, was the daughter of King Ferdinand of Spain. The strategy employed by the English and French, then, was to avoid an open contest and encourage instead, excursions conducted by individuals or mercantile companies acting for personal or corporate gains and not officially for national or royal objectives.

Beach inlet and Matanzas River, south of St. Augustine, site of the Huguenot massacre of 1564 that established Spanish supremacy in Florida for nearly three centuries (Photo by Gabriela E. Figueredo)

Smuggling

One area of incursion was smuggling. Spain, by virtue of having financed the exploration of the region, saw itself as the sole proprietor of the islands. In 1503, the government established the Casa de Contratación (House of Contracts) to oversee all mercantile transactions in the New World. Spain did not allow the colonies to trade with any other nation. Caribbean settlers were forced to buy goods from Spain, paying prices set by Spain. They also paid taxes and tariffs on each purchase. Similar conditions applied when goods from the Caribbean were sold to Spain. As a result, transactions for the colonists were far more costly than for those living in Spain. These requirements contributed to a rise in smuggling in the Caribbean.

Many smugglers were merchants who were willing to break Spain's trading laws to make a profit. Because the Spanish fleet could not police all the waters of the Caribbean, it was easy for these merchants to buy and sell goods among the colonies. Since the smugglers did not pay taxes or tariffs, they sold goods at a better price to the colonists and often offered a better price for Caribbean goods such as tobacco. In 1611 alone, 200,000 pounds of tobacco leaves from the Caribbean reached England and France, while only 6,000 taxable pounds passed through the Spanish port of Seville (P. Wood, 104).

To facilitate their enterprise, some smugglers scouted for locations where they could live and plant such products as tobacco. It was with that objective that smugglers helped settle some of the islands of the Lesser Antilles, attracting other smugglers as well as Dutch, English, and French planters. In 1629 Spain responded to the establishment of non-Spanish settlements and attacked St. Kitts, destroying dwellings and crops and shipping 700 prisoners to Europe. It was an act that reaffirmed and energized hatred of the Spanish Empire.

Enter the Pirates

Another consequence of the wealth of the Caribbean and Spain's monopoly on the region was an upsurge in piracy, as roving sea robbers sought to help themselves to some of the wealth being shipped from the Americas to Spain. The peak period of piracy in the Caribbean was from 1692 to 1725, an era referred to as the "golden age of piracy." From this era emerged the romantic notions of pirates seen in the novels of Rafael Sabatini (1875–1950), Emilio Salgari (1862–1911), and Robert Louis Stevenson (1850–94) and later depicted in the films of Errol Flynn (1909–59) and, more recently, Johnny Depp (1963–). This romantic image of pirates is more common in the United States and the United Kingdom, since pirates often covertly promoted English foreign policy aims while their victims were typically Spanish. In reality, pirates were far-from-romantic figures; they were often outlaws who in time of war served whichever nation paid for their service. In times of peace, pirates raided randomly and opportunistically, motivated by the promise of a hefty purse. Pirates risked their lives for wealth, a wealth they often foolishly spent when on land. They were known for eating to the point of sickness and drinking themselves into stupor. When they were not raiding, they were quarrelsome with each other.

There were essentially two types of pirates: privateers and buccaneers. The earliest buccaneers were bands of hunters who settled in remote areas in Hispaniola. Many of them originally came from Europe as indentured servants. Some later ran away from abusive masters. Others were unwilling to return to Europe after their contracts expired. For many reasons, they sought freedom in the wilds of the island. The buccaneers learned survival skills from the indigenous peoples, including a process for preserving meat using a wooden frame known in French as a *boucan*. From this meat, which was a mainstay of their diet, came the name *buccaneers*. In the mid-1630s, some buccaneers took to the sea.

Privateers were hired hands in the service of a nation at war with another; their orders were to attack enemy ships. All the European powers used privateers, including Spain. Privateers could keep a percentage of the plunder they took, while the bulk of the riches was intended for the patron's coffers. One advantage of using privateers was that their actions were taken on their own initiative. This allowed monarchs to claim no official knowledge of the privateers' acts in the Caribbean Sea. (Queen Elizabeth I [1533–1603] was notorious for personally funding privateers.) Another advantage was that using privateers was economical and practical. Since the privateer already owned a ship or the resources to obtain one, the sponsoring nation was freed of the need to use its own navy to harass enemy ships.

Piracy at Sea

Whatever their origin, both types of pirates were drawn to the ships of the Spanish fleet. They studied the routes followed by the ships bound for Spain, laden with gold and silver from the Americas. Initially, homebound trips were made by solitary Spanish merchant ships. After 1523, when French pirates seized a vessel loaded with gold, Spain revised its sailing policies and developed a convoy system, known as the *flota,* to deliver goods to the Caribbean and transport New World treasures to Spain. In the spring, one convoy of about 30 vessels sailed for Mexico guarded by Spanish ships known as *galeones,* or galleons, which could both transport goods and serve as warring vessels. In the summer a second fleet sailed for Panama. Between 12 and 20 warships accompanied both flotillas. In the Americas, both fleets were loaded with goods in the respective regions. They then rendezvoused in Havana, forming one giant combined fleet of up to 100 ships for the Atlantic crossing. The size of the fleet served as a defense against pirates. Instead, the pirates searched out vessels that were separated from the fleet by storms, fog, or the poor sailing skills of the captain. The pirates also plundered ships that sailed alone within the Caribbean, since the fleet system was not used to carry goods from one island to another.

Attacks were carefully planned, usually relying on the element of surprise, either by sailing with the Sun behind them or pretending to be a friendly vessel. The offensive typically consisted of broadside artillery fire followed by the boarding of the target ship after it had been secured onto the pirate ship by grappling hooks. In the din of battle, pirates could tell each other by the dangling loop earrings they wore. Sometimes the ship was captured and converted into a pirate vessel.

Often, the surviving crew members were invited to become pirates; those who refused were set adrift on a boat to survive or perish.

Piracy on Land

For a long time, the cities and harbors of the Spanish colonies, which were not as well protected as the fleets, were easier targets for pirates. Typically, once pirates entered a city, they herded the citizens into a church and demanded a ransom for their release. Prisoners were tortured until they betrayed where family possessions were hidden. In 1555, the French corsair Jacques de Sores (15?–15?) captured Havana and burned it to the ground. In 1573, Francis Drake (1540–96) raided Panama, and in 1585–86 he looted Santo Domingo.

King Philip II of Spain (r. 1556–98) and the colonial governors undertook the task of building fortresses to protect the cities. In 1586, an Italian engineer named Juan Bautista Antonelli (1550–1616), known as the "architect of the King's defense," drew up plans for the fortresses El Morro of Havana, El Morro of San Juan, and several other forts and garrisons throughout the Caribbean. Construction took decades, even centuries, as the forts were enlarged and buildings added.

The mighty fort of El Morro protecting Havana Harbor. Construction began in 1589 and ended in 1630. (Tarjeta Postal, República de Cuba. Mark Jackson's Postcards Archives)

Portion of defensive wall protecting St. Augustine, Florida. Similar walls were erected in Havana, San Juan, and throughout the Caribbean to protect cities from attacks. (Photo by D. H. Figueredo)

The typical fortification consisted of a massive fort on the top of a hill to protect the entry into the harbor, with protective walls surrounding the city. By the mid-17th century, the major cities and ports formed a sort of fortified chain. Smaller towns, however, were left unprotected and were often raided by the pirates.

Though antisocial and amoral, some pirates practiced the earliest form of democracy in the Caribbean. They chose their captain by vote and decided upon the objective of a particular mission. This system forced a captain to lobby support from the crew to win approval for

Some Caribbean Fortifications

Location	Type of Fortification	Date Built
Fort Cap-Haïtien, Haiti	Several garrisons connected by walls built by French buccaneers	1760
Fort Dauphin, Haiti	Fort on a small peninsula on Cap-Haïtien	1732
Fort Délires, Guadeloupe	Fort with towers and connecting bridge with military barracks overlooking sea and beach; constructed by Generals Charles Hovel and R. P. Labat, working for the French	1650–1780
Fort King George, Tobago	Fort with arches and esplanades built with bricks by British and French troops	1779–1803
Fort Labouque, Haiti	Towers facing the sea with a building or barracks located between the towers	undocumented; probably 1700s
Forts La Cabaña, El Morro, La Punta, and Castillo de la Real Fuerza, Havana, Cuba	Massive and complex fortification system protecting the entrance to the harbor; designed by architect Juan Bautista Antonelli	between 1589 and 1774
Fort Saint George, Grenada	Garrison built on top of a hill, on the edge of a cliff, overlooking the bay, consisting of a protective wall and towers	between 1706 and 1783
Fort Saint-Louis, Martinique	Small garrison with protective wall built with volcanic rocks	1609–1703
Kingston Harbour, Jamaica	Extensive and massive system of forts that can accommodate 98 cannons, protecting Kingston Bay	between 1740 and 1750
San Juan, Puerto Rico	Protective wall, designed and built by engineers and architects Thomas O'Daly and Juan Bautista Antonelli	1654–1765
Santo Domingo, Dominican Republic	Protective wall with fortified towers, designed by architect Juan Bautista Antonelli	1500s and 1600s

Adapted from *Fortificaciones del Caribe*. New York, UNESCO, 1997.

WOMEN PIRATES

Anne Bonny and Mary Read sailed with a pirate named Jack Rackham. Both women were English. By some accounts, Read (?–1720) was an illegitimate child. Her widowed mother dressed her in boys' clothes to pass her off as her late son so that she could receive an allowance from her mother-in-law. Other accounts suggest Read's mother's duplicity was motivated by the desire for her child to receive the advantages males had at the time. In her teens, Read joined the Royal Navy. After a stint with the English, she went to the Netherlands and, again as a young man, signed on to a ship headed for the Caribbean. The ship was attacked by pirate Jack Rackham (?–1720), who offered the defeated sailors the opportunity to join his ranks. Read accepted the offer and earned the reputation of a brave fighter. After becoming a well-known and feared pirate, she was arrested by the British. She died in prison in Jamaica in 1720.

Bonny (1697/8–?) was born in Ireland but was raised in South Carolina, where she married a sailor. The two opened a tavern that was frequented by former pirates, including Jack Rackham, who at the time was trying to lead the life of a civilian. Rackham and Bonny became lovers. When Rackham decided to return to his life as a pirate, Bonny joined him, dressed as a man. She was respected for her skills as a fighter and her ability to lead in combat. She was arrested alongside Mary Read, but there are no records of her life or death after her capture in 1720.

Salmoral, Manuel Lucena. *Piratas, bucaneros, filibusteros y corsarios en América.* Madrid: Editorial MAPFRE, 1992, pp. 239–240.

his choice of a mission. This embryonic form of democracy placed checks on the captain's power, and he was able to rule without question only at times of combat. The pirates followed a code of conduct, an accord that they signed or marked with an *x*. They were entitled for compensation when injured; the more severe the injury, such as losing a right arm, for example, the higher was the compensation provided by the participants.

Famous and Infamous Pirates: Hawkins, Drake, Morgan

As modern Mexican writer Carlos Fuentes quipped (Fuentes, 158), England's Queen Elizabeth habitually turned English privateers into knights. Queen Elizabeth placed the sword of knighthood on the

Mask of Queen Elizabeth I, Tower of London. This mask was made from life, producing a near exact likeness. Queen Elizabeth hired privateers to plunder Spanish wealth; Francis Drake was her favorite. (Photo by Daniel A. Figueredo)

shoulders of privateers John Hawkins (1532–95) and his cousin Francis Drake (1540–96), the queen's favorite, whom she dubbed "my pirate."

Hawkins was a slave trader and smuggler. In the Caribbean, he forced unwilling Spanish settlers to trade with him, threatening to destroy their towns if they refused. Hawkins's presence illustrated the difficult situation faced by many Spanish settlers who were torn between obeying Spanish rules prohibiting commerce with an English subject and their fear of Hawkins and his men. In the 1580s, Hawkins helped develop the British fleet by designing smaller, sleeker ships. During this same period, he openly promoted piracy in the Caribbean as a justifiable tool of war against the Spanish monarchs. In 1568, Spanish ships attacked Hawkins's fleet off the coast of Mexico, destroying most of his ships and capturing and executing more than 100 of his men. This incident provoked open warfare between England and Spain.

There was no more eager participant in the conflict between the two nations than Hawkins's cousin, Francis Drake. Drake, called "el Dragón" by the Spanish, terrorized Cuba and Puerto Rico. In 1572, he looted Panama, taking back to England more than £100,000 worth of loot. After circumnavigating the world, along the way claiming California for England, Drake returned to terrorize the Caribbean and the Spanish peninsula. In 1587, he attacked Cádiz, Spain, in a sort of commando raid that resulted in the destruction of 24 Spanish ships. A year later, when the Spanish Armada—a giant military fleet that carried 7,000 sailors and 18,000 soldiers—approached the English coastline, Drake, aided by a storm, defeated the mighty flotilla of 130 ships.

Hawkins's and Drake's piracy, which were considered to be acts of patriotism, enriched Queen Elizabeth's treasury. The profits helped Queen Elizabeth pay England's national debt, and the booty converted London into a center of trade and commerce.

A lesser patriot and on-and-off pirate was Henry Morgan (1635–88). In the 1660s, the English granted Morgan a letter of marque, or license, to harass the Spanish. In 1668, with 12 ships and nearly 500 privateers under his command, Morgan plundered the town of Porto Bello on the Caribbean side of Panama. In 1671, he macheted his way through the isthmus jungle and attacked Panama, a confrontation that pitted 2,000 of his buccaneers against 3,000 Spanish soldiers. News of the daring raid sent waves of fear throughout the Caribbean, especially with the report that Morgan massacred dozens of Spanish soldiers by locking them in a cell and blowing them up.

Unfortunately for Morgan, between the time he was granted the letter of marque and his attack on Panama, Britain and Spain reached an agreement regarding the Caribbean. Under the terms of the Treaty of Madrid, signed in 1670, Spain recognized British possessions in the Caribbean. As a result, England began to suppress the actions of the buccaneers and privateers.

King Charles II (1630–85) ordered Morgan to London for a reprimand. The reprimand appears to have been a gentle one, however, for the king admired Morgan's audacity. Shortly afterward, he knighted the pirate and appointed him deputy governor of Jamaica. Perhaps Charles thought it would be easier to end privateering if a former pirate was in charge of policing the Caribbean.

Returning to Jamaica, Morgan made the transition from pirate to government official, offering amnesty to those who were ready to quit and hanging those who refused. Under his leadership,

Type of pistols used by British privateers and soldiers during the 16th century (Photo by Daniel A. Figueredo)

41

warehouses and stores were erected in Port Royal, as well as hundreds of taverns. Today, a popular rum is named for Morgan. The label depicts a black-bearded swashbuckler dressed in red and holding a sword— another example of the idealization and commercialization of pirates.

The Treaty of Madrid signaled the beginning of the end of piracy. Pirates would continue to plunder for a few more decades, but other European nations followed Spain and England in treating pirates as enemies of all nations. More important, by signing the treaty, Spain agreed to end its monopoly in the Caribbean and to recognize the territories Great Britain occupied during the previous century. This gave Britain a motive to end piracy in the region.

Other Nations Settle the Caribbean

Despite Spain's claims to the Caribbean under the Treaty of Tordesillas, other European powers had a presence in the area. The Dutch, English, and French were successful in making dents in the Spanish monopoly in the Caribbean. Forced to defend major ports such as Havana and San Juan and to protect the treasure fleet, the Spanish directed their attention to the largest of the islands: Cuba, Hispaniola, Jamaica, and Puerto Rico. The smaller islands, which the Spanish considered less valuable, were abandoned. These islands served as entry points for Spain's rivals—first buccaneers and privateers, then merchants, leading eventually to a presence in the Caribbean for England, France, and the Netherlands.

Though slow in settling their newly acquired possessions, the English, the Dutch, and the French soon saw the value of the islands beyond points from which to attack the Spanish. Agriculture—particularly the development of sugar plantations—commerce, and mining became attractive. Such activities were to define colonial life in the Caribbean in the centuries to come.

Settlement of the British Colonies

The first English settlements in the area were established in the Bermudas, located in the North Atlantic, east of South Carolina and north of the Caribbean. This came about not by design but by accident in 1609 when a ship under the command of Sir George Summers (1554–1610) was wrecked off the islands. The English claimed possession of the islands in 1612, but actual colonization did not begin until 1624. Colonies in the Caribbean followed, including St. Kitts, Montserrat, and Nevis. However, there was constant turmoil on these islands as a result of war with the Spanish and competing French claims.

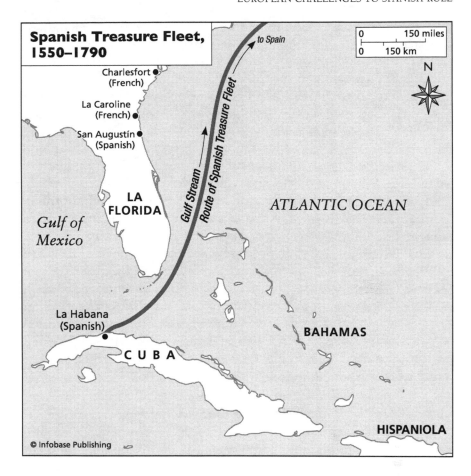

The biggest prize for the English was Jamaica. In 1655, English forces sent to conquer Hispaniola were soundly defeated. The British fleet, afraid to return home without a victory, opted to attack Jamaica. The island was ill equipped to meet the challenge of 8,000 British soldiers disembarking from 38 ships. The Spanish settlers surrendered and accepted passage back to Europe. However, Spain did not relinquish its claim to the island until 1670.

The Dutch and Danish Arrive

The Dutch arrived in the Caribbean, not to colonize, but to fight the Spanish and to obtain salt for the herring industry in the Netherlands. The Dutch West India Company was created in 1621 to supervise Dutch sailors' forays to the Caribbean. In 1623 the company sent a small fleet of three ships to the Caribbean. The number of expeditions and the size of the fleet increased in the next five years. By 1628, 30 ships a year sailed from the Netherlands. As a result, what began as warfare evolved into a highly profitable mercantile adventure for the Dutch.

In 1631, the Dutch West India Company took over the southern part of the island of St. Maarten. Its objective was twofold: establishing a naval base to monitor the movements of the Spanish fleet and setting up a salt plant. Two years later, the Spanish reclaimed the island, and the Dutch moved on to Curaçao, Aruba, and Bonaire. Other settlements were established on Suriname and Guyana.

In 1648, the Spanish quietly abandoned St. Maarten, and the Dutch returned. Curaçao became a major center in the slave trade. Slaves brought from Africa were often taken first to the island to become acclimatized before being sold to settlers in the Spanish and British Caribbean islands.

Denmark imitated the Dutch model by establishing the Danish West India and Guinea Company in 1671. Danish colonists settled St. Thomas in 1672 with a charter issued by King Christian V of Denmark-Norway. In 1683 they expanded to St. John, competing with England for the island. In 1733 they bought St. Croix from the French West Indies Company.

French Claims in the Caribbean

The French arrived through the establishment of several companies similar to the Dutch West India Company: the Compagnie de Saint Christophe (St. Christopher Company), established by Cardinal Richelieu (1585–1642), the Compagnie des Îles d'Amérique (Company of the American Islands), and the Compagnie des Indes Occidentales (West Indies Company), all founded between 1626 and 1664. Their objective, as dictated by a charter drafted in 1626, was to colonize the Lesser Antilles. In that spirit, 300 Frenchmen settled in St. Kitts in 1627. Less than a decade later, in 1635, the island served as the jumping-off point for the colonization of Martinique. That same year the French took possession of Guadeloupe. In 1665 France gained possession of St. Croix (later sold to Denmark), and in 1697 it acquired Saint-Domingue, which became the French side of Hispaniola, from the Spanish via a treaty.

Governance of the Caribbean

The various European nations had different reasons for setting up colonies in the Caribbean, and different nations had widely varying numbers of colonies and colonists in the region. Spain went to the New World to conquer. The Dutch, French, and English, on the other hand, originally did not envision permanent settlements. They went to the Caribbean to plunder Spanish wealth and raid Spanish colonies. Over the years, each country developed its own style and approach to governing its Caribbean possessions.

The Spanish Style

Spain went to the New World to conquer, colonize, and exploit. Such disposition included an attitude that was different from the approaches used by the European powers that envied Spain's possessions in the New World. Spain intended to establish permanent settlements and economic enterprises, doing so even in the Caribbean, where early on the islands served only as beachheads for other conquests or as a rendezvous point for the fleet bound for Spain. A need for administrative procedures and for administrators to oversee the colonies soon emerged. To address that need, Spain set up laws and bureaucratic systems. By 1524, the Council of Indies was established with the purpose of advising the king and appointing church officials to the New World. The council dictated who was and was not allowed to travel to the New World and oversaw the Christian conversion of the indigenous peoples. The council also managed the Casa de Contratación, which controlled business in the colonies. Both institutions aided and complemented each other, but the council was essentially a tool of politics, while the Casa was a promoter of business.

Viceroyalties were administrative units, representative of the Spanish monarch, created to govern in the name of the king the large holdings of colonial possessions from Mexico to the tip of South America and the Caribbean. The viceroyalty responsible for the Caribbean was established in 1535; based in Mexico City, the viceroyalty of New Spain also administered Mexico, Panama, the Philippines, and Venezuela. The king appointed the viceroys, who governed in the king's name and wielded enormous civic and military power. The viceroys, in turn, appointed regional governors who appointed local *alcaldes,* or mayors. The mayors operated in conjunction with a town council, called a *cabildo.* Members of the councils were supposed to serve for a specific term of office, but family relations and economic and religious influences determined who served in the *cabildo* and their length of service. In time, as political positions came to mean economic gains, settlers tried to buy political posts to gain monetary rewards. The practice of graft and favoritism became firmly entrenched.

Over the decades, the Spanish would make minor changes regarding which administrative position reported to which entity, or department, and would employ a variety of titles or names. But ultimately, responsibility for the fate and welfare of the Caribbean rested with the king. It was a hierarchical structure with the king at the top of the pyramid: "The original system of power in Spanish America was . . . a vertical autocracy, governed from afar through paternalistic laws which were rarely implemented, while at the local level practical arrangements between landowners and political bosses assured the harsh and often inefficient exploitation of land and labor" (Fuentes, 137).

In theory, the monarch's commands were law, and his subjects were bound to obey. His administrators were charged with implementing royal decrees without question, but in practice the system worked very differently. It could take anywhere from three months to a year for a decree to arrive in Havana or San Juan, and by then the circumstances surrounding it might make it irrelevant. The royal decree might also run counter to the political or business interests of the local government official and the local elite; this made enforcement difficult, if not impossible. As a result of these factors, local administrators allowed themselves a great deal of autonomy, as reflected by the popular phrase *Obezco pero no cumplo*—(I obey but do not comply) (Collier, 307).

This ruling philosophy fostered alliances between Crown officials, known as *peninsulares* because of their birth on the Iberian Peninsula, and Creole merchants born in the Americas. Over time there was a great deal of intermarriage between the two groups, and the children of these unions became the elites of the New World.

Local rulers built cities and towns, beginning first on Hispaniola in 1502. The city plans followed a grid pattern created in Spain and evenly applied throughout the colonies. There was a plaza, or central square, which was usually a park. The church stood on one side of the plaza, and city hall stood on the other, often facing the church. There was typically a military or militia headquarters on the main square as well. Houses radiated away from the central plazas, edging on narrow sidewalks with a large barred window and an enclosed courtyard. Settlers were allotted land for cultivation on the outskirts of town. At the end of the day, the Spanish residents returned to their homes in the city. On Saturday evenings and Sunday afternoons they met in the park or on the plaza. This settlement pattern, based on a preference for urban dwelling, became characteristic of Spanish America from colonial times onward (Comisión Económica, 17).

How the English Ruled

At first, the English authorized private individuals to colonize and establish settlements on some of the islands of the Caribbean. For example, St. Christopher, or St. Kitts, was the dream of a Puritan, Thomas Warner (?–1649), who in 1624 convinced London merchants to finance the settlement of 100 men on the island and who was subsequently appointed governor and knighted. Similarly, Barbados was claimed in 1625 by an English captain who financed the settlement with funds from a merchant who created a company for that purpose. These proprietors, called lord proprietors, governed with the advice of an assembly.

Charter colonies were the next step in colonial administration. In this case the king granted a settlement charter to a private enterprise—usually a trading company—rather than to an individual. Such colonies were managed more like a business than a colonial outpost or settlement, a practical approach that in theory discouraged strong rule by one individual.

This changed in the 1600s, when the English monarchy decided it wanted to exert more control over its Caribbean colonies. Governors were then directly appointed and dispatched by the king. The governor, in turn, appointed a council of 12 members. The council, composed of representatives from different constituencies, asserted the right to speak for the colony, collect local taxes, and monitor expenditures. In Jamaica, the colony itself was divided into vestries where local representatives were responsible for the local administration of the parishes. To serve on the council, a representative had to be a property owner and white. The council established local laws, and the governor was responsible for enforcing them.

The English governor was not as powerful as his Spanish counterpart. He was required to consult with the council and was not always able to impose his will, especially since the council approved all laws before the governor signed them. Essentially, his power was kept in check by the council.

There were instances, though, when English rule was not evenly implemented. After taking over Trinidad in 1797, as an experiment the British king instructed the governor to rule without an assembly or council. Former Spanish administrative posts, such as the alcalde and the *cabildo,* were abolished. The stage was set for an individual of strong character to exert his will. That was what one governor, Colonel Thomas Picton (1758–1815), chose to do, angering the planters who called him authoritarian as he reorganized the police, increasing their authority over the populace. To curb Picton's power, the British monarch created a three-member commission with all members sharing equal power.

A salient characteristic of the English style of administration was an emotional and cultural detachment from the Caribbean, as evidenced by the high percentage of planters and landlords who exploited the islands but made England home. Scores of prominent British families made their wealth in the Caribbean while an overseer or manager administered their possessions. While in residence on the island, the English made a point of distinguishing themselves from the local population by maintaining their European customs in a tropical environment. It gave the colonists a sense of security in the midst of what were typically slave plantation societies that operated by completely different rules.

As a result, English settlers spent vast sums importing luxury items from Europe. They imported large amounts of flour because they did not like such tropical substitutes as cassava and plantains. English wines and liquors were favored over rum. They missed the beef and lamb of their homeland but made do with imported salted meats. Some persisted with the tradition of partaking of the main meal of the day between noon and 2 P.M., even though the Caribbean heat was usually at its peak during those hours. The custom of wearing waistcoats and periwigs was maintained, despite the higher temperatures. The English viewed food and dress in hierarchical terms; to partake of local cuisine and utilize native dress was seen as beneath them. The stereotype of the wealthy English planter who earned his money in the West Indies was so prevalent that the image was popularized in stage plays and dramas. Typically, the wealthy planter was portrayed as ill mannered as a result of bad habits picked up in the Caribbean.

Such detachment fostered a type of 17th-century architecture typified by places such as Port Royal, Jamaica, where more than 800 houses were crowded together on a thin peninsula facing the harbor, competing for space with scores of taverns and inns. Such a setting did not encourage the presence of families but of adventurers. While Spain chose bricks and mortar to build edifices, England employed wood and mud, easily destroyed. In 1692, an earthquake followed by a tsunami wiped out and submerged Jamaica's Port Royal.

The French Way

The first French colonies in the Caribbean were in violation of Spain's claims to the region. Knowing that Spain likened French intrusion to acts of piracy, the goals of the settlers were to establish modes of

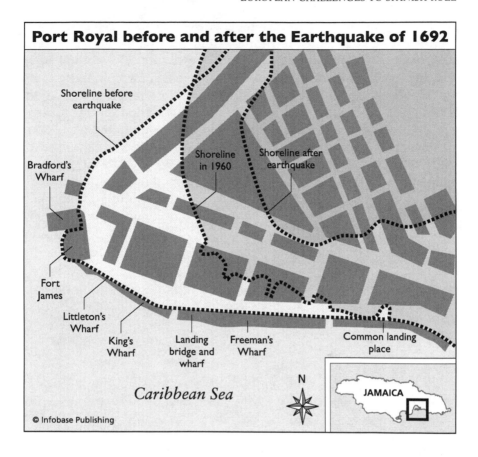

Port Royal before and after the Earthquake of 1692

Shoreline before earthquake

Bradford's Wharf

Shoreline in 1960

Shoreline after earthquake

Fort James

Littleton's Wharf

King's Wharf

Landing bridge and wharf

Freeman's Wharf

Common landing place

Caribbean Sea

N

JAMAICA

© Infobase Publishing

escape in case of an attack by the Spanish and ways to raid and pillage Spanish ships. These settlers were more adventurers, such as the buccaneers, and less colonizers; often they would leave their possessions to join expeditions attacking Spanish harbors in the Caribbean or South America. To maintain order, the companies that founded the colonies appointed governors who received a salary but were, in fact, members of the French upper class and wealthy in their own right.

The new acquisitions were placed under direct French monopoly through a policy known as the Pacte Colonial, or colonial accord. The policy required settlers on the islands to trade only with the French navy, representing France. Colonists in the French islands could not manufacture goods they could purchase from France, while France was obliged to obtain all its tropical products only from the French Caribbean. It was an ironic development, considering how fervently the French criticized Spain for enforcing a monopoly on the colonies.

49

In 1664, the French Crown took possession of Guadeloupe and Martinique, among other territories, from the companies and made them part of the French Empire. Royal power was represented by a governor and an intendant, the former in charge of the military, the latter responsible for legal matters and finances. Both reported directly to the king and had no authority over each other. Their power was further reduced by lobbyists in Paris who advocated for planters and merchants with business interests in the Caribbean. Since the French king needed the products of the islands, the tendency was to yield to the planters and merchants. For example, in 1717, the council in Martinique, composed of representatives of the planters, forced both the governor and the intendant out of office.

In Guadeloupe and St. Martin, a few farmers and planters with large land holdings were the shapers of local politics. But in the most precious Caribbean possession, Saint-Domingue, local power rested in the hands of overseers and managers. This occurred because, as with the English colonials, plantation owners preferred metropolitan life, seldom living permanently in the colonies. City building, therefore, was not a priority. Even Port-au-Prince, Saint-Domingue's official capital, was a far cry in

View of Martinique (From *Down the Islands,* by William A. Paton, New York: Charles Scribner's Sons, 1887, p. 102)

urban development from Havana and San Juan. The historian C. L. R. James cites the 18th-century writer Moreau de Saint-Méry's description of the streets of Port-au-Prince as "sewers" and goes on to state that "If it rained at night, one could not walk in the town the next day, and streams of water filled the ditches at the side of the street in which one could hear the croaking of toads" (James, 31). For the colonists there was a preference for houses in the country and an even stronger desire to return to France.

Dutch and Danish Companies

As mentioned earlier, the Dutch had no desire for permanent colonies in the Caribbean. For them, the Caribbean was primarily an economic opportunity. They concentrated their efforts on harassing Spanish shipping and trading in smuggled goods.

This effort was run by the Dutch West India Company, administered by a board, the Heeren XIX (19 Lords). By the late 1620s the government gave the company the power to administer the Dutch colonies, maintain an army, handle legal matters, and make treaties with foreign nations. The government mandated that the company and its colonial activities were to be governed by a series of managers.

Denmark's colonies in the Caribbean were also initiated by a company, the Danish West India and Guinea Company. However, the company struggled to attract investors. In 1754 the Danish king bought all the shares in the company and appointed royal governors to manage the islands of Saint Thomas, Saint John, and Saint Croix.

Emerging Capitals and Culture

With the increase in population and international trade, cities in the Caribbean began to evolve as centers of culture and finance and to form an identity that in turn shaped the self-identify of the colonists.

In the 1760s, Havana, Cuba's capital, was a walled city with a population of 75,618, larger than most other cities in Latin America. There were churches, monasteries, a printing press, and a university (Hernández, 17), and between 1776 and 1851 four major theaters were erected in Havana. In 1792, the Sociedad Económica de Amigos del País (Economic Society of Friends of the Country) was founded to promote education, commerce, industry, history, literature, and the fine arts. Through its scholarships, Cuban students were able to travel and study in Madrid and Mexico. The society funded charitable organizations and published economic and cultural journals. Members of the society, representative of elite families and Cuban intellectuals, became influential political figures during the independence movements of the late 19th century. In 1812, at least 12 newspapers circulated throughout Havana. By the mid-1800s, travelers to Havana described it as having one of the finest theaters in the world, El Teatro de Tacón (Dana, 21).

In the 1700s, Puerto Rico had a total population of over 150,426 (Ribes Tovar, 205) spread throughout the island. Most inhabitants lived on small farms and earned a living from agriculture, but about 8,000 of them lived in San Juan. By 1784, the streets of the city were paved. Residents were involved in the military or trading, or they were connected with business that serviced the ships that stopped in the harbor. For entertainment, they favored games of cards. In fact, these games proved so popular that the local government organized the selling of cards as a means to make money for the public treasury. Games of cards were sold at two or four Spanish reales, equivalent to 25 or 50 American cents, with a 6 percent tariff collected for the local government.

The first books published in Puerto Rico, appearing in San Juan in 1806, were two volumes of poetry, *Poesías* and *Ocios de Juventud* by the Spanish poet Juan Rodríguez Calderón (dates unknown). This showed an early interest by Puerto Ricans in poetry, a genre widely cultivated during the 19th and 20th centuries. For news, residents purchased copies of the weekly *La gaceta,* published for the first time in 1807. The first theater was built in 1811. In 1824, the governor, General Miguel de la Torre (1786–1838), authorized a tax for the construction of a municipal theater in San Juan that still stands today under the name of Teatro Tapia. Just as important as the construction of facilities were theatrical organizations that traveled throughout the neighborhoods on the island staging Spanish classics. Visiting theatrical companies from Spain staged popular *zarzuelas,* a combination of comedies and operettas.

Music was a driving cultural force, especially in churches, where choirs and religious organ music accompanied the mass. During the Christmas season, *aguinaldos,* or carols, were widely heard in the streets, at churches, and at family gatherings.

In the Spanish-held part of Hispaniola, Santo Domingo's growth as a capital and cultural center was impeded in 1801 when Haitian forces from the other part of the island invaded. The Haitians shut down the university and attempted to impose French and African culture on the people of Santo Domingo. The invaders formed a theatrical society to perform French comedies, a cultural indoctrination that Dominicans resisted by avoidance. Before the invasion, musical performances sponsored by the Catholic Church occurred throughout the year on holidays or religious days. From 1771 to 1779, the Spanish governor, José Solano y Bote (1725/26–1806), sponsored cultural activities in the gubernatorial palace. From 1822 to 1844, during the second Haitian occupation, the university was shut down once again, and residents avoided religious events. However, Spanish aristocrats continued to meet, often in secret, to read books, write poetry, and conduct cultural activities that reaffirmed their ties to Spain.

In Port-au-Prince, Haiti, development was hampered by the Haitian Revolution. However, after Haiti became independent in 1804, Port-au-Prince eventually became the capital of the new nation. Recovering from 10 years of fighting during the revolution, the Haitian elite in Port-au-Prince formed literary societies modeled on the literary salons that flourished in Paris during the monarchy. At these societies intellectuals discussed politics and engaged in poetry and writing competitions. One group, the Cénacle of 1836, attracted would-be writers from the countryside and planted the seed of Haiti's national literature.

In Port-of-Spain, Trinidad, and in Kingston, Jamaica, music was particularly revered. It was the cultural expression of the slaves and the planters, who often attended the slaves' musical celebrations. Public entertainment was scheduled for religious holidays, such as Christmas. The streets were packed with processions of dancers beautifully dressed in muslin and silk. They wore masks and mimicked white settlers. There was singing and the use of a variety of African-origin instruments: flutes, banjos, and different varieties of drums. These processions led in the 20th century to the establishment of the famous national carnivals of the British Caribbean.

An Evolving Cultural Identity

In the Spanish colonies religious drama was promoted and encouraged early on, although the authorities were less enthusiastic of pioneering forms of social protest literature. One such example was the work of playwright Cristóbal de Llerena (1540–1610?), a cleric in Santo Domingo, who criticized the alcalde and the church for their slow reaction in 1586 to the threat posed to the capital by Francis Drake, who eventually sacked the city. Throughout the 1600s, Havana residents preferred comedies that were slightly bawdy, prompting the church to forbid their performance. In the early 1800s, in Port-au-Prince, the palace served as the site for theatrical productions that depicted events from the Haitian Revolution or incidents in the life of a Haitian leader. Such productions were probably among the first instances in the Americas of dramatic performances involving black actors, writers, and stage crews.

THE MUSIC OF THE SLAVES

Music flourished early in the Caribbean: first the *areytos* performed by the Tainos before 1492, then the music the Spanish brought during colonization, and lastly the music performed by slaves. It is often forgotten that slaves found escape through music and dance.

"Slaves ... danced and sang at work, at play, at worship, from fear, from sorrow, from joy. Here was the characteristic form of their social and artistic expression. It was secular/religious. There was no real distinction ... between these worlds in the way that a post-Renaissance European was likely to understand. And because this music and dance was so misunderstood, and since the music was based on tonal scales and the dancing on choreographic traditions entirely outside the white observers' experience ... their music was dismissed as 'noise,' and their dancing as a way of (or to) sexual misconduct and debauchery. On the other hand, the political function of the slaves' music was quickly recognized by their masters—hence the banning of drumming or gathering where drumming took place—often on the excuse that it disturbed ... neighbours."

Brathwaite, Edward Kamau. *Folk Cultures of the Slaves in Jamaica.* London and Port of Spain: New Beacon Books, 1981.

In 1850, the first play written by a Puerto Rican, Alejandro Tapia y Rivera (1826–82), was staged in San Juan. Titled *Roberto d'Evreux,* it was a retelling of the famous love affair between Queen Elizabeth I (1533–1603) and Robert Devereux, second earl of Essex (1556–1601), whom she executed for conspiring against her. At the same time, the play served as a platform to present royals as humans full of folly. Spanish authorities did not approve of the author's sentiments and forced him to write a version that was less critical of the nobility and aristocracy.

These cultural endeavors helped foster a sense of identity within the Caribbean and emphasized the developing differences between colonists born in Europe, who preferred European culture and thought it superior to anything produced in the Caribbean, and the Spanish *criollo* and the British and French Creole, who were developing a culture of their own and which they saw as the equal of Europe's. An example of this manifestation was a poem by a Cuban general named Manuel Zequeira y Arango (1764–1846). In the poem *"A la piña"* (Ode to the pineapple), written in the late 1700s, the poet uses lofty descriptions of a pineapple to emphasize the beauty of the Caribbean in general and of Cuba in particular. In doing so, he rejects the European attitudes of cultural and physical superiority. This posture was not appreciated by colonial authorities, for the cultural divide was easy to perceive in the poem, which ends with the stanza, "the pineapple, the pride of my country," meaning Cuba and not Spain, a potential act of rebellion and a wish for separation from colonial rulers. The colonial rulers were correct in their interpretation, and the rebellions and wars of independence of the 19th century provided them with ample proof.

4

INDUSTRY AND SLAVERY
(1500–1850)

Europe intended to enrich itself in the Caribbean, but European settlers did not intend to do the work needed to acquire those riches. From the beginning, racism and oppression were features of European colonies in the Caribbean, as Eric Williams pointed out in *From Columbus to Castro: The History of the Caribbean* (1970): "the conquistadores . . . first . . . fell on their knees, and then they fell on the aborigines" (E. Williams, 30).

The underlying belief of most Europeans was that the indigenous peoples of the Caribbean were not the equals of Europeans: They were heathens, less than human, and lacked souls. According to that way of thinking, imposing a labor system on the Tainos was an avenue to civilization, a way of instructing them in the art of discipline and bringing them closer to Christianity. Spain's *encomienda* system was intended to be that avenue, but the demise of the Tainos and the protection bestowed on the survivors by the Spanish king ended this ignoble experiment in the Caribbean.

However, there was still a need for laborers. Commerce in the Caribbean, which initially centered on mining and the search for gold, shifted in the 16th and 17th centuries to agriculture. Tobacco and sugar emerged as the dominant crops.

The Brown and the White: The Beginnings of the Tobacco and Sugar Industries

Although laws were passed forbidding colonists in the Caribbean from relocating to the mainland, the Spanish Crown knew that laws alone could not keep the settlers on the islands. There had to be another attraction, another source of wealth. Sugar held that promise.

The sugar industry that would in time define the Caribbean had humble beginnings. Columbus introduced sugarcane to Hispaniola on his second voyage in 1493, but at that time mining was seen as more important than farming. In 1503, in the town of Concepción de La Vega, on Hispaniola, a settler began to cultivate sugarcane and produce molasses. In 1514 a *trapiche,* a horse-powered mill that crushed sugarcane, was set up in the same town. Two years later an *ingenio,* a sugar plantation and refinery, was established in which water powered the sugar mill, reducing labor and producing twice as much sugar and molasses as the *trapiche.* Twenty years later there were 40 or 50 *ingenios* in Hispaniola, each employing between 80 and 100 slaves and costing about 10,000 gold ducats, approximately $75,000, to set up, though there is no data on the actual income made by *ingenios.*

The industry required cattle to feed the workers and to pull the carts that hauled cane from the fields to the *ingenio.* Land and water were needed for planting. It was an expensive proposition and one that at the beginning the Spanish Crown subsidized: "The Crown pardoned all debts of those engaged in growing sugar. Later, slaves, tools, and supplies necessary to produce sugar were made exempt from foreclosure. . . . To further ease the credit problem in order to stimulate sugar production, the Crown also authorized a sum for direct loans to finance the construction of sugar mills" (B. Williams, 43). It was a profitable proposition: Planters could earn over 6,000 gold ducats a year.

The idea spread. In Puerto Rico, settlers experimented with the planting of sugarcane, and in 1523 the first sugar mill was set up near San Germán. By 1528 five *ingenios* were running. During the same decade, Jamaica established 30 *ingenios.* In Cuba, however, the sugar industry took hold slowly, as colonists there focused on the cultivation of another crop: tobacco.

Tobacco Appears

Soon after his arrival in the Caribbean, Columbus saw the Tainos inserting a long rolled leaf into either their noses or mouths and inhaling and exhaling smoke. Friar Bartolomé de Las Casas learned that the Tainos used a plant they called *cohiba* or *cojiba* as part of a religious ceremony and for healing purposes. In the 1560s seeds of this plant were taken to Spain, where in 1571 a physician, Nicolo Manardes (?–?), wrote a treatise identifying 36 medical conditions, such as headaches or blisters, that could be alleviated by the use of the plant. A French diplomat and scholar, Jean Nicot (1530–1600), introduced it to Parisian

In the 18th century, Cuban tobacco became the best known in the world. (Ministerio de Agricultura, Habana. Mark Jackson's Postcards Archives)

society and named the leaf *Nicotiana tabacum*—tobacco. By the early 1600s there was a growing market for tobacco in Europe and the American colonies. For example, in 1609, Cuba shipped over 15,000 pounds of tobacco to Spain. Four years later, the amount of tobacco being shipped increased to more than 400,000 pounds.

Cultivation in Cuba spread throughout the island with the establishment of small farms called *vegas*. The potential for wealth stirred interest in Spain, where the king saw another possible avenue to collect taxes and tariffs. In 1717, the Real Factoría de Tabacos was established to purchase from the *vegueros,* the tobacco farmers, all the tobacco produced in Cuba, restricting direct sales to other Spanish colonies. The *vegueros* saw this new monopoly as a harsh economic measure instituted by the Crown and immediately led an uprising against it. The tobacco growers resisted these measures sporadically for several years. In 1723, the Crown executed 12 insurgent tobacco growers.

To avoid the interference of the colonial government, some tobacco growers decided to relocate to a region known as Vuelta Abajo in western Cuba (present-day Pinar del Río). There the growers found better soil for the cultivation of tobacco. The product produced there, described as having a richer aroma, was considered superior to the tobacco cultivated in other areas of Cuba and on other Caribbean islands. By the end of the 17th century, tobacco from Cuba was more popular in Great Britain—which paid dearly for it, since it was often obtained through smuggling—than the leaf from Virginia in Britain's American colonies.

During this time, tobacco was increasingly popular in Cuba: "The quantity of tobacco smoked in Cuba amazed all visitors; even elderly women smoked . . . even lunatics in the Mazorra asylum chain-smoked cigars" (Thomas, 134). It had become a Cuban trait, a characteristic of Cuban society and ethnicity, which consisted of the whiteness of sugar (those of European descent) and the brownness of tobacco (those of African descent).

Introduction of Slavery

Tobacco and sugar are both labor-intensive crops. The Spanish settlers were not willing to venture into the sugarcane fields to cut and carry cane, and the indigenous peoples had been largely exterminated by the Spanish. An alternative work force was required.

White Laborers

The first solution to the need for laborers was the importation of white laborers, usually either indentured servants, redemptioners, or convicted criminals. Indentured servants were often immigrants who were too poor to travel to the Caribbean on their own. To pay for their passage, they signed a contract in their homeland in which they agreed to serve a master on the islands for a set amount of time. Once the contracted time was up, they could return to Europe or remain in the Caribbean.

Redemptioners were would-be colonists who were too poor to pay for passage, but they did not have labor contracts arranged in advance. They promised themselves to the ship's captain in return for their passage. Upon arriving in the Caribbean, they tried to find a friend or employer to redeem them by paying the captain. If they were not able to pay, the captain sold the redemptioners to other captains or merchants.

The third source of white laborers were convicts, who were shipped to the colonies for a specific length of time, usually seven to 10 years. The reason for the imprisonment could be anything as minor as stealing a silk scarf from a lady, and the sentences meted out were not always appropriate to the crime. In the Caribbean, convicts were kept in a compound inside the plantation and were supervised by an overseer. Upon completion of the labor term, the convicts were granted their liberty and sometimes passage back home. Many of these individuals would eventually join the ranks of the buccaneers upon their release or if they were able to escape.

Abuses in the acquisition and transportation of white servants were part of the system. Unsuspecting candidates were sometimes kidnapped at a seaport, either by force or by being plied with liquor by the kidnapper. Contractors often extended a servant's contract through legal reinterpretations of the contract or claims that the servant had not met all contractual obligations.

Despite the abuses, this system ultimately proved costly to planters and merchants. A servant expected a plot of land at the termination of the contract. When legal disputes arose, the servant sued the master, and a court battle ensued. The planter bought the servant's services for a limited time; the planter did not buy the servant, only the service. And indentured servants could escape and mingle in with other colonists in a town or go off to sea.

The Beginnings of the Slave Trade

European merchants and settlers sought a better way to supply the labor needs of the Caribbean. The colonists turned to a suggestion made by Las Casas in his defense of the Tainos: He suggested that Africans were a good fit for the Caribbean climate, were known for being capable of hard labor, and were not as susceptible to disease as the Tainos. It was a suggestion that Las Casas regretted years later. It is a mistake, however, to put the blame for the scourge of slavery on Las Casas alone. In the 15th century, African slave labor was already in use in European colonies near Africa, such as the Canary Islands, so it is likely that Spain, sooner or later, would have turned to African slavery with or without the inadvertent prompting of Las Casas.

European colonists wanted cheaper labor to toil on the plantations. African slaves met those requirements: "The money which procured a white man's services for ten years could buy a Negro for life." (E. Williams, 19). There was already a system in place. Africa, an immense continent with hundreds of states, included warring nations that benefited from the capture of enemies who could be sent away as slaves. Some tribes or states eventually went to war with the sole purpose of capturing slaves. Those slaves were sent first to Portugal, which had long-established trading agreements with African chieftains, and from there to the Americas.

In the 1600s, the Dutch entered the slave trade. Between 1662 and the end of the century, the Dutch West India Company emerged as a chief provider of slaves to the Americas. By 1775 the Dutch were responsible for transporting over 100,000 slaves to the Americas.

(opposite page) Deck of slave ship with slaves arranged as cargo. Slaves did not have room to stretch. (North Wind Archives)

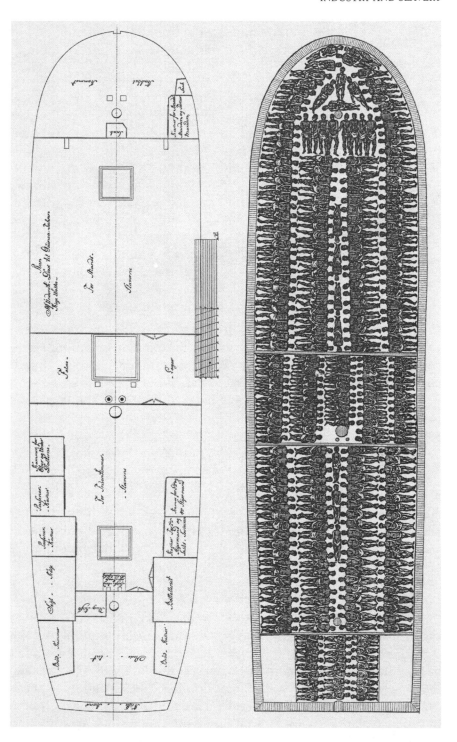

Caribbean Destinations of Slaves from the 16th to Early 19th Centuries	
Colony	Slaves
Barbados	494,200
British Leewards	304,900
British Windwards and Trinidad	362,000
Danish Caribbean	124,700
Haiti	787,400
Jamaica	1,077,100
Spanish Caribbean	791,900
Adapted from: Postman, Johannes. *The Atlantic Slave Trade.* Westport, Conn.: Greenwood Press, 2003.	

The French were latecomers to the slave trade. In the 1700s, France opted to supply their Caribbean colonies by obtaining slaves directly from Africa, taking them to France, and then shipping them to Guadeloupe, Martinique, Saint-Domingue, and St. Martin. By the end of the 1700s, France was responsible for shipping 1.25 million slaves to the Caribbean.

Triangle of Misery

The Portuguese were the first to recognize the economic potential of the slave trade. At first they collected slaves in ports along the African coasts, then shipped them to the Iberian Peninsula. This method was costly, slow, and inefficient and was soon modified. Beginning in 1518, slaves were taken directly to the Caribbean. A triangle of misery emerged.

Called the triangle, or triangular, trade, the business of shipping slaves to the Americas involved three distinct stages. In the first stage, European merchants took trade goods such as guns, knives, jewelry, spirits, and tobacco to Africa and traded these for slaves. From Africa, the slaves were shipped across the Atlantic to the Caribbean, often making their first landing in the Dutch colony of Curaçao. From there, the slaves were taken to other islands, Brazil, and England's northern American colonies (which later became the United States). In the Caribbean, plantation owners purchased the slaves and in turn sold

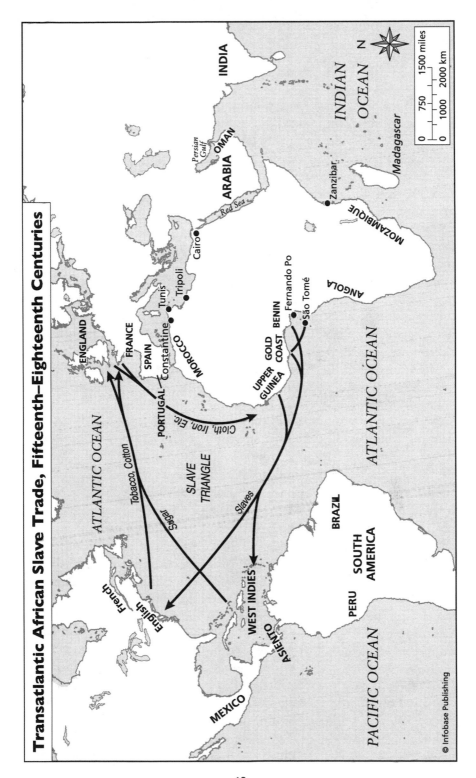

Transatlantic African Slave Trade, Fifteenth–Eighteenth Centuries

INDIA

INDIAN OCEAN

Madagascar

Persian Gulf

OMAN

ARABIA

Red Sea

Zanzibar

MOZAMBIQUE

Cairo

Tripoli

Tunis

Constantine

ANGOLA

Fernando Po

São Tomé

BENIN

GOLD COAST

UPPER GUINEA

ENGLAND

FRANCE

SPAIN

MOROCCO

PORTUGAL

Cloth, Iron, Etc.

ATLANTIC OCEAN

SLAVE TRIANGLE

Tobacco, Cotton

Sugar

Slaves

Slaves

French

English

WEST INDIES

ASIENTO

MEXICO

BRAZIL

SOUTH AMERICA

PERU

PACIFIC OCEAN

ATLANTIC OCEAN

N

1500 miles

2000 km

0   750

0   1000

© Infobase Publishing

63

the merchants coffee, sugar, rum, and tobacco. These merchants then completed the triangle by taking those products to Europe.

The slaves began their journey to captivity when they were seized in the interior of Africa and sold to slave traders. Slave ships carried anywhere from 100 to 500 slaves, depending on the size of the vessel. Groups of slaves were fastened together and brought to the coast, where they were kept confined until a ship was ready to take them. On board the ship, slaves were shackled together and jammed into the lower decks with so little space that they did not have room to stretch out an arm in any direction.

The journey to the Caribbean, called the Middle Passage, lasted two to three months. Diseases that afflicted slaves on the crossing included malaria, yellow fever, and intestinal disorders such as the bloody flux, marked by blood in the stool. In the early years of the slave trade, 15 percent of the slaves died before reaching shore. By the 1800s this rate dropped to 5 percent due to improved medical treatments and better use of space on the ships—changes made not out of kindness but to protect the slave trader's investment.

Upon arrival in the Caribbean the slaves were sold in auctions and taken to their final destination, usually a sugar or tobacco plantation. When they were bound for destinations beyond the port of entry, the slaves stayed in locations such as Curaçao to become acclimatized to their new surroundings, a phase known to the slave traders as "seasoning."

The Growth of Slavery

By the 1600s, about 60 percent of the settlers in the Caribbean were white; the rest of the population consisted of African slaves and surviving Tainos and Caribs. Spanish restrictions on trade with other nations and Spain's own desire to keep the African population lower than the white European population limited the slave presence on the islands. The British and the French were also mindful of the threat posed by an overly large slave population and enacted similar measures.

Over the years, however, the European powers threw caution aside. The demographic change was first apparent in Barbados as small farmers were replaced by sugar planters with large estates. By the 1670s, the white population stood at 17,000, while slaves numbered 37,000. Over 1,000 slaves a year were brought to Barbados. By the end of the 17th century, the island's slave population numbered 50,000. This pattern was repeated throughout most of the Caribbean.

The most dramatic development occurred in Saint-Domingue. In 1789, affected by the booming sugar industry, the population of the island included 460,000 slaves and 30,000 whites. Most of the slaves were born in Africa, and most of the whites were born in France. Cuba was next in total of slave holdings, with 50,000 slaves in 1790, a population that had increased to 239,000 by 1817. From 1811 to 1867, a total of 637,000 slaves were shipped to the island (Martínez Fernández, 113). Puerto Rico was an exception to this trend. In 1827, the slave population there numbered about 34,240 compared with 320,000 whites and people of color. This was because most farms there were small, in part due to the island's mountainous nature and lack of valleys or long, flat tracts of land. The Puerto Rican landscape was not favorable for sugar planting but was ideal for coffee cultivation.

The need for slave labor was constant. Work in the sugarcane fields was exhausting, and slaves often suffered from heatstroke. Accidents occurred in the mills, where malfunctioning equipment killed or incapacitated workers. From 1600 to 1850, an estimated 10 million to 15 million slaves were shipped to the Americas, with about 4 million going to the Caribbean. The main slave transporters were Britain, with 28 percent of the market; France, 13 percent; Denmark, 12 percent; and Spain and the Netherlands, which were responsible for about 4.5 percent each (Postma, 36–37, 41). Portugal supplied over 40 percent of the slave market, but its principal destination was Brazil.

Plantation Slave v. Urban Slave

In the British West Indies, about 60 percent of the slaves on plantations worked in the fields. Field hands were placed in groups involved in planting, weeding, and cutting of sugarcane. Placement was determined by the age and vigor, but not the gender, of the slave. About 10 percent of the slave force worked at milling and refining sugar, and about 20 percent transported the cane to the sugar mill or the market. The rest worked in the house as servants. Women participated in all aspects of sugar production, excused from work only when they were pregnant and near labor.

In the French possessions a similar labor structure was used, with the exception that one category—the *grand atelier* or "great gang"—consisted of men, usually young, assigned the tasks of clearing forests for planting and removing roots and tree trunks. Children between the ages of eight and 12 were placed in *petit atelier* groups with the task of weeding the fields. About 10 percent of the men worked in the mill and another 10 percent in craft and skilled trades.

In the Hispanic Caribbean, the labor process was similar. All field slaves worked together, regardless of gender. They were supervised by

Slaves for sale, waiting in a shed (North Wind Archives)

an overseer carrying a whip, who was usually a poor white or a person of color. During the harvest, slave gangs could be forced to work up to 24 hours at a time, with Sunday allowed as a day of rest. Slaves who did not work in gangs were assigned tasks. Such slaves were not directly supervised and, on occasion, were fortunate enough to receive some free time.

Life as a field slave was generally brutal and short. Many planters, rather than encouraging natural reproduction among the slaves, simply replaced slaves when they died as a result of the difficult working conditions. Many considered that their initial investment in the slave was paid off by the sixth or seventh year, so anything after that was pure profit. The planters also tended to import replacement slaves rather than invest in health and sanitary conditions that would prolong the lives of their laborers.

Conditions for city slaves were probably somewhat easier because their labor was connected to a trade, such as carpentry, or a function, such as driving a coach. Where a skill or a talent was involved—sewing, for example—replacement was not as easy as replacing a sugarcane cutter. In Havana, there was the instance of an aristocratic woman who so favored a young slave for his gift of mimicking languages that she allowed him to memorize poems and sermons and often thought of the boy, named

Juan Francisco Manzano (1797–1853), as an adopted son. The boy would grow up to become an important poet.

The proximity afforded by city life and service within the household was not always benign. "The slave was under constant supervision of the master and therefore subjected to greater and more capricious punishment and humiliation. . . . This was particularly true of the female slave . . ." who could be sexually abused, without recourse to protestations, and maltreated by the master's jealous wife (Patterson, 175).

Whether in the field or in the house, the country or the city, a slave was not deemed a human being, certainly not the equal of a white person. Slaves were defined by law as both a person and property. They were to work as needed by the master and could be sold like a piece of furniture. Slavery was hereditary, usually through the mother's side, and slaves could be inherited as part of an estate. When the master was in financial arrears, the slave could be sold. Codes, such as France's Code Noir (Black Code), were written to protect the slaves—they were investments, after all—but the level of protection varied from European power to power, and the codes were not always followed by the masters.

Slaves developed a variety of resistance strategies. Resistance ranged from the mundane, such as breaking tools or contaminating the master's food with bodily fluids, to outright disobedience and rebellion. Some slaves committed suicide to extricate themselves from their cruel living conditions. Some women used herbs and plants to abort their fetuses rather than bear a child who would become a slave.

Slaves strove to preserve some of their African cultural traditions. Many pretended to adopt Christianity as their faith but secretly continued to worship their traditional African deities. As a result of this cultural resistance, hybrid religions, blending elements of African and European traditions, emerged, including Santeria in the Spanish Caribbean, Vodun in the French Caribbean, and Candomble in Brazil. Today, these faiths are practiced by millions of followers throughout the world.

Runaway Slave Communities

Many slaves escaped by running away. Runaway slaves, called Maroons (from the Spanish *cimarrón*, "runaway"), fled into the woods and the mountains. If a runaway slave was captured, punishment ranged from amputating a limb to execution, based on the number of times the slave had attempted to escape. Successful runaways tended to band together,

THE WAY OF THE SAINTS

Santeria combines Catholicism with African traditions, with the slave attributing to a Catholic saint traits of an African god, thus creating an African-Catholic saint. But Santeria also maintains that gods and spirits could manifest themselves through humans after a lengthy ceremony where a person would serve as a vessel of entry for a supernatural being. Many Christians believe that santeros, Santerian priests, worship the devil. Santeros deny such conceptions and maintain that santeros aim to help others.

Santeria expert Miguel A. De La Torre explains it: "Santeria is an amorphous and practical religion that promises immediate, tangible power in dealing with life's hardship.... The focus is not on understanding the sacred forces of orishas [the Santeria gods]; rather, it is concerned with how these universal forces can be used for the betterment of humans."

De La Torre, Miguel A. *Santeria: The Beliefs and Rituals of a Growing Religion in America.* Grand Rapids, Mich., and Cambridge: William B. Eerdmans Publishing, 2004, pp. 189–190.

Santero dancers performing a ritual that dates back to the sugar plantation era of the 19th century (Photo by William Luis)

forming communities that were modeled on the African villages of their childhood or on the barracks or compound where they lived on the plantations.

The sites Maroons typically chose for villages tended to be deep in the forest and usually surrounded by swamps. As the communities matured, the Maroons were able to expand their agriculture into the cultivation of rice and vegetables. They planted trees and used palm leaves to craft ropes and hammocks. Contacts with smugglers and buccaneers allowed the Maroons to trade for products.

Runaway slaves known as Maroons were brave fighters; many of the communities they built survived into the 20th century. (North Wind Archives)

Constant pursuit by Europeans often discouraged slave women from joining the men in their isolated communities. As a result, Maroons on some of the islands kidnapped Carib women. Eventually, a peaceful relationship with the Caribs allowed nonhostile access to women. Because of their scarcity, women were very influential in Maroon society. In the 1730s, a Maroon woman named Nanny (1680s–1730s) founded the municipality Nanny Town in Jamaica's Blue Mountains and became a legendary fighter. She was reportedly so brave and strong that she could stop bullets with her buttocks, which she then retrieved and reused against her attackers. Though little is known about Nanny, it is believed that she led the Jamaican Maroons from about 1725 to 1740.

Maroon settlements in Jamaica can be traced as far back as 1655, the year the British took over the island. Many slaves fled into the mountains to join already established groups of runaway slaves and hunters. The Maroons harassed the British, employing guerrilla warfare techniques such as raiding plantations at night and disappearing into the forest before sunrise. During such raids, slaves joined the Maroons, and slave women were often taken by the Maroons. The British fought the Maroons for over eight decades, a major endeavor that slowed down the development of sugar plantations. In 1739 the governor finally decided to call for a truce. The Maroons signed a treaty that granted them autonomy and gave them 15,000 acres of land in a mountainous area called the "Cockpit Country." In turn, the Maroons agreed to not accept any more runaway slaves and to help the British track down escaped slaves and fugitives from justice. There was a second war in 1793, but this time the British used hunting dogs purchased in Cuba to track down the Maroons. More than 500 Maroons were captured and expelled from Jamaica to Sierra Leone. In Jamaica, there are still surviving remnants of the Maroon communities populated by the descendants of runaway slaves. In the Sierra Maestra in eastern Cuba, there are also remnants of former runaway slave communities.

Sugar and Salt: Developing Industries

By the 1700s, sugar was king in the Caribbean. The industry dominated and defined Barbados, Jamaica, and Saint-Domingue. For Great Britain and France, sugar became the precious metal equal in value to the gold and silver produced by the Spanish Empire.

Although sugarcane was first introduced to the Caribbean by Columbus, it was not until the 1640s that sugar plantations became important sources of income for planters. This was the beginning of a period referred to as the Sugar Revolution due to the insatiable appetite in Europe, and especially in Great Britain, for sugar: "Sugar habit . . . increased most rapidly in England. In 1700 . . . Britons ate 4 pounds of sugar a year. By 1750 per capita consumption doubled" (Rogoziński, 107).

Sugar in the British Colonies

Barbados responded to the demand. Between 1664 and 1665 28 million pounds of sugar were shipped to England (B. Wood, 47). Barbadian planters learned the craft of sugarcane planting and refining from Dutch settlers, who learned it in Brazil. The Dutch, who settled in northeastern Brazil, were successful planters, importing and using West African slaves. When the Portuguese expelled them from Brazil in 1656, the Dutch took their African slaves and the methods of sugarcane planting and production to Caribbean islands such as Barbados. The interruption of sugar production in Brazil benefited Barbados's role in the sugar industry as it rose to meet the demand.

The boom in Barbados increased the island's population. By 1670, there were 70,000 people living on 166 square miles, with about 75 percent of the population consisting of slaves. Within the white population, there were just over 700 major sugar planters. The typical planta-

Typical sugar plantation in the British West Indies (Mark Jackson's Postcards Archives)

tion consisted of about 100 acres "of which forty were planted to cane, forty allowed to lie fallow, twenty used for pasture, provisions, and as a nursery for canes" (E. Williams 1984, 113). There was a mill for grinding sugarcane and buildings for manufacturing.

Limited land mass and overuse of the soil, though, fated Barbados to a short reign as the king of sugar. By the mid 1700s Jamaica had become England's most important Caribbean colony. In 1740 Jamaica produced 36,000 tons of sugar a year. The sugar, partially processed, was sent to England for processing and distribution throughout Europe and the American colonies, where molasses and rum from Jamaica were particularly popular. Jamaica became England's main sugar provider, enriching planters there. In 1759 Britain's capture of Guadeloupe provided a competitor in the sugar market. Jamaican planters, many of whom lived in London and formed a West Indian lobby that was well funded with money from the Caribbean, complained to the king and Parliament. The Jamaican planters won. Their appeal for mercantile protection was one reason for England's return of Guadeloupe to France in 1763.

France Enters the Sugar Market

The sugar industry was not the sole domain of Jamaicans. Saint Thomas and Nevis entered the market. There was also Martinique. But the most successful of all competitors was the French colony of Saint-Domingue, which was destined to be the king of the sugar colonies until the 19th century.

By the 1750s, Saint-Domingue was producing 61,000 tons of sugar, while Jamaica was producing 36,000 tons (Klein, 59). From a slow beginning in the cultivation of cotton, indigo, and coffee and a slow growth in the slave and white populations, Saint-Domingue, on the French side of Hispaniola, was by the 1780s the richest colony in the world, and Saint-Domingue planters were considered the most efficient producers of sugar. There were 460,000 slaves on Saint-Domingue, the largest population in the Caribbean, and over 800 sugarcane plantations. Because the soil was richer than in Jamaica or Barbados, workers in Saint-Domingue produced twice as much as the same number of workers in Jamaica: "French sugar cost one-fifth less than British, the average yield in Saint-Domingue and Jamaica was five to one" (E. Williams 1984, 122). Therefore, French planters could undersell their counterparts in the Caribbean by 10 to 20 percent. It is estimated that near the end of the 18th century, Saint-Domingue produced 30 percent of the world's sugar (Klein, 90). The colony generated 40 percent of France's foreign trade.

It was a market that drew over 1,500 ships a year to Port-au-Prince. Saint-Domingue traded not only with France but also with the American colonies. Wine, salted meat, linens, and clothing arrived in Saint-Domingue, ordered and purchased by the planters and merchants. These goods gave the settlers an appearance of luxury and wealth envied by their neighbors in the Caribbean and their countrymen in France.

Nineteenth Century: Cuba's Entry

The British occupation of Havana in 1762 introduced new trading partners to Cuba, such as Great Britain and the American colonies, and the arrival of 10,000 slaves that were purchased by sugar plantation owners throughout the island. The 70 sugar plantations already in existence now had a larger workforce. But it was the Haitian Revolution of 1791 that served as a catalyst for the mass importation of slaves to Cuba. With Saint-Domingue out of the market, Cuban planters saw the opportunity to fill the vacuum. French planters and technicians fleeing Haiti flocked to Cuba, bringing their expertise with them. Spanish planters from Hispaniola, afraid of a Haitian invasion, followed their French counterparts to Cuba. Spain helped by allowing the transportation of more slaves to the island and importing capital, machinery, and technicians.

The first few decades were spent modernizing sugar mills for the use of steam power. Between 1780 and 1836, production increased from 18,000 tons to 113,000 tons a year. In 1840 Cuba was further aided by the emancipation of slaves in Jamaica, which led to a diminished labor force on that island's sugar plantations. As sugar prices rose from 4 to 14 cents per pound by mid-century, Cuba became the world's largest producer of sugar, providing 29 percent of the market. In 1870 Cuba reached its 19th-century plateau: over 700,000 tons, or 41 percent of the world's output (Klein, 93).

During the 19th, century Europe found another source of sugar in sugar beets; however, Cuba's sugar industry survived this development

Inside a sugar mill in Cuba during the 1800s (From *Cuba's Struggle for Freedom,* by Gonzalo De Quesada and Henry Davenport Northrop, s.n., 1898, p. 428)

by increasing its output through the implementation of new technologies. These included building the first railroad system in Latin America in 1837, with 768 miles of track in use by the 1860s. Other innovations included filtering the crushed sugarcane and the use of mechanized pans to receive the flowing juice. The administrative process of centralizing the sugar refinery in large factories, called *centrales,* and allowing *colonos,* independent planters, to grow and cut their own sugarcane fields accelerated the manufacturing process. Nevertheless, the primary factor behind the success of the sugar industry in Cuba, as in the other islands, was the labor provided by the slaves.

Salt Industry of St. Martin

In St. Martin, salt was the equivalent of the sugar industry. There are several salt ponds on the minuscule island. The largest and best-known is the Great Salt Pond, a circular enclosure with an area of one square mile and a depth of about 28 inches throughout most of the pond. The salt was formed when direct sunlight warmed the surface of the water to 92 to 110°F, causing the water to evaporate. In the evening, the thickening salt would sink, and the layers would build up as the cycle was repeated over weeks and months in different areas of the pond. Eventually, cakes of salt would form. At that point, bands of workers, composed of slaves, poor whites, and free people of color, would collect the salt with baskets, wading into the heated water and walking barefoot on the burning sand. The work went on for about 11 months of the year. During the peak years of salt mining, from 1789 to 1961, 6,000 to 7,000 salt miners at a time worked in the pond.

Mining the salt beds resulted in a total of 200,000 tons of salt shipped to the Netherlands by the end of the 1700s. Though there are no firm estimates of the number of slaves who worked during any given year due to the destruction of St. Martin's archives in 1810 during the British occupation, about 50,000 slaves arrived on the island between the late 1600s and the end of slavery in 1795 (Sekou, 115).

As the slave presence increased throughout the Caribbean, so did the fruit of their labors. White planters grew rich, as did the European merchants who traded in products—sugar, tobacco, salt—from the islands. To the planters and merchants, the slaves were a reliable source of wealth. Little did they imagine how that source would come to end less than a century later.

5

REVOLUTIONS IN AMERICA, FRANCE, AND HAITI (C. 1700-1850)

When European nations found themselves at war, possessions in the Caribbean were used as bargaining chips. As military strategies changed in the 1700s, European nations began to develop ways of conducting warfare far from home. Conflicts in Europe now played out in the Caribbean Sea, no longer with a pirate ship attacking a lone merchant vessel or isolating a stranded ship from the flotilla, but with large fleets battling each other. The Seven Years' War (1754 and 1756–63) was the result of European concern over a consolidation of military power by Great Britain and Prussia. Coupled with this was the animosity between Great Britain and France over territories along the Ohio River in the North American colonies, territories that both nations claimed. As the two powers positioned their forces along the river in 1754, war erupted. The war was fought in Europe, coastal Africa, India, North America, the Philippines, and the Caribbean. Many historians consider this conflict the first global war.

The American Revolutionary War, which raged from 1776 to 1783, led to a bigger conflict, with the French and Spanish supporting the North Americans against the British. An unexpected outcome of the Revolutionary War was France's bankruptcy, which in turn ignited the French Revolution of 1789–99. More than any other conflict in Europe, the French Revolution helped change the way of life of the Caribbean islands.

But if there was a conflict that served as a military rehearsal for the emergence of Great Britain as a world power, the candidate is a little-known war with a curious name: the War of Jenkins' Ear.

Jenkins' Ear: The War of 1739

An ear started off a conflict that embroiled British and Spanish forces on the high seas of the Caribbean and along Florida's coastline. The ear belonged to a mariner named Robert Jenkins (1700–?). In 1738, at a hearing of the House of Commons in London, Jenkins presented a bundle of dried skin that he said was his ear. He claimed that it had been sliced off in 1731 by a Spanish coast guard captain named Juan de León Fandiño, who boarded his vessel miles away from Spanish possessions. Many observers at the time doubted Jenkins's account of the incident and his claim that he kept the ear in his possession for seven years. Some did not think he lost his ear at all, especially since he wore a wig at the hearing and did not remove it to reveal a scar. Nevertheless, Jenkins's account inflamed passions among Londoners, who demanded vengeance.

An enactor portraying Spanish or Spanish-Cuban infantryman in the Castillo San Marcos, St. Augustine, Florida, c. 1740 (Photo by D. H. Figueredo)

The war that came about capped the tensions that had flared on and off for decades between the Spanish and the British regarding smuggling in the Caribbean. Spain hired Spanish privateers who manned *guarda costas,* vessels that sailed along the coasts of Cuba, Hispaniola, Jamaica, and Puerto Rico, with the mission of boarding British ships. The Spanish claimed that foreign ships belonged to pirates and confiscated whatever goods were on board. The British claimed the Spanish were pirates who were plundering goods destined for Great Britain. Thus, whether or not Jenkins's story was true, it was enough to send the two nations on the path to war.

On October 23, 1739, Great Britain declared war on Spain. In the next two years, the British dispatched 8,000 men and nearly 80 ships to the Caribbean. It was the first time Britain

Cannon used against James Oglethorpe in 1742 when he attempted to take St. Augustine for the British for the second time during the War of Jenkins' Ear (Photo by D. H. Figueredo)

conducted a transatlantic campaign that required the service and administration of officers at home, in the Caribbean, and in the American colonies (Syrett). One of the battlefields in this war was the Florida coastline, as the European powers fought for control of Saint Augustine.

This war did not settle old disputes and did not alter the balance of European power: The British maintained their American colonies, and the Spanish remained in Saint Augustine. It did, however, demonstrate to the British that they could conduct and maintain transatlantic operations (Syrett) and that the use of larger forces was required to capture an overseas city. The experience encouraged a grander scheme 20 years later.

British Occupy Havana, 1762

As part of the Seven Years' War, Great Britain, fighting against Austria, France, Portugal, the Russian Empire, Spain, Sweden, and Saxony, captured the islands of Guadeloupe in 1759 and Martinique in 1762. In June 1762, British forces reached the port of Havana and laid a siege that lasted 42 days. On August 13, 14,000 British soldiers rushed El Morro Castle through a breach in a wall while the infantry attacked the edge of the city. After occupying the fortress, the British turned the cannons on the city itself, destroying numerous residences.

At first the Cubans feared and distrusted the British. But the occupiers proved wiser than Spanish administrators and soon implemented changes that made life easier for Cubans, beginning with the abolition of taxes. The occupation, rather than restricting Cubans, gave them a sense of liberation: "The British . . . opened the port to unrestricted commerce, sold merchandise and slaves at reduced prices, . . . [gave] Cubans their first taste of legal trade with all countries." (P. Foner, 42). More than 1,000 ships unloaded cargo with merchandise from Europe and the American colonies and then loaded to take back to Europe Cuban tobacco and sugar. The grasp of the Catholic Church was relaxed as Protestant services and Freemasonry, a secret fraternal and nonreligious society, were introduced. The latter would prove of great importance during the wars of independence of the 19th century, as the vast and secret network of communications from one Masonic lodge to another provided Cuban rebels with a means of conspiring against the Spanish.

With the British came an increase in the slave trade, which gave a boost to the sugar industry in Cuba. There was also an unexpected development: an increasing awareness of a Cuban identity as separate from Spanish traits, called *Cubanidad,* or Cubanness. *Cubanidad* emerged in several ways. It was the by-product of Cuban militiamen and volunteers fighting the British under the command of Cuban officers and Cuban civic leaders without instruction from the Spanish authorities. The free-trade policies of the British made many elite Cubans aware that their economic interests were not the same as those of the mother country. Over the next 100 years, this divergence of interests increased along economic, cultural, and social lines, leading to an eventual dissolution of the bond between Cuba and Spain. This growing sense of *Cubanidad* was expressed by Cuban writer Martin de Ulloa (1716–95). Upon the British departure from Cuba, he was asked whether he preferred to be a Spanish or a British subject. Ulloa replied that it mattered little because he was neither Spanish nor British but Cuban (Santovenia, 202).

The occupation ended in 1763 with the signing of the Treaty of Paris, which brought an end to the Seven Years' War. The British returned Havana to Spain in exchange for Florida, which they viewed as a natural appendage to the North American colonies. France yielded to Britain its North American territories except for Louisiana and New Orleans, which it ceded to Spain.

America's War of Independence

The Seven Years' War demonstrated Great Britain's naval power and military might, a fact that worried North American patriots who in 1776 rebelled against King George III. The North Americans saw the need to enlist foreign allies in their struggle and turned to France, still reeling from giving up its territory on the North American continent, and Spain, still seeking vengeance for the attack on Havana and the loss of Florida. Three years before Spain declared war on Britain in 1779, Cuban spies were in Florida gathering information for the North American rebels. They also helped to send money from France and Spain to the colonial troops. In the fall of 1779 the Spanish governor of Louisiana, Bernardo de Gálvez (1746–86), led several expeditions against the British, winning victories along the Mississippi River and in Florida. In 1781 the French and Spanish in Cuba secured 1,200 livres, the equivalent of $300 million (R. Hernández, 24), needed by George Washington and the Continental Army to continue with the war. The Spanish, encouraged by Gálvez, contemplated the recapture of Jamaica from Britain.

The principal contestants in the Caribbean Sea were the British and the French, involved in a naval game of chess where opposing fleets journeyed from island to island, fought near harbors, and gave each other chase. In September 1778, a French fleet from Martinique captured the lightly fortified British island of Dominica, located between Guadeloupe and Martinique. In December the British invaded French St. Lucia, defeating the island's defenders. A French fleet sailing from North America arrived later with intentions of ousting the British. For 10 days, more than 70 British ships and 5,000 soldiers fought against 12 French ships and 7,000 troops. Though leading several gallant charges against the fortress that defended the bay, the French commander, Admiral Jean-Baptiste Theodat, comte d'Estaing (1729–94), was unable to defeat the British and was forced to sail away. In July of the same year, the same commander took British Grenada and successfully defended it from a counterattack led by the British navy.

In 1780 there were indecisive battles off Martinique, and in 1782 there was a major encounter between the British and the French, known as the Battle of the Saints, off Dominica. In this encounter, the British fleet, under Admiral George Rodney (1718–92), boxed in between the harbor and the French, broke through the defensive line of the French, fired on enemy ships they isolated, and captured the French commander, Admiral François-Joseph De Grasse (1722–88). The defeat forced the Spanish and French to reevaluate, then abandon, designs for

HOW GEORGE WASHINGTON'S BRIEF STAY IN BARBADOS HELPED THE REVOLUTIONARY WAR

George Washington and his brother, Lawrence, headed to the West Indies in the winter of 1751: "The decision of the Washingtons to travel ... to Barbados was strengthened by family ties. Lawrence's wife, one of the prominent Fairfaxes of Virginia, was related to Gedney Clark, a well-established resident of Barbados. The brothers rented a house on the outskirts of Bridgetown on an encampment overlooking Carlisle Bay. Dinner invitations interspersed with engagements at the theater, fireworks displays, and horseback rides in the country to visit various plantations kept George occupied. However, Lawrence [suffering from tuberculosis] did not respond to the treatment of local doctors. George himself contracted smallpox and was laid up for three weeks. While the smallpox scarred him, it also gave him immunity from this major scourge of the eighteenth century. In later years, when smallpox decimated the American forces fighting for independence, George, as their leader, went unscathed and was the first to inoculate his troops when a vaccine became available."

Kiernan, James Patrick. "George Washington's Barbados Connection." *Americas* 53, 3 (May/June): 5

an invasion of Jamaica. This was the last major battle in the Caribbean during the American Revolutionary War.

The economic repercussions of the Revolutionary War were felt throughout the Caribbean. Many of the colonists, even in the British possessions, sympathized with the Americans' desire for liberty and their protests against colonial economic monopolies. For Cuba, Hispaniola, and Puerto Rico, the Spanish alliance with the American rebels signaled the allowance of American and French ships into their ports. In the British Caribbean, temporary blockades and the inability of British ships to bring goods to the islands led to famine in Jamaica and Antigua and a food shortage in Barbados. The food shortage affected the most vulnerable disproportionately, such as the 15,000 slaves who starved to death in Jamaica (E. Williams 1984, 226). On the other hand, the independence of the North American colonies in 1783 created a new market for Caribbean goods and an eager trading partner.

However, the victory of the Americans over the British Empire had a wider political and ideological significance for the Spanish Caribbean. It sent a clear signal that colonial powers could be overthrown by their oppressed subjects.

The French Revolution in the Caribbean

The cries of "Liberty! Equality! Fraternity!" that reverberated in the streets of Paris in 1789 echoed throughout the French Caribbean. The French Revolution, which lasted from 1789 to 1799, fueled fires of rebellion in Guadeloupe and Martinique and revolutionized Saint-Domingue, on the French side of Hispaniola. News of the French Revolution, like news of other developments in Europe and North America, reached the islands through rumor and from travelers visiting the Caribbean before official reports arrived from Paris (Banks, 198, 219). In 1789, when the French National Assembly declared all whites equal and with the same right to own property, the governors in Guadeloupe and Martinique welcomed the news. But in Martinique, poor whites sided with the French Republic, while wealthy whites chose royalty. Similarly, in Guadeloupe, republicans and royalists grew further apart, with royalists often plotting the murder of republican officials (Dubois, 98).

In the meantime, black slaves in Martinique and Guadeloupe observed the events in silence and waited their turn. "They had heard of the revolution and had construed it in their own image: the white slaves in France had risen, and killed their masters, and were enjoying the fruits of the earth. It was gravely inaccurate, but they had caught the spirit" (James, 81).

In March 1791, a new governor and fresh troops from France restored order in Martinique and ended street fighting and skirmishing in the countryside. That same year, the National Assembly in Paris removed the French king from the throne; a year later, the king and his family were executed. In response, the governors of Guadeloupe and Martinique declared their support for the monarchy, an act that signaled independence from Republican France. Slaves in Guadeloupe rebelled. After killing 23 whites, they presented themselves before the colonial authorities and proclaimed their innocence, explaining that their actions were directed only against royalists. This was an explanation the supporters of the French Revolution on the island and republicans in Paris accepted.

Promonarchy planters in Guadeloupe and Martinique sought the support of the British. Early in 1794, more than 6,000 British troops invaded Guadeloupe, Martinique, and St. Lucia, military actions that seemed successful. But in June 1794, the French returned to Guadeloupe with 1,150 men under the command of an enigmatic figure named Victor Hugues (1774–1826), an efficient administrator and fearless fighter. Hugues rallied 2,000 slaves, and together the French soldiers and the slaves forced the British out of Guadeloupe. Hugues then sent agents to the neighboring islands to encourage slaves to rebel against the British, who by now had more than 90,000 troops dispersed throughout the Caribbean.

The weakest point for the British was their intervention in Saint-Domingue, where, encouraged by white French planters, the British prime minister sent 20,000 men to intervene in the Haitian rebellion that began in 1791. In September 1793, British forces sailed from Jamaica to Saint-Domingue. A year later they were in control of all major ports in Saint-Dominque.

It was not a successful campaign, however, as the British were constantly attacked by Haitian forces using guerrilla warfare techniques. Exhausted and unable to get reinforcements, the British acknowledged defeat in 1798 and signed a peace treaty with Toussaint Louverture, the Haitian leader. The five years in Saint-Domingue cost the British 14,000 dead, with about 1,000 men killed in combat and the rest felled by malaria, yellow fever, diarrhea, and other diseases.

The Guillotine Comes to Guadeloupe

Victor Hugues brought the guillotine to Guadeloupe, where he carried it from town to town as he sought enemies of the revolution and condemned to death over 700 traitors. The guillotine became a symbol of the whimsical nature of the revolutionary process. In France, many of the Jacobins who sent the enemies of the French Revolution to the guillotine were themselves guillotined when accused by former colleagues of being counterrevolutionaries. In the Caribbean, the ups and downs of the guillotine reflected the changes in how Hugues approached the abolition of slavery. In 1794, Hugues favored abolition of slavery and freed the slaves who fought with him against the British. He later switched to gradual emancipation as a way to ensure employment to fuel the island economy and maintain the country's productivity. The freed men who objected to Hugues's policy were then forced by Hugues himself to work for an unspecified period. Those who protested were accused of being counterrevolutionary and threatened with the ever-present guillotine.

The underlining motivation for Hugues was neither idealism nor freedom for the slaves but the need to keep the plantations in operation. Hugues felt that without the labor of slaves there would be no plantations, since freed slaves tended to relocate to towns and villages and work at trades such as carpentry. Thus, in 1802, when the plantation economy required the presence of a large workforce, Hugues found no difficulty in implementing the new orders from France: to reestablish slavery.

From Guadeloupe, Victor Hugues moved to French Cayenne on the South American mainland, where his rule as a colonial administrator was close to that of a tyrant. His transformation from liberator to oppressor embodied what one scholar described as "the broader tale of revolution and its limits," meaning that once in power, the idealist revolutionary became a reactionary bureaucrat intent on preserving revolutionary measures (Dubois, 195). In that respect, Hugues was a precursor to such 20th-century Caribbean revolutionaries as Maurice Bishop of Grenada and Fidel Castro of Cuba.

Haiti: The First Black Republic

In the 18th century, Saint-Domingue was the richest of all the colonies in the Caribbean and one of the richest in the world. The great Trinidadian writer C. L. R. James sums up the wealth of the colony this way: "By 1754, there were 599 plantations of sugar and 3,379 of indigo. . . . In 1767, [Haiti] exported 72 million pounds' weight of raw sugar and 51 million pounds of white, a million pounds of indigo and two million pounds of cotton, and quantities of hides, molasses, cocoa and rum. . . . Nor was it only in quantity that [Haiti] excelled but in quality" (James, 45). At the time, the colony generated about 40 percent of France's foreign trade. It was a prosperity envied by all, especially England and Spain. But it was a prosperity based on the flawed institution of slavery.

The white planters in Saint-Domingue lived in luxury, often better than their counterparts in Europe. But they did not work for these riches. The labor, the sweat, and the agony fell on the backs of thousands of African slaves stolen away from their homeland and shipped like beasts of burden to Saint-Domingue. Yet the white planters did not acknowledge and did not appreciate the work of the slaves, dehumanizing them and abusing them for the slightest fault, such as dropping a bucket of water. If the planters refrained from causing permanent damage, it was because to do so could impair or destroy the slave, the principal source of labor and their chief investment.

Aware of the need to keep the slaves healthy and strong, France enacted the Black, or Negro, Code (Code Noir) in 1685. This code provided guidelines for the humane handling of slaves, specifying the diet they should be fed, the religious instructions they were to receive, how many lashes a slave could receive for misbehaving, the proper punishment for theft, and so forth. The code advocated punishment for planters who willfully incapacitated or murdered their slaves. It, however, was seldom enforced. Hundreds of violations, even killings, went unpunished. One notorious case was that of a plantation owner named Le Jeune who in 1788 murdered four of his slaves he suspected of attempting to poison him and tortured two slave women he accused of being part of the conspiracy. Le Jeune told all his slaves that he was planning to murder them. When the frightened slaves reported the incident to the governor and a hearing was scheduled on the case, the white planters in the region testified on behalf of Le Jeune. Even though the evidence was against Le Jeune, the court voted in his favor and, furthermore, ordered that the blacks who accused and testified against him were to be given 50 lashes. It was evident that whites could get away, literally, with murder.

The slaves were not passive recipients of injustices, however. Some committed suicide. Some ran into the woods and formed Maroon societies. A few plotted to kill their white masters. In 1720, a runaway slave named Mackandal (1715–58), through a series of secret organizations with ties to plantation slaves, enlisted up to 1,000 individuals to mass murder the whites by poisoning their food.

Plantations were infiltrated by Mackandal's men, who convinced the slaves at some of the locations to join the conspiracy. Ultimately, the plot failed when Mackandal was betrayed, captured, and burned alive, but the spark lit by Mackandal's rebellion was not extinguished. In 1791 the repressed hatred and anger of the slaves engulfed Saint-Domingue in flames.

Seeds of Rebellion

In 1789, there were two aristocracies in Saint-Domingue: the aristocracy of land and the aristocracy of skin. The former was based on wealth; the latter was based on whiteness. Those who were white, regardless of socioeconomic background, were on top; those who were not were at the bottom. The wealthy whites at the top of the social hierarchy were known as the *grand blancs*. Between them and the black slaves at the bottom were poor whites, called the *petit blancs;* the mulatto population, known as *affrinchis,* who were the freed offspring of a white and a black or free-born people of color. This latter term also referred to African slaves who earned their freedom as well as mulattoes. The mulattoes in Haitian society were tied to both races, although they frequently identified with the white Europeans.

There were racial classifications based on an individual's ancestry to determine a person's "blackness," but the fundamental concept was that all that was white was superior to all that was black. This was the general pattern in the colony, although it was not unusual in some regions for poor whites and poor people of color to compete for employment or in small businesses. Some free people of color owned land and slaves.

The black and mixed population greatly outnumbered the whites. In the 1780s, there were 28,000 whites, 22,000 *affrinchis* and free people of color, and 460,000 black slaves. This demographic imbalance between oppressors and oppressed was a prescription for rebellion and revolution. The whites held the power. The mulattoes, identifying lighter skin color with power, tended to side with the whites. The free people of color were often divided in their loyalties. In fact, many of the colonial militias consisted primarily of free people of color and mulattoes. Without weapons and education, the slaves could not challenge the whites, but many remembered Mackandal and dreamed of removing the chains of slavery.

Revolution in Paris

The opportunity for freedom came from the other side of the Atlantic. In 1789, the French Revolution shook the foundations not only of France but of the rest of Europe as the rebels convened a National Assembly, limited the power of the king, abolished the feudal system, and claimed the rights of all men before the government. An abolitionist society in Paris, Les Amis des Noirs (friends of the blacks), began to dispatch to Saint-Domingue literature claiming liberty and equality for all people. In 1790, a mulatto leader, Vincent Ogé (1750–91), responded to the call for freedom by leading a rebellion of 200 free people of color and former slaves in the north of Saint-Domingue. Ogé was not advocating equality for slaves but only for free people of color. Furthermore, he was not asking for separation from France but only to be treated the same as any Frenchman. The planters captured Ogé and executed him.

Ogé's execution prompted the National Assembly in Paris in 1791 to pass a decree offering equality to all free people of color in Saint-Domingue. Within months, however, the assembly yielded to pressure from white aristocrats who did not support equal rights for the free people of color, demonstrating that the assembly was more interested in the welfare of the white population than in the rights of all people. The message was clear: Regardless of the French Revolution, whites were still on top. The reversal of the decree set the stage for a civil war between whites and the free people of color, a rift that was soon exacerbated by slave revolts.

The Genius of Toussaint Louverture

A strong leader was needed to fight for the freedom, the equality, and the rights of the slave population of Saint-Domingue. That leader emerged in the person of Toussaint Louverture. Born on May 20, 1743, Louverture was the son of a slave believed to be a descendant of an African king. He was born into the ownership of a kind master, Bayon de Libertad, who took a liking to him and allowed him to use his library. Louverture's godfather was a priest who taught him to read and write and introduced him to Latin. The youth became a medical practitioner before the age of 20. His ability to discuss the classics and philosophy with his master delighted the latter so much that he allowed Louverture to supervise 40 acres of the plantation and a dozen slaves. When rebellion broke out a few months after the death of Ogé, Louverture helped his master escape to the United States before joining the rebellion.

Toussaint Louverture, liberator of Haiti (North Wind Archives)

The rebellion was planned on the night of August 14–15, 1791. The leader was a Vodun priest named Boukman (?–1791). After a Vodun ceremony where the participants supposedly slaughtered a pig and drank its blood, the conspirators, about 200, pledged death to all whites. Known as the Bois Caïman Ceremony, this event is one of the cornerstones of modern Haitian history.

A week after the ceremony, nearly 50,000 slaves joined the plot and set out for the plantations in the north of Saint-Domingue. They burned more than 1,000 plantations, slaughtered men, raped and murdered women, and decapitated children. Surprised and terrified, the white planters, who had not thought the blacks able to organize on such a large scale, hid. A few days later they reorganized. Taking advantage of the rebels' weariness and the fact that some slave units disbanded, the whites began their attack, killing any black person they came across, rebel or not. Dozens of decapitated black heads were placed on stakes around plantations. Hundreds of slaves were crucified, and many more were hanged in the streets. One head planted on a pole was that of the Vodun priest Boukman, who was killed in action on November 7, 1791. A sign on the post read, "This is the head of Boukman, chief of the rebels."

The revolution continued for the next 13 years, with different leaders in charge of different groups, mostly in the north of Saint-Domingue. The whites and mulattoes often fought together against the slaves, while many free people of color supported the slaves. The first two groups wanted power for themselves and wanted to maintain slavery; the blacks wanted the abolition of slavery. In France, monarchists and republicans continued to battle each other in the assembly and on the streets on whether to keep the monarchy or enforce the rights of all men. They shared, however, one concern: to keep Saint-Domingue a colony.

Fighting for Freedom

Toussaint Louverture's objective was the abolition of slavery. Between 1791 and 1794 he organized and trained an army of 4,000 slaves. According to historian Martin Ros, he gained the troops' loyalty in three ways: knowledge of medicinal herbs that allowed him to treat the soldiers' wounds and to help cure their ills; knowledge of French, Spanish, and rudimentary Latin so that he could easily converse with whites, especially in seeking information; and discipline (Ros, 57–58). The black leader trained his soldiers to endure long marches loaded with backpacks and weapons in the tropical heat, to go without water and food for long stretches of time, and to obey and respect officers in command.

Spain and England watched Louverture and the rebellion with great interest. The British, who feared similar uprisings throughout the

DID THE HAITIAN REVOLUTION BEGIN IN A VODUN CEREMONY?

Though the ceremony at Bois Caïman is a foundational text in the teaching of history in Haiti, there are scholars who question whether the event occurred at all. The initial accounts of the gathering at Bois Caïman were written by Frenchmen, some sympathetic to the whites and others in support of the slaves. The first account, published in 1814, was written by a white man, Antoine Damas, who had not witnessed the ceremony but obtained the information from the interrogation of captured rebels. He described the participants as ignorant and equated the ceremony to primitive rituals. Haitian historians of the 19th century also shied away from a description of the event, either because they were Catholics who rejected Vodun or were Francophiles who wanted to identify the Haitian Revolution with French idealism, not African traditions.

Nevertheless, an account written in 1853 by Beaubrun Ardouin served as the basis for the textbook renditions that appeared in Haiti in the early 20th century. By the 1940s, Haitian children were taught about the ceremony as a true event. Some argue that the influence of an African-based belief system is central to understanding the political significance of the meeting. Léon-François Hoffman wrote, "Those who dismiss ... Bois Caïman ... argue that only after the thirst for blind revenge and destruction was canalized and Boukman's hordes trained ... into regular Western-type armies did the revolt turned into revolution. They ... [argue] that the plantation slaves ... can only act effectively under the leadership of the overseers." Hoffman then adds that "those who glorify the ... legend ... revere the charismatic leader, divinely inspired to be the interpreter of the will and instinct of the people."

The conclusion is that whether or not the ceremony took place, African beliefs influenced the slaves' desire for freedom.

Hoffman, Leon-François. *Haitian Fiction Revisited*. Pueblo, Colo.: Passeggiate Press, 1999. pp. 159–180.

Caribbean, supported the white planters, while Spain supported the rebels. In 1793, Louverture joined the Spanish and led them to several victories and the capture of several cities. In the summer of 1793, however, France's representative on the island, Léger-Félicité Sonthonax (1763–1813), abolished slavery in Saint-Domingue. In this, he was following instructions from France, which anticipated that abolition would entice the slaves to the French side to help defeat the English and Spanish invaders. The move worked; Louverture left the Spanish to support commissioner Sonthonax.

Under Louverture's leadership, the Haitians defeated the Spanish forces. Then, in 1797, the black leader expelled the British invaders. Four years later, Louverture's forces occupied the Spanish side of the island. In virtual command of the whole of Hispaniola, Louverture formed a commission to help him govern and draft a constitution that claimed loyalty to France but gave autonomy to Saint-Domingue. He appointed himself governor for life.

Napoléonic Forces Invade Haiti

In France, Napoléon Bonaparte (1769–1821) came to power. He grew uncomfortable with Louverture's popularity and influence. Concerned that the end of slavery meant financial disaster for the plantation economy of Saint-Domingue, in 1802 Napoléon ordered 22,000 French soldiers under the command of his brother-in-law Charles-Victor Leclerc (1772–1802) to invade the colony, remove Louverture from power, and reestablish slavery. In May of that year, Napoléon's forces surrounded Louverture at his stronghold in Crête-à-Pierrot. The black general surrendered and retreated to his plantation. He probably anticipated that the tropical heat and local diseases, such as yellow fever, would soon debilitate the invaders, placing him and his troops in a good position to take up arms once more and defeat the invaders. However, this did not occur.

In June 1802, Louverture was tricked into meeting French officers, who proceeded to arrest him. As he was rushed off to a ship and then to Europe, the black general said, "In overthrowing me, you have cut down . . . only the trunk of the tree of liberty. It will spring up again by the roots for they are numerous and deep" (James, 334). In the spring of the following year, Louverture died in a French prison.

Victory for Haiti

Napoléon, though, could not claim victory in Saint-Domingue. Shortly after Louverture's arrest, his second-in-command, Jean-Jacques Dessalines (1758–1806), sought a temporary alliance with the French invaders.

Napoléon Bonaparte tricked and arrested Louverture, but to no avail, for his elite troops were soundly defeated by Haitians. It was the first major defeat suffered by Napoléon's army.

As soon as yellow fever paralyzed Leclerc and his troops, with Leclerc himself succumbing to the disease, Dessalines renewed the rebellion. In December 1803, the French were finally defeated, and Dessalines proclaimed Saint-Domingue a free republic, naming the new nation Haiti. The choice of the name for the new republic symbolized a desire to accentuate the pre-European, Amerindian roots, since "Haiti" was how the Tainos referred to the island. The Haitian Revolution is a singular event in world history. It is perhaps the only time in history that a slave population launched a successful revolution. It sent a powerful message to the rest of the world that the racial ideologies used to oppress slaves and other non-European populations were built on a foundation of lies.

In January 1804, Dessalines and his followers drafted Haiti's declaration of independence. The principal author was Louis Boisrond-Tonnerre (1776–1806), Dessalines's adviser and secretary. Tonnerre, recalling the horror of slavery and the abuses perpetrated by whites on blacks, exclaimed, "For our declaration of independence, we should have the skin of a white man for parchment, his skull for an inkwell, his blood for ink, and a bayonet for a pen!"

Shaped by an era of violence where only the strong could rule, Dessalines grew dictatorial and in September 1804 proclaimed himself Emperor Jacques I of Haiti. He ordered the execution of nearly all whites on the island and created a system of agricultural forced labor. There was opposition to his rule, and several of his lieutenants planned his assassination. On October 17, 1806, Dessalines was murdered and his body dismembered.

WRITTEN ON WHITE SKINS: HAITI'S DECLARATION

Haiti's Declaration of Independence is actually called "Act of Independence of Haiti." It was signed in the town of Gonaïves in northern Haiti. Part of it reads thus:

"Today, January 1, 1804, the General in Chief of the indigenous army, along with the generals of the army, convene to take measures that will lead to the happiness of the country ... to make known to foreign powers the resolution to render the country independent, and to enjoy a freedom established through the blood of the people....The generals ... have sworn to posterity, to the entire universe, to forever renounce allegiance to France, and to die rather [than] live under its domination."

Schutt-Aïné, Patricia, and the staff of Libraire au Service de la Culture. *Haiti: A Basic Reference Book; General Information on Haiti.* Miami and Port-au-Prince: Librairie au Service de la Culture, 1994, p. 66.

A Divided Haiti

The republic of Haiti entered the 19th century divided: mulattoes against blacks and the northern region against the southern part of the nation. Henry Christophe (1767–1820), who had been a general under both Toussaint and Dessalines, declared himself king of Northern Haiti. His former comrade-in-arms Alexandre Pétion (1770–1818), who was supported by the mulattoes, ruled in the south.

In the north, Christophe renewed the plantation system of agriculture, which helped create an elite black aristocracy. He created a Haitian currency, invited European intellectuals to help develop educational reforms, and built monuments and a palace. In the south, Pétion distributed land to former soldiers and encouraged cultivation on small plots. He attempted to create a republic and lent his support to the war of liberation in Venezuela, inviting liberator Simón Bolívar (1783–1830) to the south of Haiti.

In 1815 Bolívar visited Pétion. Bolívar explained his dream of liberating his country from Spanish rule and then the rest of South America, and be asked Pétion to support the enterprise and to provide him with "money, arms, ammunition, ships, and food." In return, Pétion asked

Bolívar to free the slaves in all the states he should liberate. Bolívar agreed, adding that he would take such action in the name of Pétion, thus building for the Haitian a monument of freedom in South America. Pétion, however, declined the honor; all he wanted was liberty for the slaves. Historian Gerhard Masur pointed out: "With this agreement for the emancipation of the slaves Pétion and Bolívar achieved world historical significance. Before Abraham Lincoln had raised his voice in the Anglo-Saxon world these two men on a little island in the Caribbean proclaimed the application of the principles of liberty and equality to an anonymous host of slaves" (Masur, 272–273).

When Pétion died of malaria at the age of 48 in 1818, a mulatto named Jean-Pierre Boyer (1776–1850) assumed the presidency. Well liked by the people, Boyer was able to unite the north and south of Haiti in 1820 after Christophe's death. (Christophe committed suicide, using a silver bullet, at the age of 57.) In 1822, Boyer, pursuing Louverture's dream of creating one nation out of the two countries occupying Hispaniola, annexed the Spanish side of the island. By the time peace came to Haiti in the 1820s, more than 100,000 blacks had been killed in the effort to create a free republic.

The United States Shuns the Black Republic

During the Haitian Revolution, the United States kept a wary eye on the colony, willing to help the French planters defeat the rebels not because they were rebels, but because they were blacks. Americans feared that the slave rebellion would spread to the United States. After Haiti became a republic, the United States refused to acknowledge its existence. In 1806 U.S. president James Madison (1751–1836) banned trade with Haiti. This embargo continued until 1809.

In 1826, the United States did not want Haiti to participate in an international conference held in Latin America. When this first inter-American congress took place in Panama, no representative from Haiti attended. The United States still maintained that Haiti's independence was illegal and did not consider the black republic part of the Americas.

At the same time, the United States benefited immensely from the Haitian Revolution. The instability during the revolution forced France to focus its economic and military resources on Haiti and to give up its claims in the continental United States. Thus, in 1803 France sold the Louisiana Territory to President Thomas Jefferson (1743–1826). In the acquisition, the United States gained Arkansas, Missouri,

After years of refusing to recognize Haiti as a free republic, the U.S. government did so in 1862 during the presidency of Abraham Lincoln.

Iowa, Minnesota, the Mississippi River, North Dakota, South Dakota, Nebraska, portions of New Mexico, Montana, Wyoming, Oklahoma, Texas, Kansas, and Colorado. In 1862, under President Abraham Lincoln (1809–65), the United States finally recognized the republic of Haiti, and trade started in earnest.

6

SLAVE REBELLIONS, ANTISLAVERY MOVEMENTS, AND WARS OF INDEPENDENCE (C. 1700–1850)

From the beginning of the conquest until halfway through the 19th century, slave traders and white planters perceived themselves as superior beings who ruled over less advanced creatures, first the indigenous population, then African slaves. By force and intimidation, sanctioned by European powers, the traders, planters, and slaveholders filled their coffers and lived a life of comfort. As long as they were white and free, even those who were not wealthy saw themselves as superior.

It was a way of life they envisioned as unchanging. After all, there were slaves in the Bible, and "institution[s] of servitude" existed early in the world's history (Barnes, 22). But even at the beginning of the conquest of the Caribbean, there were some, like Friar Bartolomé de Las Casas, who questioned the concept of white superiority over the rest of the world and condemned slavery as an evil institution. Over the centuries, slaves and others who agreed with Las Casas worked together and separately to end the world that slave traders and white planters cherished.

While it is certain that white religious leaders played a role in bringing an end to slavery by leading abolition campaigns in Europe and the United States, the role of slave resistance was long underestimated. A more balanced interpretation of the end of slavery and the slave trade needs to take into account abolitionist efforts, slave resistance, and evolving industrial technologies that made slave labor less necessary. All these factors were key to the unraveling of slavery in the middle of the 19th century.

Slave Rebellions

There were slave rebellions, many rebellions. Between 1735 and 1834 there were at least 57 rebellions throughout the Caribbean, an average of one uprising every other year, and a formidable achievement considering that the slaves were oppressed under conditions intended to break the spirit of resistance. Rebellions occurred on plantations and on ships. There were individual acts of resistance and small acts of disobedience, often interpreted by white overseers as sheer ignorance or lassitude on the part of the slaves. Scholars and writers classify these under the general heading of day-to-day resistance. These acts encompassed everything from breaking tools and poor work habits to befouling the food of the masters. Slaves also resisted by fleeing either on a short-term basis or to permanent runaway slave communities known as Maroon towns, *palenques* (Spanish), or *quilombos* (Portuguese). Slaves with considerable technical knowledge and skill occasionally used temporary flight, known throughout the Caribbean as *petit marronnage,* as a bargaining tool for better conditions. The flight of a number of slaves at the same time on their way to a permanent slave community, typically in the aftermath of a revolt, was known as *grand marronnage.*

Scholars of an earlier era often viewed acts of day-to-day resistance as characteristic of black inferiority or the effect of the lack of a Christian upbringing (Bush, 4). But, in fact, when a slave lied, deceived the master, or did not accomplish assigned tasks, the cause was often deliberate insubordination. Black women were active participants in the acts of everyday rebellion. "Many Europeans in the West Indies declared women slaves to be more troublesome than men. . . . Women slaves of all classes used many ploys to frustrate their masters and avoid work. Sometimes they feigned sickness." (Bush, 53, 62). There was also poisoning, an approach that house slaves could use because they prepared meals and had access to medicine cabinets, liquor, and other household items. Though there are no figures on actual poisonings—the same symptoms could be the manifestation of disease and not poison—the planters lived in fear of being poisoned.

A more self-destructive act of resistance was self-mutilation and suicide. There were instances of women slaves making cuts on their arms, wrists, or legs, binding the wound, and applying dirt to provoke sickness. Suicide was attempted on slave ships by leaping into the ocean with legs or arms bound or holding weights to make them sink.

Slave ships were occasionally the setting for revolts, often unsuccessful. Perhaps the most famous rebellion on a ship occurred onboard the *Amistad,* off the coast of Cuba. In 1839, a prince from Sierra Leone

Former president John Quincy Adams successfully defended the slaves who mutineered aboard the ship Amistad in 1839.

known as Joseph Cinque (c. 1813–79)—a Spanish variation of his actual name, Singbe—organized a rebellion with 54 natives from Sierra Leone and a young girl. The slaves seized the ship's crew of six and killed the captain and the cook. After 57 days at sea, the *Amistad* was seized by an American coast guard vessel. A trial followed in which former president John Quincy Adams (1767–1848) represented the slaves. Since the slaves were purchased illegally by a Spanish slaver in violation of international trade laws established in 1807, their acquisition was ruled illegal by the court and their sale voided. The slaves won their case and were returned to Africa in November 1841.

Rebellions on land were more common. At first, in the 1500s, many planters did not seriously consider the possibilities of large-scale uprisings because the number of slaves was relatively small. The ratio of slaves to Europeans (10 to 1 at most) was not inordinately high, given that Europeans had access to most of the weapons. Another factor was that the planters did not hold the intellectual capacities of their captives in high regard. The planters were confident that the novelty of the setting, the language barrier among the slaves, the separation from family, the hours of long labor, and the constant threat of intimidation were sufficient to dissuade slave revolts. Another technique practiced by the planters was to sow dissension among the slaves by pitting house and field slaves against each other. Sometimes members from rival tribal communities in Africa were made to supervise each other in the fields, an arrangement that fostered old resentments.

But in the 1600s, as sugarcane became the dominant crop in the Caribbean, the potential for armed conflict increased because of the need for a large workforce to cut the cane. On some islands, the ratio of slaves to free residents increased dramatically, in some cases reaching 50 to 1. These islands became powder kegs waiting to explode. Some colonies took steps to reduce the potential for rebellion. For example, in Barbados, planters formed a large militia and encouraged British warships to make frequent stops to the island.

Nevertheless, rebellions erupted. There were uprisings in Barbados in 1649, 1675, and 1692. The 1675 rebellion involved more than 100 slaves from plantations across the island. Betrayed by a female slave named Fortuna, the conspirators were captured. Half of them were executed. The rest were punished and sent back to the plantations. The 1692 rebellion involved more than 300 slaves, nearly one-third of whom were executed. During the second half of the 18th century, there were eight rebellions in Jamaica; during the first half of the 19th century, six rebellions were reported in Cuba. As noted in an earlier chapter, Haiti was the scene of the only successful slave revolution in the history of the modern world.

One of the bloodiest uprisings occurred in Grenada. Many historians think of Fedon's Rebellion in Grenada as that island's version of the Haitian Revolution (Rodriguez, 266). As in Haiti, the struggle in Grenada involved free people of color, slaves, the British, and the French. Though the rebellion started in 1795, its evolution dated to 1763, when the British took Grenada from the French. The British imposed English as the official language and forbade native born white Grenadians from holding public office. Free people of color were not allowed to vote, serve in the military, or acquire land. Julien Fedon (?–?) was one of those free people of color.

Fedon was familiar with both the French and Haitian Revolutions. In 1795, he sought support from French Republican agents, who were using Guadeloupe as a base, in planning a rebellion against the British. Fedon assumed the role of commandant-general of the revolutionary army, which included 7,000 slaves (of the 14,000 on the island) and nearly 200 whites and free people of color. Surprising British troops and civilians on March 1, Fedon took over three villages, forcing the colonists to flee to the capital. In less than a year, Fedon's army controlled all of Grenada except for the capital.

In June 1796, the British captured Fedon's camp and summarily executed all the black slaves and free people of color. The whites who supported Fedon were sent into exile on other Caribbean islands. Fedon disappeared, a mystery yet to be solved. The rebellion cost Great Britain nearly 3 million pounds sterling in losses, demoralized the white population, and ended Britain's designs to create a sugar colony on the island. After 1796, colonists in Grenada concentrated on the development of small farms and abandoned the notion of a plantation economy.

The British faced another massive rebellion 20 years later on an island they thought pacified: Barbados. In 1816 the Easter Rebellion involved the southern half of the island. Its leader was an African slave named Bussa. The uprising lasted three days and cost 500 to 1,000 slaves their lives. The insurrection forced British officials in London to persuade the island's governor and the council to implement policies to improve the lot of Barbadian slaves. In 1825 the island's parliament passed the Consolidation Law, which allowed slaves to own property and testify in court and reduced the fees paid by slave owners willing to emancipate their slaves.

Characteristics of the Rebellions

Recent arrivals from Africa, *bozales,* were more willing to rebel and organize uprisings than slaves born in the Caribbean, creoles. In the Haitian Revolution, recently arrived slaves, often warriors fresh from battle in Africa, played a big role in organizing military strategies against the European troops and local militias sent against them. Religious activities offered inspiration and organized avenues for rebellion. Obeah and Vodun priests held a mystical sway over their congregations. They helped plan meetings and enforce secrecy. The otherworldly nature of the religion, promising a return to Africa after death, encouraged open rebellion, for it was better to die and have a free afterlife in Africa than to live in slavery.

Christian religion also helped shape rebellions. One 19th-century pastor wrote, "The Christian religion lends no sanction to slavery; that it is not adverted to in the New Testament either as a good and desirable relation, or as one that religion would have originated for the good of society. . . . It would be clearly impossible to find a hint . . . to prove . . . that either Christ or his apostles would have originated slavery, or that they regarded it as a good and desirable institution" (Barnes, 341). (At the same time, many planters used religious passages from the Bible to justify the correctness of slavery, interpreting scripture to fit their political and economic needs.) In 1831, a rebellion in Jamaica evolved out of a meeting of Baptist slaves who used the Bible as a basis, especially one of Paul's observations that a subject cannot serve two masters. For Christian slaves, Jesus was the benign master who offered freedom and eternal life; the planters were the evil masters who stole the life from the slaves. In the 1830s, British planters blamed missionaries for encouraging slaves to rebel. In turn, the missionaries were encouraged to support abolition by the cruel manner in which rebellions were crushed, such as an 1831 insurrection in Jamaica in which 300 slaves were given hasty trials and then hanged in the public square in Montego Bay.

Abolition/Slavery Narrative

Toward the end of the 18th century, abolition literature began to appear in England and in the northeastern United States; it then spread throughout the Caribbean. Printed in newspapers and broadsides, abolitionist literature, also called antislavery literature, was dedicated to a political objective: the end of slavery. However, some of the abolitionist writers wrote out of a need to escape slavery or to make something of a living once they found themselves free. Probably the best known work from the Caribbean is the autobiography *The Interesting Narratives of the Life of Olaudah Equiano, or Gustavus Vassa, The African, written by himself* (1787) by Olaudah Equiano.

The first to write a slave narrative entirely on his own, Equiano was an extraordinary man who bought his own freedom, sailed as part of a scientific expedition, and then wrote, published, and sold an account of his life, which became an 18th-century best-seller. When he died, Equiano left his children an inheritance of about $150,000—an enormous sum by the standards of the day. Equiano was probably born in 1745 in present-day Nigeria. When he was about 11 years old, he and his sister were captured by slave traders. The two were separated. When Equiano was 12, he arrived in England. From there he was shipped to Barbados, where he witnessed the selling of slaves as if they were animals and the deliberate separation of friends and families by the white colonists.

Equiano was taken to Virginia, where he was sold to a Royal Navy officer who named him Gustavus Nassa, a common strategy used to deny slaves their identity by denying them their

Equiano was an extraordinary man who bought his own freedom and fought to end slavery. (Schomburg Center for Research in Black Culture, The New York Public Library)

original names. As personal servant to the officer, Equiano took part in the Seven Years' War (1754 or 1756–63). In England, the officer allowed Equiano to attend schools, where he learned to read and write. To Equiano's surprise, the officer sold him to another captain who took Equiano to Montserrat; there he was sold again to a Quaker merchant.

Sailing throughout the islands of the Caribbean with the merchant, Equiano began to buy and sell merchandise and saved 40 pounds sterling, the amount needed to buy his freedom. He returned to England as a freedman and worked as a hairdresser before becoming a seaman; he sailed the Mediterranean, went on an expedition to the Arctic in 1772, and spent some time with Miskito Indians on the Caribbean coast of Central America. In 1783 he befriended the abolitionist Granville Sharp (1735–1813). In 1787 Equiano was appointed "commissary for stores" in charge of acquiring provisions for an expedition to resettle freed slaves in Sierra Leone. Equiano realized that the enterprise was doomed to failure due to poor planning and widespread theft by many of the white organizers. When he made these observations public, he was reprimanded and removed from his post. The expedition failed, and Equiano was vindicated.

Around this time, Equiano began to write his memoir with the intention of stirring "a sense of compassion for the miseries which the Slave-Trade has entailed on my unfortunate countrymen" (Equiano, iii). To print the book he sought funds from abolitionists. Contributors included the prince of Wales and the duke of York. Once the memoir was published, Equiano promoted it through lectures and discussions throughout England, Wales, Scotland, and Ireland. The narrative was a bestseller. It was reprinted eight times in Great Britain and later published in the United States. In 1792, Equiano married a white English woman and had two daughters. During the 1790s, he devoted his energy to campaigning against slavery, using his book and his own life as an abolitionist document. He died in 1797.

The narrative effectively denounces the inhumanity of all those involved in slavery, draws ethnographic scenes of life in Africa during the 18th century, and offers one of the first travelogues of the Caribbean. Equiano's account of his conversion to Christianity is an excellent example of religious literature. The text is held together, though, and made engaging by Equiano's persona: likeable, imaginative, and modest. He finishes his autobiography thus: "What makes any event important, unless by its observation we become better and wiser" (Equiano, 255).

Just as effective and well received was the work of Mary Prince entitled *The History of Mary Prince, a West Indian Slave, Related by Herself.*

The volume was published as an antislavery tract in 1833. Mary Prince was born in Bermuda in 1788. She worked in the salt mines in Bermuda and Antigua, where chemicals damaged her feet. In 1826, she married a free black man but was still held as a slave by her owner, John A. Wood, who abused her physically, often stripping her naked and beating her. In 1828, Wood and his wife traveled to England, taking Prince with them. Mary Prince seized the opportunity to escape, seeking shelter in a Moravian church in London. Mary Prince narrated her story to Reverend Thomas Pringle (1789–1834), a poet, who edited the narrative. The memoir depicted the horrors of slavery from a very personal viewpoint while also serving as a document of resistance. According to scholar Sandra Pouchet Paquet, the narrative presented "personal freedom . . . as the moral and legal right to determine one's identity as a birthright" (Paquet, 32).

The narratives of Prince and Equiano contained strong Christian motifs evocative of the British religious classic *Pilgrim's Progress* (1678). The texts often served as the basis for sermons given at Protestant services in England, helping to fuel the abolitionist movement.

TESTIMONY OF SLAVERY

For generations, the experience of slaves was discounted and minimized. Slaves were depicted as acted upon but seldom as actors In shaping history. That changed in the aftermath of the Civil Rights movement in the United States, when slave narratives were widely recognized as valuable historical sources. Today the emphasis is on examining the testimonies of both white masters and slaves.

"If scholars want to know the hearts and secret thoughts of slaves, they must study the testimony of the blacks. But, since the slaves did not know the hearts and secret thoughts of masters, historians must also examine the testimony of whites. Neither the whites nor the blacks had a monopoly on truth, had rended the veil cloaking the life of the other, or had seen clearly the pain and joy bounded by color and caste.... Consequently, whether we focus on the slave or the master, we must systematically examine both black and white testimony."

Blassingame, John. Introduction to *Slave Testimony: Two Centuries of Letters, Speeches, Interviews, and Autobiographies*. Baton Rouge: Louisiana State University Press, 1977, p. xiv.

The Antislavery Movements of the 19th Century

In the 1790s, abolitionists promoted the end of the slave trade through the lobbying efforts of the Society for Effecting the Abolition of the Slave Trade, founded in 1787 in England, and the Societé des Amis des Noirs (Society of Friends of the Blacks), founded in 1788 in France. The British society conducted research on slave conditions in the colonies and on the Middle Passage by interviewing 20,000 sailors, documenting cruelty at sea and unsanitary conditions for both the sailors and the slaves. The society, composed of Anglicans and Quakers, concluded that slavery was simply against the will of God.

Members of the French organization believed that France was setting an example for the world by applying the principles of equality to the slaves. The Societé des Amis des Noirs disseminated French translations of abolitionist texts and sponsored lectures in which speakers affirmed that it was more economical to hire laborers for specific jobs than to keep slaves. In 1790, the society was able to place delegates in the National Assembly in Paris. Internal chaos in France and the French and Haitian Revolutions made the society's promotion of an end to slavery ineffective. In 1794, the society did gain a victory of sorts when the National Assembly abolished slavery; however, the victory was short-lived, and slavery was reinstituted in 1802.

In the meantime, in 1807, the British passed laws to end the slave trade. Britain then tried unsuccessfully to persuade the Portuguese and Spanish to follow suit. These countries maintained that since Britain lost its North American colonies and was no longer intent on developing large plantations, the British Empire saw no need for slaves. In their view, ending the slave trade would be a painless decision for Britain.

From 1810 onward, the abolitionist movement changed strategy from advocating for a remediation of the conditions of slavery to espousing full emancipation for all slaves. In 1823, the Anti-Slavery Society was formed in London with the objective of protecting slaves from inhumane treatment and developing plans for their gradual emancipation. In the 1820s the British Parliament approved measures that would allow slaves time for religious practice, keep slave families together, minimize physical punishment, and make it easier for slaves to buy their freedom by allowing them to save money they made on their own.

British colonists protested these measures. Jamaican planters observed that such practices would place them at a disadvantage with their competitors in the Spanish Caribbean. They claimed that Spanish planters could continue to maltreat their slaves to increase production, while British planters would be handcuffed by being forced to consider the living conditions of their slaves. Despite the objections of the planters, the abolitionist tide continued to build. Finally, in 1832, Parliament passed the Emancipation Act, ending slavery in all British possessions. The act included a compromise to appease the Caribbean planters by allowing them a five-year transition period from slavery to freedom.

In Cuba and Puerto Rico, the antislavery movement was home-grown; unlike the British government, the Spanish government did not support abolition. Cuban and Puerto Rican intellectuals and abolitionists used literature as a weapon. The inhumanity of slavery was decried in works such as the 1839 novel *Francisco: el ingenio o las delicias del campo* (Francisco: the sugar plantation or the delights of the countryside) by Cuban Anselmo Suárez y Romero and the 1867 drama *La cuarterona* by Puerto Rican Alejandro Tapia y Rivera. In 1867, Segundo Ruíz Belvis, also from Puerto Rico, wrote a brilliant argument against slavery, *Proyecto para la abolición de la esclavitud en Puerto Rico* (Proposal for the abolition of slavery in Puerto Rico). One strategy to end slavery, promoted by the Cuban economist José Antonio Saco (1797–1879), was importing white workers from Spain to slowly replace slave labor. This was to be accompanied by hiring former slaves as paid laborers.

Abolition of Slavery: A Time Line	
1792	France (reinstituted and abolished slavery several times until 1848)
1794	Haiti
1807–1808	slave trade abolished in United States and Great Britain
1822	Dominican Republic
1824	Spain
1833	entire British Empire
1848	Denmark territory in the Caribbean
1848	St. Martin
1865	United States
1873	Puerto Rico
1886	Cuba
1888	Brazil

Based on several sources, including: Sekou, Lasana M. *National Symbols of St. Martin.* St. Martin: House of Nehesi Publishers, 1996, 1997; Williams, Eric. *From Columbus to Castro: The History of the Caribbean.* New York: Vintage Books, 1970, 1984.

Saco believed that the economic incentives of free labor would benefit the economy as a whole. He proposed the emigration of European workers not only on economic grounds, but on racial ones as well, as he was concerned that Cuba might become an "Africanized" nation.

Since Spain was being pressured by England to consider abolition, proslavery Cubans, fearing Spain might eventually yield, lobbied the United States to acquire the island. Nothing came of these plans. Cuban rebels fighting for independence during the late 1800s freed many of Cuba's remaining slaves. This led the Spanish to implement a gradual abolition plan in Cuba and Puerto Rico. Slavery ended in Puerto Rico in 1873 and in Cuba in 1886.

The Chinese of the Caribbean

Planters hoped that with the end of slavery most slaves would remain in the plantation economy by working as wage laborers. This held true in some cases, but in many instances former slaves left the plantations and pursued new lives in cities and towns, where many worked as tradesmen or in shops, hotels, and restaurants. Soon the need arose for laborers in the sugar industry. The solution was to import East Indian and Chinese workers.

Chinese emigrants, eager to escape unrest at home and hoping for better economic opportunities, responded to the call for workers. About a quarter of a million Chinese emigrated to the Caribbean. Some 125,000 of them went to Cuba, 18,000 went to the British Caribbean, and the rest were dispersed throughout the French islands and Suriname (Lai, 3).

The Chinese laborer, typically a man, signed a contract for five to seven years of labor and was provided free transportation and clothing. The standard labor contract included an exit clause that allowed the laborer to terminate the contract upon payment of the transportation costs to the contracting agency. These costs were prorated based on how much time remained on the contract. For example, a laborer who ended the contract during the first year was expected to repay $75, in the second year $50, and so on. Arrangements were occasionally made to provide a salary advance, about $20, to the laborer's family in China.

The life of a Chinese worker was not much better than the life of an African slave, with the contractor assuming the role of a slave master. Abuses were common, since the contractor viewed the Chinese worker as inferior to white Europeans. In the 1870s, the Chinese government suspended emigration to Cuba until 1877, when China and Spain negotiated better treatment for Chinese workers. As part of the new agreement, Chinese laborers were free to leave when they wished. The forced abduction of workers was also prohibited.

Chinese laborers started by working in the sugar plantations. By the end of the 19th century, they had began to move into towns, where they often bought small shops supplying goods to plantation workers and the rural poor. The Chinese made a practice of selling small quantities of a given product at an economical price, allowing customers to spend as little as possible. When customers did not have sufficient cash, the Chinese owners often allowed purchases on credit, keeping a tally from which amounts were deducted as the customer made payments. There were also instances when Chinese store owners lent money to their clients. The stores were characterized by long hours of service, from dawn to midnight, with work provided by relatives and close friends.

The Arrival of East Indians

In 1845, 225 East Indians, the first laborers from India, arrived in Trinidad, the beginning of an emigration that by 1915 accounted for a population of 143,000 East Indians; in Jamaica, there were about 39,000 by the end of the century. Like the Chinese, the East Indians, eager for economic opportunities as well as encouraged by the British to reduce unemployment in certain areas in India, such as the state of Uttar Pradesh, signed a contract: five years of service for men, three years for women. The contract was renewable. After 10 years of work, the laborer was offered a subsidized return to India. It is estimated that one-third returned.

The laborers worked in the sugarcane fields and cotton farms, living on the plantation but eventually moving out to form their own communities, "leaving the estates until, by setting themselves up as peasant proprietors, they had . . . achieved a measure of economic independence. With

East Indian woman in Trinidad, late 19th century (From Down the Islands, by William A. Paton, New York: Charles Scribner's Sons, 1887, frontispiece)

105

East Indians were recruited to work in sugar plantations in Jamaica and Trinidad, as replacement for slave labor. (From *Down the Islands,* by William A. Paton, New York: Charles Scribner's Sons, 1887, p. 207)

the achievement of this independence and the establishment of village life, came the social establishment of the Indians" (Tikasingh, 12). In their villages, the East Indians maintained their own traditions, practicing either Hinduism or Islam.

In Trinidad, East Indians began to emerge as an economic force in the period between 1870 and 1900. Over the next 20 years, East Indians went from owning 50,000 acres of land in 1900 to over 90,000 by 1921. In Jamaica, the small East Indian population cultivated rice as a means of earning financial independence. As they moved away from the sugar plantations, they formed villages on the edges of swamps. The East Indians planted sugarcane, which they sold to the sugar mills, and rice, which they used for themselves as well as to earn extra income, since rice stems could be used as feed for pigs. With the income this provided the East Indians paid the rent for their houses and plots and managed to keep some money for themselves. Remaining in rural areas, the East Indians in Jamaica and in Trinidad did not mingle with the rest of the population. In Trinidad, this changed in the 20th century when East Indians challenged Afro-Trinidadians for political power.

Morant Bay Rebellion

The end of slavery did not immediately transform social relations on the islands. The racial and ethnic divisions that typified slavery continued to typify postemancipation societies, with whites still on top of the economic and political pecking order. Discrimination flourished, and opportunities for economic advancement were limited for blacks. In the British Caribbean, for instance, there were 750,000 freed slaves, but there was little they could do with that freedom. For example, eligibility to vote for the legislative assembly responsible for levying and collecting taxes required property ownership, something not available to most former slaves. In Jamaica in 1863, out of a total population of 440,000, only 1,457 people were eligible voters. Tension and resentment simmered in the Caribbean as a result of these inequalities.

On October 7, 1865, during a judicial proceeding in Morant Bay, a disruptive black spectator was arrested. A crowd came to the man's defense and rescued him from the militia. A black preacher named Paul Bogle (1822?–65) was suspected of inciting the crowd, so on October 8, eight black policemen set out to arrest him. Bogle's supporters intercepted and disarmed them. Bogle sent the officers back to Morant Bay.

On October 11, Bogle and 400 men armed with guns, pikes, and bayonets marched into town, where they had a verbal confrontation with the justice of the peace. The militia shot at Bogle and his men, who responded by throwing rocks and forcing the militia and the local official into the courthouse. Enraged, Bogle's men set fire to the building and beat to death those attempting to escape.

The rebels looted Morant Bay, burning down all the buildings in the center of town. After releasing the prisoners from the jail, the rebels headed into the countryside with a pledge to kill all the whites in the parish. Soon, the island of Jamaica was gripped in fear as people anticipated a rebellion similar to the Haitian Revolution. Governor Edward Eyre (1815–1901) dispatched troops to the area. The soldiers shot anyone who was black, whether or not they were participants in the rebellion. Bogle was captured and killed. In the 20th century Bogle's treatment by colonial authorities was sympathetically treated in the lyrics of Jamaican singer Bob Marley's "So Much Things to Say." Bogle remains a heroic figure in Jamaica to this day.

During the rebellion on October 11, 22 civilians and officials were killed and 34 were wounded. During Eyre's reprisals, nearly 900 alleged rebels were executed, and 1,000 houses belonging to the rebels and sympathizers were destroyed (Cundall, 245).

The British governor also arrested a planter named George William Gordon (1820–65), the son of a Scottish planter and a slave, for his alleged role in the rebellion. An accountant who was a friend of Bogle's, Gordon was influential in the parish, attended a Baptist church that served the poor of the area, and was a member of the Legislative Assembly. He sympathized with the plight of peasants and was critical of the governor and town officials. Gordon once called the governor a dictator and advocated his removal from office by force. On October 23, the governor put Gordon on trial. The jury found him guilty of inciting the Morant Bay Rebellion and sentenced him to death, despite the fact that he was not in the area when the incidents occurred. Gordon's body was left to decompose, hanging from a post before the burned courthouse.

Governor Eyre's violent suppression of the rebellion displeased the British Parliament. He was removed from office, and the island's government was replaced by direct Crown rule. In Great Britain, however, the press described the rebellion as a riot led by unruly blacks. This provided ammunition to racist politicians who claimed that blacks in Jamaica were not ready to rule themselves. For nearly a century, the Morant Bay Rebellion was viewed as an act of criminal behavior and not as a political uprising. It was not until the novel New Day, by Vic Reid, appeared in 1949 that the events were narrated from the perspective of the rebels. The novel led scholars to reexamine the events of October 1865 and realize the importance of the Morant Bay Rebellion in planting the seeds of political consciousness in the Jamaican population, a consciousness that would come into full bloom in the middle of the 20th century.

Spain's War of Independence

Due to political differences in the Spanish court, in 1808 King Charles IV (1748–1819) of Spain passed on the throne to his son, Prince Ferdinand (1784–1833). Napoléon Bonaparte (1769–1821), eager to expand his empire and sensing disunity within the Spanish court, intervened, forcing the father king to offer the crown to Napoléon's brother Joseph Bonaparte (1768–1844). On May 2, 1808, the Spanish people rebelled against Napoléon, a conflict known as the War of Independence or the Peninsular War. As a result of this war, the Spanish Crown lost effective control over and communication with its American empire. The Spanish colonies formed independent juntas to rule themselves. In 1813 the Spanish, with help from the British, defeated the French invaders. The conflict led to the first Spanish constitution. The Constitution of 1812 established parliamentary rule and limited the authority of the monarch. However, in the intervening years the colonies learned to live without guidance from the mother country. By 1824, the great Spanish Empire was history.

The Most Loyal Islands

At the end of the 1700s, as a result of economic and administrative reforms, Spain was ruling more efficiently than ever. However, the Napoleonic invasion created a power vacuum in Spanish America and revealed festering tensions between the mother country and the colonies. Spain's inability to run the colonies directly while it was occupied by French troops set off a wave of nationalism and independence movements across the Spanish Empire. When it was all over, only the islands of Puerto Rico and Cuba remained Spanish.

The colonies broke away in rapid succession. Venezuela declared its independence in 1811. Colombia followed in 1819 and Peru in 1821. Guatemala, Nicaragua, Honduras, Costa Rica, and El Salvador established the United Provinces of Central America in 1821. Ecuador and Mexico broke away in 1822. In 1824, Simón Bolívar (1783–1830) defeated once and for all the Spanish forces in South America.

Historians and scholars have often asked why Puerto Rico and Cuba remained loyal to Spain. Part of the answer lies with the slave system, particularly in the case of Cuba. The slave system stunted nationalist aspirations in Cuba because local planters feared a Haitian-style revolution and relied on Spanish troops to keep the slave system in place. The flight of Spanish loyalists to Cuba and Puerto Rico also affected the decision to forgo immediate independence.

As a result of this immigration, the population of Cuba and Puerto Rico grew dramatically. In Puerto Rico, the population went from 150,000 in the 1780s to 400,000 in the early 1800s, with about 80 percent of the people settling in the countryside. They included about 400 Corsican immigrants who were allowed into Puerto Rico under the Cédula de Gracia (Royal Decree of Graces) of 1815, which was designed to attract settlers from parts of Europe other than Spain. They settled in the southwestern part of the mountainous countryside of Puerto Rico, where they planted coffee, sugarcane, and tobacco; by the 1860s, seven out of 10 coffee plantations on the island were owned by Corsican families (Casablanca, 19). The *cédula* gave immigrants certain benefits. These included an allotment of six acres of land per family member, three acres per slave, and the right to become Spanish citizens. These benefits discouraged newcomers from supporting rebellious plots against Spain.

Refugees to the island from the wars of independence in other colonies were also averse to rebellion. The independence movement was further slowed by the political rights granted by Spain in 1809. As a result of the Napoleonic invasion of the peninsula in 1808, Spanish citizens formed juntas, a government consisting of a military or civilian coalition or both, on the Iberian Peninsula to combat the invaders. In 1809, the junta in Cádiz, seeking allies against Napoléon, declared Puerto Rico a province rather than a colony, with full representation before the Spanish Cortes, or parliament. The island's representative helped draft the liberal constitution of 1812 and demanded that, should Spain be defeated by France, Puerto Rico should have the right to declare independence. Such advances made Puerto Ricans seriously contemplate whether or not to part ways with the mother country.

Yet these political concessions were short-lived. After Napoléon's defeat in 1813 the Spanish monarchy was reestablished, and the constitutional government was dismissed. The return to absolutism was a key factor in the decision by many of the Spanish colonies to seek independence. Political unrest continued in Spain. In 1820 the monarch, the restored King Ferdinand VII, was forced to bring back some of the earlier constitutional reforms. The struggle between monarch and political elites continued, and in 1823 the king again revoked constitutional gains. The king sent governors and captain-generals with unchecked powers to Cuba and Puerto Rico; these governors and captains ruled the islands as if they were monarchs. Their harshness encouraged exactly what they wished to oppose, separatist movements.

Imperial Rule in Puerto Rico

Spain, concerned that the wars of independence on the continent would spread to Puerto Rico, gave rights with one hand and took them away with the other. While notifying Puerto Rico of its change to provincial status, the junta instructed governors to rule as if under a state of siege, with permission to suppress individual liberties as needed. In addition, the Spanish Parliament placed Puerto Rico under special laws, removing constitutional rights and forcing Puerto Ricans to pay up to a half million pesos to Spain to help the mother country recover from the losses suffered during the Napoleonic invasion.

From 1822 to 1837, the military governors ruled whimsically and impulsively (Wagenheim, 54). Governor Miguel de la Torre (1786–1838) implemented the regime of the three B's: *baile, botella, baraja* (dance, bottle, cards), encouraging dancing, drinking, and gambling on the assumption that the diversions would distract Puerto Ricans from political activities. Other governors also enacted mercurial edicts: a decree that punished the unemployed for being lazy; a ban on mustaches and goatees; a requirement that blacks remain indoors after 11 P.M.; and a decree that said people could not move from one residence to another, travel throughout the island. Words such as *dictatorship* and *tyranny* were not permitted in print. During the 1830s and 1840s, at least three major newspapers were shut down by the Spanish authorities.

Several conspirators were betrayed and arrested during this period. They included María Mercedes Barbudo (1780–1825), a Puerto Rican woman who was one of the independence pioneers of the Hispanic Caribbean. Barbudo used her home as a center for discussions of independence and for the dissemination of revolutionary tracts and writings, distributing anti-Spanish propaganda published in South America and in the United States. In 1824 Governor de la Torre deported her to Cuba, where she later died in exile.

Beginning of the Abolition Movement in Puerto Rico

With an agricultural economy based on small farms and diversified crops, which included coffee, maize, rice, tobacco, and sugarcane, Puerto Rican landowners had no need for extensive holdings of slaves. The slave population on the island was not as large as in other Caribbean islands. In 1827, the population included 162,311 whites and 34,240 slaves; in 1872, there were 618,150 whites and 31,635 slaves. In comparison, Cuba had 279,689 whites and 239,694 slaves

EARLY CUBAN REVOLUTIONARY LITERATURE

The first Cuban newspaper to openly seek independence was *El Habanero*, published in exile in Philadelphia in 1823 and 1824 and in New York between 1824 and 1826. Edited and published by Cuban exile Father Félix Varela, the paper was smuggled into Cuba, where it caused a sensation. The Spanish government denounced the publication of *El Habanero* and ordered a stop to its circulation. The governor even authorized the assassination of Varela.

The newspaper is credited with inspiring Cubans to seek a break against colonial rule. Varela is also credited with writing *Jicoténcal* in 1826, the first Latin American novel published in the United States. The work criticized Spain's conquest of the Americas.

Leal, Luis, and Cortina, Rodolfo J. Introduction to *Jicoténcal,* by Félix Varela. Houston: Arte Public Press, 1995, pp. xiv–xv.

in 1817, and 833,157 whites and 344,615 slaves in 1867 (E. Williams 1984, 291).

In 1865, Julio Vizcarrondo (1830–89), a Puerto Rican living in Spain, founded the Sociedad Abolicionista Española (Spanish Abolitionist Society). The society established branches throughout Spain and published an antislavery journal, *El abolicionista español* (The Spanish abolitionist). In 1867, a commission from Puerto Rico traveled to Spain to plead for the abolition of slavery. One of its members, Segundo Ruíz Belvis (1819–67), wrote an antislavery manifesto, *Proyecto para la abolición de la esclavitud en Puerto Rico* (Project for the abolition of slavery in Puerto Rico). The combined efforts of these patriots influenced Spain in its decision to abolish slavery in Puerto Rico in 1873.

Seeds of Rebellion in Cuba

In Cuba, the first conspiracy against Spain was organized in 1809. The plotters drafted a constitution whereby suffrage would be based upon property ownership, and Catholicism would be recognized as the official religion. It was hoped that this would attract the support of the wealthy classes and conservative Cubans. This plot was not supported by the landowners, who feared that independence would bring about the end of slavery. In 1810–11 there was a rebellion planned by slaves who were inspired by the Haitian Revolution. It was suppressed with the execution of its architect, José Antonio Aponte (?–1812), a free black carpenter. Conspiracies, often including slaves, abounded and were violently suppressed throughout the 1820s.

Three political movements emerged during the 19th century: reform, autonomy, and annexation. The reform movement proposed freedom for the island to trade with all countries, the maintenance of slavery and the slave trade, and the conversion of Cuba into a Spanish province. In the 1830s, the reform movement dropped support for the slave trade while allowing for the maintenance of slavery. The autonomous movement, modeled on the regime established in Canada by the British, promoted the end of slavery, equal political participation with Spain, freedom of trade, freedom of the press, and the right to hold political meetings. The autonomists did not advocate a formal break with Spain.

Annexationism was probably the biggest movement during the early 1800s. Promoted by slave owners, the annexationists wanted Cuba to become a slave state of the United States, which would allow for the practice of slavery. Two approaches were considered. One included the acquisition of the island by the United States, with prices ranging from $100 million in 1848 to $310 million in 1854. Another approach endorsed military action, with a Cuban leader taking over the island, calling for its independence, and then annexing it to the United States. This was the initial objective of one of Cuba's most memorable and controversial patriots, General Narciso López (1797–1851).

General López: Independence or Annexation?

Related to wealthy Cuban families, López, a native of Venezuela, fought with the Spanish troops in South America against liberator Simón Bolívar (1783–1830). In Cuba, López married into wealth and was attracted to the annexationist cause. Some historians suggest that López began as an annexationist but later considered joining the struggle for full independence. He was a popular figure in the American South, where he was seen as an important advocate of adding Cuba to the United States union as a slave state. The press of the era, particularly in the southern states, precursors to the Hearst journalism of 1898, advocated for war against Spain and portrayed López as a romantic adventurer.

In 1848, after participating in a conspiracy against the Spanish government in Cuba, he fled to New Orleans, where he plotted the invasion of Cuba. In 1851, López and 400 men landed on the northern side of Cuba. His troops included Cuban patriots as well as Americans who were veterans of the U.S. and Mexican War of 1846–48. After disembarking in Cuba, López was captured and sentenced to death. Minutes before he was garroted in a public execution in Havana in 1851, López shouted, "My death will not change the destiny of Cuba."

The Raising of the Cuban Flag

López carried and raised for the first time in Cuba the island's national flag. Lopez conceived the flag, which incorporated the pyramid symbol used by Freemasons and stripes in blue and white with a solitary star in the center of the pyramid. The flag was sewn by Emilia Teurbe Tolón (1828–?), the wife of coconspirator Miguel Teurbe Tolón (1820–57). The lone star signified Cuba's sovereignty, though some historians have observed that the one star in the Cuban flag was meant to be incorporated with the other stars in the U.S. flag, reflective of López's plans for annexation. Seventeen years after López's execution, Cuba's Republic-in-Arms, fighting the Spanish government during the Ten Years' War (1868–78), selected the flag as the island's national banner.

Haiti Invades Santo Domingo

For the Dominican Republic, then called Santo Domingo, the initial independence struggle was not against Spain but against its neighbor, the black republic of Haiti. In 1795, Spain ceded two-thirds of Hispaniola to France by the provisions of the Treaty of Basel. The treaty ended a war that Spain conducted with other European allies to end the French Revolution. The problem was, though, that Spain lost to France as French troops defeated Spanish troops and invaded Spain. Spain offered to exchange Santo Domingo (the Spanish part of Hispaniola) for the withdrawal of French forces from Spain. France agreed. However, the French government was slow in claiming the island. Toussaint Louverture decided to take possession of Santo Domingo on behalf of the French, doing so in 1801. His first act was to proclaim the abolition of slavery.

In 1802, when Emperor Napoléon attempted to reconquer Haiti and reestablish slavery, French troops on the Spanish side of the island united with Dominican forces to expel Louverture. In 1805, Haitian emperor Dessalines, the successor to Louverture, attempted an invasion of Santo Domingo but was repelled. As Dessalines retreated into Haiti, he torched several cities along the way. Seventeen years later, Haitian president Jean-Pierre Boyer (1776–1850), leading a force of 12,000 soldiers, was successful in occupying the Spanish side of Hispaniola.

The Haitian occupation of Santo Domingo lasted from 1822 to 1844. Boyer immediately freed the slaves, about 9,000, and granted them land taken from the Spanish planters who escaped to Cuba and Puerto Rico. He imposed French as the official language and shut down the University of Santo Domingo, the oldest in the Americas.

Independence from Haiti

In 1838, well-to-do Spanish-Dominicans under the leadership of Juan Pablo Duarte (1813–76) formed a secret society called La Trinitaria, the Trinity, with the objective of obtaining independence. The conspirators sought an alliance with Haitian political reformers who opposed the rule of President Boyer. When internal developments in the black republic forced Boyer into exile, his successor, Rivière Hérard, attempted to imprison the Trinity conspirators, forcing Duarte to flee the island. In 1844, 105 Dominican patriots signed the Manifestación de la Parte Este (Declaration from the Eastern Section), claiming independence from Haiti. This was not accepted by the Haitian government. Over the next decade, the Haitians conducted military campaigns against the newly formed Dominican Republic. This history of aggression would be used to fan the flames of anti-Haitianism in the Dominican Republic in the 20th century.

The Haitian military campaigns involved more than 40,000 Haitian soldiers against 15,000 Dominicans. Despite their numerical superiority, the Haitian forces were not supported by their compatriots, who feared that the cost of the conflict would drain the national economy. Furthermore, internal divisions prevented a succession of Haiti's presidents from forming a united front against the rebellious Dominicans.

Spain Follows Haiti

After independence from Haiti, two Dominican presidents, Pedro Santana (1801–64) and Buenaventura Báez (1812–84), took turns ruling the country from 1844 to 1861. Each man's primary goal was becoming powerful and wealthy. Expressing concerns about another Haitian invasion and afraid that internal turmoil could remove him from power, Santana invited Spain to annex the republic in 1861. Spain did so with the help of 20,000 soldiers brought from Cuba and Puerto Rico. Dominicans fell into two camps, those who supported the annexation out of loyalty to Santana and those who saw in it the recolonization of their country, a shameful act, especially because it was initiated by a fellow Dominican.

Supporters of the move anticipated political stability and equal footing in Spain by making the Dominican Republic a Spanish province. But Spain treated its new acquisition as a rebellious colony, implementing dictatorial laws that censored printing, forbade Protestant services, and shut down Masonic lodges. Rumors soon circulated that the Spanish planned to enslave black Dominicans and ship them to Cuba and Puerto Rico.

The first rebellion against the Spanish occurred in 1863, igniting a civil war. The conflict ended two years later after Santana's death (from natural causes) and Spain's retreat from the Dominican Republic. The war left the country bankrupt. Many Dominican cities were destroyed. Agriculture in the country came to a virtual standstill. The defeat of Spain, however, reaffirmed Dominican sovereignty and engendered pride in the fledgling nation. The Dominican victory was a clear signal to Haiti that any further aggression would be repelled. The war also sent a message to Puerto Rican and Cuban independence fighters: Spain could be defeated.

The war of restoration in the Dominican Republic nurtured individualistic rule by regional leaders who united local forces and were able to maintain control of their regions. In Latin American and the Caribbean this personalistic style of leadership is known as *caudillismo,* or loyalty to a strong political figure, and the local leaders are frequently referred to as *caudillos.*

Dominican presidents of the 19th century were typically the strongest of the regional caudillos. Many Dominican caudillos who fought against Spanish forces employed guerrilla tactics to expel the invaders. They recruited local youths and relied on knowledge of the terrain without forming coalitions with other regional leaders. Such strategies made local leaders more powerful, ruling without aid from the capital or the national government.

The caudillos who came to power at the end of the 19th century and through much of the 20th century were intent on accumulating wealth and reaping personal benefits, disregarding the public good and the nation at large. It was not until the 20th century and the construction of a national road system that the Dominican Republic developed more fully into a nation-state where regional interests were subjugated to a national agenda.

These dictatorial traits were not unique to the Dominican Republic. The strongman became a standard figure in the politics of Cuba and Haiti and, in a slightly different version and perhaps less dictatorial, in the Anglophone Caribbean during self-rule and after independence.

7

PUERTO RICO, CUBA, AND THE SPANISH-CUBAN-AMERICAN WAR (1850–1900)

In the 1860s, Spain treasured Cuba and Puerto Rico, the source of considerable wealth through high taxes and tariffs. The planter aristocracy on the islands felt economically abused yet did not seek a rupture with Spain, the mother country. In Cuba, the planters feared that a break with Spain could bring an end to the slave trade and also lead to a black insurrection similar to the Haitian Revolution. In Puerto Rico, the planters were afraid that the United States might take possession of the island. There was also a cultural identification with Spain: The Hispanic islands were Catholic, the language was Spanish, and the traditions and family values were rooted in Spanish customs.

The islanders did have grievances. They wanted the tariff system reformed and demanded representation in the Cortes, the Spanish parliament, as well as equality with Spaniards. Spain, however, was in no position to entertain these reforms. In 1868, a revolution overthrew Queen Isabella II (1830–1904), and a new king, Amadeo of Savoy (1845–90), was placed on the throne. The new Spanish government, confronting its own political uncertainties and battling dissent, responded to the requests from the islands with harsh measures that included increasing the power of the military, shutting down the press, outlawing political meetings, and increasing taxes and tariffs.

Spain would come to regret these measures.

Puerto Rico

In the 1850s, Puerto Ricans dissatisfied with Spanish rule began to plot a revolution. Apart from the dissatisfaction with unfair taxation and high tariffs, Puerto Ricans also wanted an end to what they saw as manifestations of Spanish tyranny, which, besides slavery, included the *libreta* system, which made serfs out of laborers. It was put in place in 1848 by the Spanish governor. Under this system, laborers who lived and worked on a plantation could not venture off the grounds without the planter's permission. The *libreta* was a notebook that had to be in the laborer's possession at all times. Laborers had to account for their movements by indicating on their *libreta* time off from work, time away from the plantation, and the time of return. Through the *libreta*, planters knew everything about laborers. Such restrictions on personal freedom were seen as manifestations of Spanish tyranny.

A committee traveled to Spain to plead for the abolition of slavery. Segundo Ruíz Belviz (1819–76), a member of the committee, presented an antislavery manifesto, *Proyecto para la abolición de la esclavitud en Puerto Rico* (Project for the abolition of slavery in Puerto Rico), in which he described the ill effects of slavery on economics, society, and the family structure. One of his principal arguments was that since Puerto Rican agriculture was based on small farms rather than large plantations, as found in Cuba and Jamaica, there was no need for slavery. Furthermore, the island had the distinction of having a white population that was greater than the slave population: 328,806 whites versus 31,635 slaves. By ending slavery, Ruíz Belviz believed the former slaves could be hired as workers, and the promise of paid labor would serve as an incentive, thus augmenting productivity.

El Grito de Lares

A physician named Ramón Emeterio Betances (1827–98), who was opposed to slavery, founded an abolitionist society in the 1850s. Through the society, he and other wealthy members purchased new-born slaves and freed them. Betances authored antislavery tracts that angered the government, resulting in his exile by the Spanish authorities. In the Dominican Republic, Betances wrote a proclamation of freedom, known in Puerto Rico as "The Ten Commandments of Free Men," demanding the abolition of slavery, freedom of speech, freedom of religion, freedom of the press, and the right to assemble. While preparing his return to the island to lead an insurrection, Betances and his fellow conspirators were betrayed. The authorities in the Dominican Republic, observing neutrality accords, confiscated the boat obtained to transport Betances and the weapons for the uprising.

On September 23, 1868, even without Betances, the rebellion took place. Revolutionaries took over the town of Lares and raised a banner, the island's first flag. A provisional government was established, slavery was abolished, and a pile of the hated *libretas* was torched. As the rebels moved on to another town, a Spanish militia surprised them; after a battle, the rebels were dispersed.

Although the insurrection, known as El Grito de Lares, lasted just one day, it had a long-lasting effect on Puerto Rico and Spain. In the words of one nationalist writer, it was the day that "Spaniard became Spaniard and the Puerto Rican, Puerto Rican" (Corretjer, 61), indicating the island's political rupture with the mother country.

Aftermath of the Insurrection

The insurrection led to the end of slavery in Puerto Rico. In 1869, in response to the Lares rebellion, the Spanish government began the process of abolishing slavery with the desire of reducing Puerto Rican grievances against the colonial authorities. Finally, in 1873, the slaves were freed, though they were required to work for their former masters for a period of three years.

After the Grito de Lares rebellion, there was tranquility in Puerto Rico. Reforms were implemented that afforded the island a sense of self-rule. Puerto Rican leaders and intellectuals debated whether to seek autonomy from Spain or assimilation with the mother country.

In 1887 there was a setback as a new governor, believing liberal Puerto Ricans who wanted independence were plotting against the government, ordered hundreds of arrests. Many were then tortured or murdered in prison. In November of that year, the governor planned to execute prominent autonomist leaders, but protests from the Puerto Rican population and the neighboring island of St. Thomas alerted the Spanish Cortes, who removed the governor from office.

The movement toward autonomy continued, and in 1897, Spain accepted the political compromise, the brainchild of Puerto Rican leader Luis Muñoz Rivera (1859–1916). Puerto Rico was now granted provincial status, and Puerto Ricans were able to participate in local elections. The deal with the Spanish provided for a military governor in Puerto Rico who could rule only with the approval and support of elected Puerto Rican officials. The island was permitted to make treaties with foreign powers and could even accept or reject treaties with Spain.

Cuba's Ten Years' War

Cuba's destiny was quite different. From 1868 to 1878, war raged on the island. Prior to the 1860s, Cubans refrained from participating in open conflict against Spain. There were two main reasons for this. The first was the large Spanish army presence on the island. The second was the fear among the Cuban planter aristocracy that war could bring about the abolition of slavery. Since black slaves were the sole workers in the sugar industry, this would jeopardize the whole industry. Instead of rebelling, Cubans attempted to work through the Spanish Cortes for greater autonomy and an end to high tariffs and taxes. Their requests were ignored.

El Grito de Yara

In October 1868, after hearing of the Lares rebellion in Puerto Rico, Cuban plantation owners in the province of Oriente began their own rebellion, known as El Grito de Yara, led by a rich planter named Carlos Manuel de Céspedes (1819–74). An army of 12,000 insurgents, known as *mambises,* was formed. As the rebellion spread to the center of Cuba, a constitution was written, a house of representatives was established, and Céspedes was elected president of the republic-in-arms. Poor whites, free blacks, mulattoes, slaves, and Chinese immigrants joined the ranks of the rebels. They fought under two generals known for bravery and brilliant battle tactics, the Afro-Cuban Antonio Maceo (1845–96), called "the bronze titan," and the Dominican Máximo Gómez (1836–1905). Gómez was the strategist, Maceo the dashing commander. Under their leadership, by 1873, the *mambises* controlled Oriente Province in eastern Cuba.

By the mid-1870s, however, divisions stalled the *mambises*'s progress. Conservative members of the provisional government opposed Gómez's audacious plan of marching toward Havana. They also feared Maceo's rising popularity among Afro-Cubans. Disagreements over Céspedes's management of the revolutionary government forced him to resign. In 1874 Céspedes was killed by Spanish troops.

In 1877, Spain dispatched to Cuba an aggressive military leader, General Arsenio Martínez Campos (1831–1900), and increased the Spanish army to 70,000 men. In the capital, Spanish volunteers created a paramilitary force of nearly 20,000. In October 1877, Martínez Campos captured the new president of the republic, Tomás Estrada Palma (1835–1908). Martínez Campos began negotiations for a truce.

General Antonio Maceo opposed a truce. Meeting with Martínez Campos, the Afro-Cuban general demanded the immediate abolition of slavery and independence for Cuba. The Spanish leader did not yield, and the war, under Maceo's leadership, continued for a few months until the Cuban army was defeated by the Spanish forces. Maceo was allowed to leave Cuba for Jamaica.

ROMANTIC HEROES: CARLOS MANUEL DE CÉSPEDES AND PERUCHO FIGUEREDO

Carlos Manuel de Céspedes, the Cuban leader in the Ten Years' War, embodied the contradictory nature of Cuba's abolitionists. A wealthy landowner whose ancestors had lived in Cuba since the early days of the colony, Céspedes was a slave owner who freed his slaves so that they could join the war against Spain, serving under his command. When he proclaimed the rebellion, he announced the end of slavery on the island. Later on, to satisfy white planters who wanted freedom from Spain but did not support abolition, he modified his position, advocating for the gradual end of slavery. In 1870 he again revisited his stance and, as president of the republic-in-arms, announced the abolition of slavery.

One of his closest allies was Perucho Figueredo (1818–70), a member of Cuba's aristocracy. Upon hearing of Céspedes's call to arms, Figueredo left his home in Bayamo, saying: "I will join Céspedes and will go with him either to glory or the scaffold."

With Céspedes in charge of the insurgents, Figueredo helped in the capture of Bayamo. Mounted on his horse, Figueredo penned a battle hymn modeled on "La Marseillaise," France's national anthem, which became popular during the French Revolution. When 2,000 Spanish troops returned to retake the city, the people of Bayamo sang the hymn as they fled to the countryside.

Figueredo was captured in 1870 and sentenced to death. A messenger from the Spanish general offered to free him if he promised never to fight against the Spanish again. Figueredo responded: "I would hope not to be bothered in the last moments that I have left of life."

Figueredo's battle hymn is Cuba's national anthem today. Céspedes is regarded as the island's founding father.

A truce was signed in 1878, but separatists within the Cuban army rebelled in August. There were several clashes against Spanish forces. However, the rebellion was not supported by the Cuban planter aristocracy. They were convinced by Spanish propaganda that the insurrection was a race war, with Afro-Cubans planning to establish a republic similar to the one in Haiti. By October, the uprising had failed.

The 10-year conflict cost about $300 million (Thomas, 269). The Spanish and the Cubans suffered combined losses of 200,000.

1878: Pax Iberiana

In 1878, an uneasy peace came to Cuba. The Partido Liberal Autonomista (Liberal Autonomist Party), whose members were predominantly from the middle class, was founded. This political party favored autonomy for Cuba while at the same time arguing that the island should remain part of Spain. Its members promoted rights for Cubans as well as Spaniards, including freedom of speech, freedom of the press, and free assembly. The autonomists also advocated for the abolition of slavery, which finally occurred in 1886. By that time, many of the slaves had already been freed, either by rebels during the independence war or by a Spanish government amnesty for slaves who took part in the conflict.

In the mid-1880s, the sugar industry was mechanized to address the end of slavery, falling sugar prices, and the developing sugar beet industry in Europe. To centralize sugar production, plantation owners acquired large land holdings upon which they constructed or expanded railroad systems. In 1881, electric and telephone services were established in the capital.

During this period, Spain adopted different attitudes toward Cuba and Puerto Rico, choosing to be more liberal and flexible with the latter and dictatorial with the former. The captain-generals of Cuba banned public gatherings. Criticism of Spain and the government was likely to lead to imprisonment or exile.

Cuba's War of Independence

Six years after the end of the Ten Years' War, political conditions in Cuba remained unchanged, and the dream of liberty and independence still beckoned. Wealthy exiles in the United States responded by promising funding for a new revolution. In 1892, the poet and orator José Martí (1853–95) founded the Partido Revolucionario Cubano (Cuban Revolutionary Party) in New York City. Its objectives were to fight for Cuba's independence and establish a republic on the island, as well as liberate Puerto Rico from Spanish rule.

One of the cornerstones of Martí's philosophy was Cubanidad, or "Cubanness." This was an expression of Cuban nationalism that sought to play down racial differences on the island. Martí was a forceful opponent of racism and saw discrimination against Afro-Cubans as a danger to the development of a Cuban national identity and a threat to the island's independence. He hoped to establish a color-blind society in Cuba, free of the racial ideologies built up by years of slavery.

He infused the independence movement with this ideology of Cuban nationalism.

José Martí

José Martí became the symbol of the struggle for independence. He traveled throughout the Americas promoting the Cuban cause. Settling in New York City in 1880, he wrote for the *New York Sun* and several Latin American newspapers. In his essays, he tried to develop a political and cultural consciousness that reflected Latin America's needs and that was not influenced by U.S. politics. In these writings, Martí cautioned Latin America against succumbing to the economic, cultural, and political influence of the United States. He worried about the tendency of some Cuban revolutionary leaders to be authoritarian and expressed concern that the United States would emerge as an imperial power in Latin America. He advocated for the creation of a Cuban republic with freedom and equality for all.

In 1891, his fame as an orator took him to Tampa, where Cuban cigar workers embraced him as a leader and applauded his call to all Cubans, regardless of race, to fight as one. The money collected by the cigar workers, including Spanish and Italian anarchists who rallied to Martí's side, helped fund the invasion of the island.

Martí was the invasion's strategist. In 1895, he authorized the uprising, penning a document in which he explained the need for a just war to bring about freedom and equality in Cuba. The insurrection, known as the Grito de Baire, took place on February 24 in Oriente Province in eastern Cuba. In April, Martí returned to his beloved island, but just a month later, on May 19, 1895, he was killed in combat. While in exile, he wrote a poem in which he expressed the desire to die facing the sun:

> *No me pongan en lo oscuro*
> *A morir como un traidor*
> *Yo soy bueno y como bueno*
> *Moriré de cara al sol*
> *(Do not hide me in the dark*
> *to die a traitor's death*
> *I am a good person and like a good person*
> *I will die facing the sun)*

When his body was found, he was reportedly on his back, and sunlight was on his face.

Fearing U.S. intervention, José Martí had hoped for a quick victory against the Spanish. However, the war went on for three more years

Cuban soldiers attacking Spanish infantry (From *United States in War with Spain and the History of Cuba,* by Trumbull White, Chicago: International Publishing Co., 1898, pp. 72–73)

under the leadership of experienced generals Antonio Maceo, Máximo Gómez, and Calixto García. Although the Spanish government had 120,000 troops, they could not defeat the Cuban insurgents who, numbering in groups of 2,000 under several leaders, used guerrilla warfare, like the Tainos centuries before. The battles between the Spanish troops and the *mambises* were fierce, with each side demonstrating great courage. Cuban rebels often led suicidal machete charges against the Spanish infantry.

Since the Cuban rebels were aided by people from the countryside, the island's military governor, General Valeriano Weyler y Nicolau (1838–1930), employed a *guerra contra guerra* (war against war) strategy. To cut off civilian support for the rebels in rural areas he used a policy called *reconcentración,* setting up concentration camps in which rural residents were imprisoned. Over 500,000 civilians were placed in the camps; some 250,000 of them perished due to poor conditions, malnutrition, and disease. Anyone or anything in the evacuated areas of the island was considered a legitimate military target, including crops and livestock. Still, General Weyler y Nicolau could not end the war, and by 1896, the *mambises* had reached the outskirts of Havana. A year later, though, Spanish and Cuban forces were at a stalemate.

These developments were closely watched by Puerto Rican patriots, such as Betances, whose desires to achieve independence were rekindled. Many observers and participants thought that the end of the war and victory for Cuba were just a matter of time. However, events took an unexpected turn in 1898.

1898: The Spanish-Cuban-American War

At the very end of the 19th century, Havana served as a catalyst for change not only for the Caribbean but for the world at large. To the north of Cuba, the United States was waving the banner of manifest destiny and eager for territorial expansion and recognition as a global power. It was a long-standing dream of the United States to possess Cuba. As the 19th century came to a close, the United States was edging toward a confrontation with Spain, prodded on by two individuals with their own dreams of glory: journalist William Randolph Hearst (1863–1951) and Undersecretary of the Navy Theodore "Teddy" Roosevelt (1858–1919).

Both men detested Spanish rule over the island and believed that it would be just and right for the United States to help bring about Cuba's freedom. But both had other motives. For Hearst, war could mean higher circulation for his newspaper *The Journal,* a rival of the more popular and distinguished paper *The World,* owned by Joseph Pulitzer (1847–1911). Roosevelt considered the English-speaking nations the most advanced in the world (Burton, 36). For him, war would allow the United States to guide Cuba out of backwardness and would affirm America's imperial power in the Caribbean. It would also provide him with the opportunity for fame and enhance his pursuit of national political office.

On the other side of the Atlantic, Spain was trying desperately to hold on to the island because of its critical importance to the Spanish economy. But in doing so, the Spanish government was antagonizing the very people, the Cubans, it wanted to keep within the empire. Instead of granting the island autonomy, Spain grew more dictatorial.

A Forgotten Heroine: Evangelina Cisneros

Traditionally, the beginning of the Spanish-Cuban-American War is identified as the explosion of the battleship *Maine* in 1898 in Havana Harbor. However, recent feminist interpretations suggest that the onset

125

of the conflict has at its roots sexuality, chivalry, and the manipulation of the human response to a woman in distress. In this instance, the woman was the beautiful Evangelina Cossio y Cisneros (1878?–1967), known in the United States as Evangelina Cisneros.

Cisneros's father, a veteran of the Ten Years' War of 1868–78, was arrested in 1895 when local police discovered him hiding weapons in a friend's house and planning to join the insurgents fighting in the countryside. When he was sentenced to death, his daughter convinced the governor that her father was too elderly and ailing for the sentence to be carried out. The governor commuted the sentence to life imprisonment. Father and daughter were shipped to a prison on Isla de Pinos (Isle of Pines), a small island to the south of Cuba. The Isle of Pines was reserved for prisoners who were not considered dangerous or who were connected in some way with the Spanish government. Some prisoners were housed in small individual huts, while others were imprisoned in a larger compound near the island's main town. Cisneros's father was assigned to a hut, and there the young woman looked after him.

While at the Isle of Pines, Cisneros, who was 17 years old, caught the eyes of the colonial warden. The attraction was not mutual. The warden relocated Cisneros's father to the larger prison, hoping to use his release as romantic leverage. The ploy was not successful, and the young woman continued to repulse the warden's advances. One evening, though, the warden somehow found himself alone with Cisneros in her hut. There are two versions of what happened next. The Spanish version claimed that the warden was tricked into the dwelling so that Cisneros and other prisoners could murder him and provoke a larger rebellion. The Cuban version, however, maintained that the warden went into the hut to rape the young woman. When she cried for help, her Cuban neighbors rushed to her rescue, beat the warden, tied him up, and left him in the countryside. The Spanish and the Cuban accounts agree that the incident led to Cisneros's arrest on charges of plotting a revolt and attempted murder of a Spanish official.

Evangelina Cisneros was sentenced to a women's prison in Havana. In 1897, news of her situation reached newspaper tycoon William Hearst. He reported on the young woman's plight in *The Journal* and started a letter campaign asking for her release. When the Spanish authorities did not respond, Hearst arranged for her rescue, sending a reporter to Havana who broke a cell window and helped the young woman escape. From Cuba, the pair sailed to the United States, where Cisneros became a symbol of Cuba's dream of liberty. She toured New York City, promoting support for the Cuban cause, and Washington, where she met with President William McKinley (1843–1901). The American public saw her treatment and arrest by the Spanish government as evidence of human rights abuses on the island. Hearst, famous for his sensational approach to journalism, encouraged public opinion in favor of U.S. involvement in the Cuban war of independence. He asserted that it was America's duty to defend an island held hostage by an oppressive regime. In other words, like Cisneros, Cuba needed to be rescued. Thus, Cisneros and Hearst provided the psychological fuel that fanned the fires of war.

In June 1898, Evangelina Cisneros married a compatriot. She returned to Cuba at the end of the Spanish-Cuban-American war and lived quietly in Havana until her death in 1967. Her story was seldom told in Cuba, and few Cuban historians wrote about her, focusing instead on such heroic leaders as José Martí and Antonio Maceo and on depictions of battles against the Spanish forces. Similarly, accounts of the conflict in the United States preferred the more cinematic exploits of Teddy Roosevelt and his famous charge up San Juan Hill. Feminists have since recovered her story and its contribution to the Cuban cause.

The interest that Cisneros's story stirred in the American reading public continued as Hearst published more and more stories about alleged atrocities in Cuba. *The Journal* covered at great length the "reconcentration" of Cubans to designated camps by General Weyler.

Remember the *Maine*

Pressure from the U.S. government and the American public prompted Spain to recall General Weyler. The governor's supporters in Havana, though, rallied in his favor in early 1898, causing a riot. Some of the rioters expressed anti-U.S. sentiment, which led the McKinley administration to fear for Americans living on the island. On January 24, 1898, President McKinley ordered the battleship USS *Maine*, anchored at Key West, to sail to Havana Harbor.

The ship arrived in Havana a day later. Spanish authorities, who wanted to avoid a direct confrontation with the United States, extended every courtesy to the crew: Cannon in the Morro Castle saluted the vessel, and the Spanish secured a safe spot where the ship could anchor in the bay. To avoid any incidents ashore, the U.S. captain, Charles Sigsbee (1845–1923), did not allow the sailors to leave the ship.

Several weeks later, on the evening of February 15, an explosion rocked the city of Havana. Engulfed in flames and smoke, the USS *Maine* sank in the harbor. The death toll was 266 American sailors. Captain Sigsbee immediately concluded that his ship was the victim of

The wreck of the USS Maine; *the explosion claimed the lives of 266 American sailors and started a war.* (From *United States in War with Spain and the History of Cuba,* by Trumbull White, Chicago: International Publishing Co., 1898, pp. 192–193)

sabotage. Even though the Spanish participated in the rescue effort and helped look after the wounded, rumors of sabotage quickly spread. In the United States, Hearst's artists drew illustrations of a torpedo placed under the ship; the newspaper headline read, "Who Destroyed the *Maine*?" Two days after the explosion Hearst answered his own question with another headline: "The War Ship *Maine* Was Split in Two by An Enemy's Secret Infernal Machine!" (Lundberg, 73).

The American public, still enamored of Cisneros and now mourning the death of several hundred sailors, clamored for vengeance. On April 21, President McKinley ordered a military blockade of the island. Four days later, he asked Congress to declare war on Spain. Rallying to the war cry, over 125,000 young men volunteered for combat. U.S. war strategy included aggressive forays not only into Cuba, but into Puerto Rico and the Philippines as well. By the end of the month, Commodore George Dewey had defeated the Spanish navy at Manila Bay in the Philippines.

Cuban patriots responded to these developments with ambivalence and doubt. Twice in the past, in 1854 and 1859, the United States expressed a desire to annex Cuba, offering to buy the island from Spain. The offer had been rejected. Some in the United States had supported filibustering expeditions. Many Cuban rebels believed that Spain was tiring of the war and that they were on the verge of independence prior to U.S. intervention. The United States was an unexpected ally that might try to rob Cuba of its rightful victory.

In July, the U.S. Navy defeated the Spanish fleet off Santiago Bay, and the marines defeated the Spanish troops inland at the Battle of San Juan Hill. The victory was seen as symbolic of U.S. might and catapulted Colonel Teddy Roosevelt, who resigned from government to take part in the war, into the international limelight. Roosevelt and his Rough Riders were credited with leading the charge up San Juan Hill, over-running enemy trenches, and turning the tide of battle. By mid-July, less than three months after its declaration of war, the United States was victorious over the Spanish in Cuba. With Dewey's victory in the Philippines, the United States gained colonies in both the Pacific and the Caribbean.

WAS THE *MAINE* EXPLOSION AN ACCIDENT?

There are many different theories about the cause of the explosion. The initial suspicion was that the Spanish placed a mine or a torpedo under the ship. However, since Spain wanted to avoid war with the United States, this does not seem likely. According to the book *Trama* (Montaner, 250), some theorized that Cuban anarchists placed the mine to draw the United States into the conflict.

However, by the 1910s, researchers were convinced the explosion was the result of an accident. In 1976, Admiral Hyman Rickover concluded that coal near the ship's engine became so hot that it created internal combustion. Since the coal was next to the room that contained ammunition, the explosion was inevitable. For Rickover, an accident caused the sinking of the USS *Maine* (Rickover, 1976).

Montaner, Carlos Alberto. *Trama*. Esplugues de Llobregat, Barcelona: Plaza & Janes, 1987.

Rickover, Hyman G. *How the Battleship Maine Was Destroyed*. Washington, D.C.: Dept. of the Navy, Naval History Division, 1976.

Occupation of Puerto Rico

On July 21, 1898, U.S. war vessels left Cuba for Puerto Rico with 3,000 marines on board. In San Juan, the Spanish prepared for the attack, keeping most of their forces within the city. Many Puerto Rican patriots were willing to fight against the United States because just a year ear-

U.S. Marines marching to battle (From *United States in War with Spain and the History of Cuba,* by Trumbull White, Chicago: International Publishing Co., 1898, n.p.).

lier Spain had granted the island political autonomy. As a result, independence fever did not burn as hot in Puerto Rico as in Cuba. Having achieved these concessions from Spain, some Puerto Rican leaders did not want to risk U.S. intervention. However, others still opposed any Spanish presence and encouraged their compatriots to rise in arms. "It's extremely important," wrote Ramón Emeterio Betances, "that when the first troops of the United States reach the shore, they should be received by Puerto Rican troops, waving the flag of independence." (Wagenheim, 88).

The U.S. Marines expected heavy resistance at San Juan, where an estimated 8,000 Spanish soldiers were stationed. On July 25, they chose to disembark on the south of the island and make their way north to the capital. As they marched inland they encountered little resistance except in the town of Coama, where the marines stormed the Spanish garrison.

In San Juan, the population evacuated while the Spanish troops prepared themselves for a confrontation in which most expected to perish. The mood was somber. It was reported that at least two Spanish artillery soldiers, despondent over the potential loss of the island, attempted suicide. The attack, however, did not take place. On August 12, the U.S. military received word that an armistice had been signed between the United States and Spain.

The Treaty of Paris

In May 1898, England approached the United States to suggest solutions to end the war between the United States and Spain. The United States was receptive to the idea of negotiations, especially because U.S. troops held a decisive military advantage over the Spanish and were likely to profit by a settlement. By mid-July, Spain, all too aware of impending defeat, asked the French government to intercede on its behalf, and Paris was selected as the site for peace negotiations. The two rivals, after consenting to a cease-fire in August, conferred through the fall. Finally, in December 1898, the Treaty of Paris was drafted and signed. The terms of the treaty included agreements on the part of both the United States and Spain. Spain was to free Cuba, with the United States assuming protection for the island; Spain was to cede Puerto Rico, the Philippines, and Guam to the United States; and the United States was to assume financial responsibilities for Cuba.

For the United States, the war and the treaty trumpeted its entrance into the world arena as a global power. John Hay (1838–1905), American ambassador to Great Britain at the time, described the conflict as a "splendid little war." It energized the American public, glad to see young men from both North and South united in joint cause against a common enemy. It softened some of the bitter memories of the American Civil War (1861–65) that wreaked such havoc on the country. For Spain, the signing of the treaty was perceived as an act of national humiliation. As for Cuba and Puerto Rico, neither was invited to participate in the peace negotiations.

America's First Objective: Yellow Fever

Upon occupying Cuba, the United States set out to build roads and improve sanitation. A priority was the elimination of the dreaded disease known as yellow fever. The disease was common in Cuba, perhaps more so than in any of the other islands in the Caribbean. When outbreaks occurred, cities turned into ghost towns as people fled to the countryside and authorities quarantined entire neighborhoods. On many occasions, buildings where yellow fever was reported were burned to the ground to avoid contagion.

The disease killed one out of five victims, though Cubans tended not to suffer as severely as visitors. In 1762, more than 3,000 Spanish soldiers posted in Havana perished during an epidemic. A year later a British fleet seized the opportunity to attack the vulnerable city. The invaders were victorious, but within months British soldiers and sailors succumbed to yellow fever.

The disease took its name from its symptoms. The first symptoms of yellow fever were weakness, a high fever, and internal bleeding. In some patients the disease progressed further. They began vomiting a thick, black, bloody substance, and their skin and eyes turned yellow. Patients who did not progress beyond the high fever usually recovered. Those who reached the vomiting phase were doomed.

In the late 1870s, a Cuban doctor, Carlos J. Finlay (1833–1915), concluded that yellow fever was transmitted by a mosquito. In 1881, he presented his findings in a study entitled *El mosquito hipotéticamente considerado como agente de transmisión de la fiebre amarilla* (The mosquito hypothetically considered the agent for transmission of yellow fever). The scientific community dismissed Finlay's findings until 1900, when Dr. Walter Reed (1851–1902), a member of the American Yellow Fever Commission, proved through a series of experiments that his Cuban counterpart was correct.

The U.S. government immediately began a campaign to eradicate the mosquito in Cuba by draining puddles, dumping oil onto bodies of stagnant water, and fumigating streets and buildings with sulfur. A satisfied U.S. Army, as represented by Major V. Harvard, a surgeon, submitted a report stating that the identification of the yellow fever agent "was one of the most brilliant discoveries of the age." The official document attributed the breakthrough to the American Dr. Reed rather than the Cuban author of the original research, Dr. Finlay.

Independence for Cuba

The United States set up military governments to oversee Cuba and Puerto Rico. In 1900 the United States called on Cubans to draft a constitution establishing a democratic government. Cuba approved a constitution in 1901, but the United States inserted an amendment known as the Platt Amendment, after its sponsor, Senator Orville Platt (1827–1905).

The Platt Amendment allowed intervention in Cuban affairs when U.S. interests were at risk. It prohibited the island from entering treaties without U.S. approval and established a naval base at Guantanamo Bay in southeastern Cuba. The amendment created great turmoil at the Cuban Constitutional Convention, and it was narrowly approved by one vote. U.S. officials made it clear that without adoption of the Platt Amendment, Cuba would remain under military occupation. The Platt Amendment defined Cuba's relationship with the United States for the next three decades and became a symbol of U.S. imperialism in Cuba and the rest of Latin America.

Cuba held its first democratic elections in 1902, choosing Tomas Estrada Palma as president. After the election, the U.S. military governor announced the end of the occupation; his departure signaled the inauguration of Cuba as a republic.

President Estrada Palma had lived for many years in the United States and was seen as pro-American. He negotiated an agreement with the United States, the Treaty of Reciprocity, that gave both nations preferential treatment in commerce when dealing with each other. The treaty helped revive the sugar industry as Cuba's main economic enterprise. This contributed to relative prosperity on the island. Estrada Palma was able to build over 300 kilometers of railroad tracks, and land values increased.

At the same time, the economic imbalance that typified the Cuban economy for much of the 20th century began to emerge. Spanish policies during Cuba's War of Independence decimated the population, which fell from 1.8 million before the war to 1.5 million after it. The war also

UNITED STATES NAVAL BASE AT GUANTÁNAMO BAY, EVOLUTION OF A COLONIAL SYMBOL

After the terrorist attacks of September 11, 2001, the United States converted a section of the Guantánamo Naval Base in Cuba into a prison camp for suspected terrorists captured in Afghanistan and other parts of the world. The decision is rich with historical irony. One of the fiercest battlefields of the cold war is now a focal point of the war on terror.

Few places in the world are as isolated and controversial as the 45-square-mile base in southeastern Cuba at the entrance to Santiago Bay. The Cuban government cut off water and overland supplies to the base in 1964 and ringed it with barbed wire fencing. As a result, all supplies for the 8,500 residents of the base are brought in by sea or air.

The tortured history of the base began in 1903, less than a year after Cuba gained its independence. U.S. influence on the island was at its peak, and Cuba had little choice but to accept the naval base, for which it received a paltry $2,000 a year. The rent went up slightly in 1934 to $4,085 annually, although the revolutionary government refuses to cash the checks as a symbol of defiance.

The administration of President George W. Bush began transferring prisoners to the base in early 2002 to what was then known as Camp X-Ray, a group of chain-link cages. A more permanent compound of

---

shattered the economy, making it ripe for exploitation by foreign interests after the war. The Cuban upper and middle classes were economically devastated by years of war. This left an economic vacuum filled by U.S. merchants and corporations. By the early 1900s, foreigners, particularly those from the United States, owned a disproportionately large share of the island's major businesses, including railroads, utilities, and sugar mills.

Between 1905 and 1933, the young republic elected four presidents. However, the island's political life was marked by electoral fraud, military conflicts, and rebellions as one political party tried to wrest power away from another, as well as manipulation by U.S. senators and diplomats.

steel cages replaced the earlier facility several months later. Much of what goes on at the detention center is classified, but there have been persistent accusations of torture and inhumane treatment of prisoners. In 2004, the U.S. Supreme Court ruled that prisoners held at the detention center could appeal their confinement in the federal courts. In another decision against the Bush administration, the Supreme Court ruled in 2006 that the detainees must be granted all the legal protections guaranteed by the Geneva Convention. These legal debates are very much ongoing, and as an effort to address the rulings, the Bush administration established military tribunals to determine whether prisoners are "enemy combatants." Recent estimates suggest there are now just under 400 prisoners housed at the facility, and several human rights organizations and Internet sites are dedicated to tracking the treatment of prisoners.

In spite of the controversies over the detention center and the future of the base in a country that does not want it, an American enclave flourishes there, including Boy Scout and Girl Scout troops and Little Legue baseball. The base includes a commissary, a bank, a college, a furniture store, gas station, hospital, dry cleaners, a bowling alley, library, a nine-hole golf course, an 18-hole miniature golf course, tennis courts, batting cages, and three swimming pools, according to U.S. Navy records. A weekly newspaper, the *Guantanamo Bay Gazette,* chronicles events in the community.

The Cuban government has refrained from making public statements about the use of the base as a detention center for suspected terrorists. In the past, the base was used to house Haitians and Cubans seeking asylum in the United States. It also serves as a refueling station for navy vessels patrolling the Caribbean.

Uncertainty for Puerto Rico

Events in Puerto Rico followed a different path. Military rule on the island ended in 1900 as the United States passed a bill called the Foraker Act. The legislation provided for a governor, to be named by the president of the United States, an executive council, composed primarily of Americans, and a chamber of delegates elected by Puerto Ricans. The latter body, though, could only exert power in the arena of local issues.

The relationship between Puerto Rico and the United States was strained. Puerto Ricans resisted efforts to adopt the English language. The U.S. government tried to anglicize the island's name and convert it to "Porto Rico." U.S. officials attempted to establish an educational system based on the English language and mandated the adoption of an American curriculum. Regarding U.S. colonization efforts, a distraught Luis Muñoz Rivera wrote pessimistically that "within half a century, it will be a disgrace to bear a Spanish name" (Wagenheim, 110–113).

8

CUBA: DICTATORSHIP AND REVOLUTION (1900–2007)

The forced departure of the Spanish Empire from the Hispanic Caribbean in 1898 opened a new era in the political evolution of Cuba and Puerto Rico. Each island struggled with the new reality of overwhelming U.S. influence and how to construct boundaries to safeguard their respective sovereignties. The path of Cuba was steeped in revolution and bloodshed as nationalist movements surfaced to challenge the political and economic elite on the island and their overly friendly ties with the United States. The Cuban path ultimately led to revolution and a rejection of the United States. A central theme of the first half of the 20th century was to answer a basic question: What does it mean to be Cuban?

The process of self-definition began in the 19th century as Cubans developed their own sense of selfhood as *criollos,* or Creoles, fostering cultural and psychological identification with the island of their birth rather than Spain and creating a Caribbean persona that eventually sought a break from Europe. There was also a segment of society, as in all the nations of Latin America, that sought to identify itself with Europe and devalue African and indigenous influences on culture and society. Many Cubans saw themselves as white and of European descent. It was common for white Cubans to discriminate against darker Cubans, especially those of African descent.

Such racism led in 1912 to a conflict known as "the race war," when black veterans of the independence wars, fearing that they were being excluded from the benefits of the new nation, took up arms against the government. The genesis of the conflict can be traced to the establishment in 1907 of a political party based on race, the Partido Independiente de Color (Independent Party of Color). The establishment of a race-based party was antithetical to the teachings of Cuban martyr José Martí, who had argued against Cuban definitions of nationhood based on skin color.

The revolt started after the Cuban Congress, fearing that it might lead to a movement to "Africanize" Cuba, outlawed the party. Party members resisted. The Cuban government moved to quickly and brutally suppress the uprising. U.S. Marines fighting alongside Cuban soldiers, under the command of white Cuban officers, massacred nearly 3,000 men, killing many Afro-Cubans regardless of whether they were involved in the struggle. It was a tragic reenactment of what the French did to the Haitians during the revolution in Haiti and what British soldiers perpetrated on Jamaicans during the Morant Bay Rebellion of 1865.

The early Cuban Republic was plagued by corruption scandals, U.S. interference, and clashes among the Liberal and Conservative Parties that amounted to little more than squabbles over patronage and access to government funds. Elections were corrupt affairs, with pervasive interference by the Cuban military. Cuba's second president, José Miguel Gómez, (1909–13), who put down the uprising caused by the outlawing of the Independent Party of Color, was nicknamed *Tiburon,* "the shark," for his propensity for using Cuban funds for his own purposes. He was followed by Conservative Party leader Mario García Menocal (1913–21), a colonel of Cuba's independence war and a prominent sugar mill administrator. Menocal managed to steal even more than Gómez and was forced to put down a rebellion led by former president Gómez aimed at removing him from power. He oversaw one of Cuba's greatest sugar booms, which coincided with World War I (1914–18)when the Allies purchased the island's entire sugar crop. Menocal was succeeded by Alfredo Zayas (1921–25). By this time, corruption was so rampant that Washington sought to impose fiscal discipline by forcing Zayas to appoint the "Honest Cabinet," a group of Cuban leaders whose goal was to reduce corruption and trim the bloated bureaucracy. It was another sign of the ability of the United States to dictate Cuban internal affairs as well as foreign policy. One notable success for the Zayas government was the decision by the United States to renounce any claim to the Isle of Pines (now known as the Isla de la Juventud). The U.S. business community had lobbied Washington since 1898 to maintain sovereignty over the island, which lies just off the coast of southwestern Cuba.

Most Cubans acknowledged that change was needed. The man they thought would bring it about was Gerardo Machado (1871–1939), another former military leader of the independence war, who pledged to spend more on public works projects and to seek an annulment of the Platt Amendment. The struggle for Cuba's future was about to take a revolutionary turn.

Machado's Dictatorship in Cuba

Cuban strongman Gerardo Machado took office in 1925 after being elected on a national reform platform. His rule lasted until 1933. His eight years in office were shadowed by the worldwide depression that began in 1929. This was a period of social unrest in Cuba, as sugarcane workers found themselves employed only two months out of the year (as a result of a 60 percent drop in sugar production), 1 million workers were unemployed out of a population of 3.9 million, and most Cubans lived on a salary of $300 a year (Martínez Fernández, 167). Labor and student protests were countered with police brutality and repression, including firing into crowds of protesters.

In the summer of 1933, Cuba plunged even further into economic and social chaos. Sugar prices, the island's principal source of wealth, reached bottom, with a pound of sugar selling for a penny in the world market. As a result of worldwide economic depression, Cuban exports plummeted from a value of $353 million in 1925 to $80 million in 1932. This economic downturn furthered the resentment against dictator Machado. The economy declined to such an extent that the government was often unable to pay employees. Rumors circulated that military positions might be eliminated, causing unrest in the armed forces.

To remain Cuba's strongman, Machado used violence to terrorize his political opponents. The violence increased as the economy declined. Secret organizations sprouted up across the island, most notably the ABC revolutionary society, dedicated to unleashing a campaign of urban warfare against the Machado government. The secret societies were organized into cells so that members knew only others in their own cell. The structure of these organizations made it difficult for the government to destroy the opposition. In addition to the secret societies, students at the University of Havana were among Machado's fiercest opponents. Their opposition led Machado to close down the university and secondary schools across the island, a move that backfired because it gave the students more time to plot his overthrow.

Cuba was to be the first test case of the U.S. Good Neighbor policy, which was aimed at increasing economic relations between the United

States and Latin America by guaranteeing that Washington would refrain from direct military intervention in the affairs of its southern neighbors. Officials in Washington, sensitive to disorder and chaos in Cuba because of the risk to U.S. investments, decided that Machado must go. In 1933 newly elected U.S. president Franklin D. Roosevelt (1882–1945) sent Ambassador Benjamin Summer Welles (1892–1961) to the island to mediate the situation and convince Machado to step down.

The very presence of Welles, who arrived in May 1933, emboldened the Cuban political opposition. One by one, political allies began to abandon Machado. Separate conspiracies were brewing among the senior officers, the junior officers, and the enlisted men in the Cuban army. In August, a general strike shook the island. The senior officers withdrew their support, and Machado left Cuba on August 12, 1933, boarding a hydroplane for Nassau in the Bahamas.

Machado's departure unleashed an orgy of violence directed at his supporters. In the following weeks, the homes and businesses of Machado's allies were burned and pillaged. Many of his closest supporters were murdered and their bodies mutilated and paraded through the streets. The presidential palace was attacked and looted by angry mobs. Today, Machado is almost universally reviled as a symbol of brutality and oppression. His was the first failed dictatorship of the 20th century, but it would not be the last.

Machado's chief of staff, General Alberto Herrera, was selected as interim president in 1933. Since he lacked the support of the military and the public at large, Ambassador Welles negotiated the selection of Carlos Manuel de Céspedes y Quesada (1871–1939), a son of Cuba's founding father, as the new president. Céspedes, a diplomat, was acceptable to the United States, but the perception that he was Washington's candidate ultimately undermined his support among the Cuban people. The new president assembled a cabinet on August 14, 1933, but in less than a month, Céspedes would be bounced from office by an unknown sergeant and a coalition of students.

Origins: The Revolution of 1933

Within the army, there was a deep divide between enlisted men and officers. Officers often achieved positions of power because of social connections and wealth. The norm within the Cuban armed forces was to discriminate against the common soldier, who was usually poor and of mixed-race origin. There were separate facilities at military bases for officers and the enlisted men, with the latter often being noticeably inferior. In a public setting, such as a theater box, a soldier was expected to leave, as a sign of deference, if an officer entered, even if both were off duty. Salary increases and furloughs were granted whimsically by officers, forcing enlisted men to ingratiate themselves with their superiors. Enlisted men often worked as servants in the homes of the officers. This caused great resentment among enlisted men.

In 1933 a rumor went around that Céspedes's government might purge the enlisted men who had previously supported Machado and that their salaries would be reduced (Thomas, 635–636). In August, a handful of sergeants began to plan a rebellion. By September, a charismatic sergeant named Fulgencio Batista (1901–73) emerged as the leader of the rebels. Of mixed racial heritage, Batista was a sugarcane worker who joined the army at the age of 20. After a decade of workmanlike service he was promoted to sergeant. As leader of the rebels, he instructed privates, corporals, and sergeants to take command of military posts throughout Havana and the rest of the island. Batista succeeded in establishing alliances with civilian groups, most importantly with the Directorio Estudiantil Universitario (Student Directory), a revolutionary organization based at the University of Havana. On September 4, 1933, the soldiers and the students ousted President Céspedes.

An executive commission of five men, a pentarchy, was created to govern the country. It quickly collapsed and led to the appointment to the presidency of a popular professor from the University of Havana, Ramón Grau San Martín (1887–1969). The most influential member of Grau's cabinet was radical nationalist Antonio Guiteras Holmes (1906–35), who was named to the post of interior minister. In the days immediately following September 4, Sergeant Batista was promoted to colonel and army chief of staff. These three men—Batista, Grau, and Guiteras—would wrestle for control of the revolutionary government through the 134 days of its existence.

Although the government was in power for a little over four months, it enacted sweeping

From humble beginnings, Batista emerged as a revolutionary, a president, and then a dictator. (From Album de la revolución cubana, Habana, 1959, postcard 11. D. H. Figueredo's Collection)

141

reforms that included the establishment of an eight-hour workday and a minimum wage. During a strike by workers, the government took over the Cuban Electric Company, a subsidiary of a U.S. corporation, and slashed electricity rates by 45 percent. In an effort to address concerns about foreign economic domination, the revolutionary government decreed that 50 percent of the workforce in a foreign company must consist of Cubans. Rural reforms included forcing sugar mills to grind more sugarcane produced by *colonos,* small independent farmers. On the labor side, the eight-hour workday and a minimum wage were established. On the international side, the government did not recognize the Platt Amendment, which granted the United States the right to intervene in Cuban affairs, and it refused to repay loans made by the Chase National Bank to the disgraced Machado government.

These reforms were not supported by wealthy Cubans and antagonized the United States, which did not recognize the revolutionary government and did what it could to encourage and foment political opposition. There were several challenges to the rule of Grau, Guiteras, and Batista. The most dangerous came from about 300 officers who led a rebellion from the Hotel Nacional in Havana. Batista ordered the army to roust the officers by bombarding the hotel from a ship and from artillery surrounding the site.

Escalating violence, as one political group fought against another, forced Grau's resignation. He was followed first by an interim president and then by a veteran of the war of independence, Carlos Mendieta Montefur (1873–1960), who was considered Batista's puppet. Batista continued to command the army while transforming himself into an astute politician. He both approved and distanced himself from acts of violence against anyone who opposed him. He publicly criticized the United States while secretly consulting the American ambassador on political and economic matters.

Although the revolutionary government attempted to implement a social agenda, the average Cuban tended to view the Revolution of 1933 as a failure. The government did not address land reforms, did not do enough to lessen U.S. economic influence in Cuba, and did not make the United States accept Cuba as an equal and sovereign nation.

Strongman Batista

After Céspedes vacated the presidential office, Colonel Batista dominated the political scene, placing several weak presidents in power. The Batista of the 1930s and 1940s emerged from the left of the political spectrum, and although a dictator, he laid a revolutionary claim to his power. Influenced by New Deal reforms in the United States and revolutionary measures enacted by Mexican president Lázaro Cárdenas (1895–1970), Batista enacted a rural education program that succeeded in building more than 1,100 schools in isolated regions of the island. Batista encouraged modest land reform and built tuberculosis clinics and other medical facilities across the island. Most importantly, realizing that he could not rule indefinitely through the military, Batista began to move toward establishing democratic institutions in Cuba.

A constitutional convention in 1939–40 drafted the new, progressive Constitution of 1940, which guaranteed a host of civil and property rights, including equality for men and women and the right of women to vote and hold elective office. Forming unlikely alliances with communists and conservatives, Batista won the presidential election of 1940 and a four-year term in office.

The Constitution of 1940 prohibited a president from seeking reelection, and Batista's handpicked successor was defeated by Grau in the 1944 election. The defeat effectively ended Batista's first tenure in power, and control was peacefully transferred to Grau. This confounded the expectations of some who believed that Batista would overturn the unfavorable results. Quite aware that it was uncommon for military men in Latin America to give up power peacefully, Cubans applauded Batista's action. He toured South America, where he was welcomed as a hero, and settled in Daytona Beach, Florida, in 1945.

Had Batista remained in Florida and away from politics, he would probably have been remembered as the democratically elected president who restored democracy and implemented social reforms. However, in 1948, he returned to Cuba after his election to the Cuban Senate; created his own party, Acción Unitaria (United Action Party); and expressed a desire to be president once again. When polls in 1952 showed that Batista could not win the elections, he ousted the democratically elected president in a coup on March 10, 1952. By destroying the democratic institutions he helped create, however flawed, Batista destroyed his past accomplishments. The Batista of the 1950s was essentially at war with his own legacy.

This time around, Batista was unable to establish legitimacy for his government. There was no credible explanation for his claim that the 1952 coup was a revolution to cleanse the Cuban government of corruption. Furthermore, he was unable to fashion an exit strategy for his regime. When he first took power he claimed the move was temporary,

143

but he remained in power for more than six years as his government and support crumbled around him. He would become a Machado for a new generation.

Batista's second regime degenerated into violence and corruption. Efforts by some of his supporters to terrorize the civilian population and break the morale of the revolutionaries seeking to oust him backfired and led to a strengthening of resistance. While Batista's direct involvement in ordering violent acts is unknown, it is clear that he did not punish those responsible for human rights violations. There were also allegations that Batista made millions from mob-run casino operations, graft, and the national lottery.

By the mid-1950s Batista's government was in deficit, with an average unbudgeted expenditure of $40 million annually (Santovenia, 191) and disparate social conditions: "The disparity between the wealthy and the poor . . . grew greater. About one fourth of all Cubans lived in poverty. . . . For peasants in the country, work was limited by the duration of the sugarcane harvest to about half a year" (E. Williams 1984, 51). The white middle class, professors, university students, and peasants began to conspire against Batista. Several leaders became prominent, but none loomed as large as attorney Fidel Castro Ruz.

Rare close-up of Fidel Castro in 1959. After his victory over Batista, his revolution became a symbol of defiance of American might. (From Album de la revolución cubana, Habana, 1959, postcard 126. D. H. Figueredo's Collection)

Fidel Castro, the Rebel

The son of a wealthy Spanish landowner, Castro (1926–) might be seen as representative of the well-to-do Caribbean politician, such as the Manleys from Jamaica, whose idealism took him from a life in corporate boardrooms to a life of action in the political arena. After attending prestigious private schools, where he proved himself a brilliant student and gifted athlete, Castro enrolled at the law school of the University of Havana in

Rare drawing of the Moncada attack on July 26, 1953. Though a failure, the attempt gave birth to the Cuban Revolution. (From Album de la revolución cubana, *Habana, 1959, postcard 24. D. H. Figueredo's Collection)*

1945, where he achieved notoriety for his intelligence as well as impulsiveness and short temper.

Castro graduated in 1950. Two years later he was campaigning for a seat in Cuba's House of Representatives when Batista's coup d'état derailed his aspirations. Castro took two steps. First he filed a legal brief against Batista, accusing him of violating the Constitution of 1940. Then he plotted to overthrow the new regime by taking over a garrison and calling on the people of Cuba to rebel against Batista and establish a new government.

The attack on the Moncada Army Barracks on July 26, 1953, was a fiasco, resulting in the death of 70 of the 120 plotters and Castro's arrest. During his trial, Castro achieved international fame when he delivered a speech, "History Will Absolve Me," now considered a classic of political rhetoric. The speech is devoid of Marxist content, leading many to speculate about when Castro became a committed communist. Sentenced to 20 years in prison, he received amnesty at the end of 22 months and sought exile in Mexico, where he continued to plan the revolution.

"HISTORY WILL ABSOLVE ME"

In his famous defense speech, Fidel Castro listed the objectives of his revolutionary government and claimed that history would recognize his role as a leader and Cuba's liberator: "The first revolutionary law would return power to the people and proclaim the 1940 Constitution the Supreme Law of the State until such time as the people should decide to modify or change it. . . . The second revolutionary law would give non-mortgageable and non-transferable ownership of the land to all tenant and subtenant farmers, lessees, share croppers and squatters. . . .

"The third revolutionary law would assure workers and employees the right to share 30% of the profits of all the large industrial, mercantile and mining enterprises, including the sugar mills. . . .

"The fourth revolutionary law would grant all sugar planters the right to share 55% of sugar production and a minimum quota of 1,000 pounds for all small tenant farmers who have been established for three years or more. . . .

"The fifth revolutionary law would confiscate all the holdings and ill-gotten gains of those who had committed frauds during previous regimes, as well as the holdings and ill-gotten gains of all their legatees and heirs. . . .

"I know that imprisonment will be harder for me than it has ever been for anyone, filled with cowardly threats and hideous cruelty. But I do not fear prison, as I do not fear the fury of the miserable tyrant who took the lives of 70 of my comrades. Condemn me. It does not matter. History will absolve me."

Castro, Fidel. *History Will Absolve Me.* New York: Lyle Stuart, 1961.

1953 to 1959: The Violent Phase

The revolutionary movement against Batista was composed of urban fighters, several guerrilla movements in the countryside, businessmen who provided financial backing, religious groups, and only at the very end the Communist Party. In 1952 the opposition parties, the Auténticos and the Ortodoxos, demanded elections. In 1953 Castro, in the attack on the Moncada Barracks, called for the violent overthrow of the regime. In 1954 Batista held elections that were considered a sham. In 1955 representatives of the traditional parties held a series of dialogues with Batista requesting new, legitimate elections. That same year two important revolutionary groups were formed: the Directorio

Revolutionario (Revolutionary Directory, DR) and the 26th of July Movement.

The Directorio was formed by university students. Its main focus was the overthrow of Batista. On March 13, 1957, Directorio members conducted a daring attack on the presidential palace in Havana that resulted in the death of more than 50 students. After this setback, the Directorio set up guerrilla operations in the Escambray Mountains of Las Villas province in central Cuba.

The 26th of July Movement, named for the day of the attack on Moncada, was led by Fidel Castro. It counted in its ranks the celebrated guerrilla fighter Ernesto "Che" Guevara. This movement was based in the Sierra Maestra Mountains, in the province of Oriente, and grew from 12 guerrillas in 1956 to more than 7,000 in late 1958. A branch of the 26th of July Movement operated in the city of Santiago de Cuba, Oriente's capital, sabotaging police stations and assassinating Batista's officers. The revolutionary forces in the mountains and the urban forces in Santiago made the province of Oriente a stronghold of the rebellion against Batista.

Castro's War

Castro returned to Cuba in December 1956 aboard a yacht packed with 82 rebels. His strategy was to disembark on a beach and make his way to the Sierra Maestra in eastern Cuba. From there he would launch a war of liberation against Batista. A little over a dozen rebels survived an initial battle against Batista's troops; however, the landing energized the urban resistance groups.

Employing guerrilla tactics, Castro taunted Batista's forces. The international attention he received when the *New York Times* published a series of articles about his daring landing and his plans to return democracy to Cuba enhanced his image as a romantic hero. Cuba's upper class, which always detested Batista, found in Castro a leader who could unite the opposition against the government. As Castro drew the wealthy and middle classes, and their funds, to the revolutionary cause, Batista found himself isolated. The U.S. public also began to turn against the Cuban government as news of atrocities made headlines. Pressure began to mount on the Eisenhower administration to sever its ties with Batista, and as a result an arms embargo was put in place.

Castro's guerrilla tactics wore down Batista's soldiers, who were young, inexperienced, unfamiliar with the countryside, and not as motivated as the rebels. Through a clandestine radio station, Castro waged a psychological war, reporting on clashes between the rebels

Rare depiction of the Battle of Las Villas, when Batista was defeated in December 1958. The battle took place within the city of Santa Clara. (From *Album de la revolución cubana*, Habana, 1959, postcard 1237. D. H. Figueredo's Collection)

and soldiers, insulting Batista and his officers, and, more important, inviting recruits and young officers to join the rebels. Although Batista had more than 33,000 men spread out throughout the island, he could not defeat Castro. Batista's own men doubted his abilities as a commander, and some of the older officers negotiated privately with Castro to switch sides.

In December 1958, Batista discovered that one of his key generals was negotiating with Castro to turn him over to the rebels. This discovery, coupled with setbacks on the battlefield and diminishing support from Washington, convinced him to flee Cuba in the early morning hours of January 1, 1959. He never returned to the island and spent the last years of his life writing book after book in a vain effort to restore his image as a revolutionary leader.

A triumphant Castro marched into Havana on January 8. He became provisional premier and promised to hold elections within six months. His likeness appeared on billboards and murals. Cubans happily nailed to the entrances of their homes signs that read, "Fidel, this is your home."

Castro Victorious

In power, Castro acted with speed. His first cabinet was composed of a cross section of all economic classes. There was no obvious hint of Marxism in the first months of the revolution, and, in fact, he described it as "humanist" in a visit to the United States in April. The first public clash with the Eisenhower administration came with the trial and execution, typically by firing squad, of more than 300 Batista supporters. The clash between the two countries was exacerbated by Castro's agrarian reform plan, which resulted in the expropriation of some large agricultural holdings held by U.S. interests. The reform plan was sharply criticized by the Eisenhower administration after several landowners complained that they were inadequately compensated for their property.

In late 1959 and early 1960 Castro and the revolution veered sharply to the left, resulting in a cold war alliance with the Soviet Union, which was eager to establish a political presence in the Caribbean to counter U.S. influence in Latin America. Support from Moscow enabled Castro to break relations with the United States and sever long-standing economic and political ties. The revolution eventually nationalized all U.S. companies, eliminated almost all forms of private property, and created neighborhood watch organizations to monitor antirevolutionary behaviors, known as Committees for the Defense of the Revolution.

In terms of the arts, the revolution established the Instituto Cubano del Arte e Industria Cinematográficos (Cuban Institute for Art and Cinematography), which to this day controls Cuba's movie industry, and encouraged the founding of literary institutions such as the Casa de las Américas (House of the Americas), which fosters intellectual dialogue with Latin American nations and publishes and distributes the work of writers sympathetic to the revolution. Castro courted Latin American intellectuals, such as Mexican writer Carlos Fuentes (1928–) and Colombian author Gabriel García Márquez (1928–) by inviting them to conferences in Cuba and subsidizing their work as writers.

Castro showed little tolerance for dissent. In November 1959 the government passed the Fundamental Law that charged individuals as counterrevolutionaries if they engaged in any activities threatening to the revolution. Counterrevolutionary activities were defined in the broadest terms, and as a result thousands of political dissidents were imprisoned or fled the island. Estimates of the number of political prisoners at any one time in the 1960s range from 15,000 to 40,000. Castro censored the press and closed down parochial and private schools.

Cubans' Flight to Miami

Between 1959 and 1965, nearly 200,000 Cubans sought exile, mostly in Miami, Florida. Eventually, more than a million Cubans would flee the country. The first wave of exiles consisted of former supporters of the Batista regime. After 1960, those who left were in disagreement with Castro's government and his failure to reinstitute the 1940 Constitution.

Outside Cuba, some of the exiles plotted against Castro. One supposedly secret operation resulted in the Bay of Pigs invasion, called Playa Girón in Cuba, in April 1961. The Central Intelligence Agency (CIA) recruited and trained about 1,300 Cubans to secure a beachhead at Playa Girón, south of Havana, and establish a provisional government. After bombing Cuban airfields on April 15, the exiles landed on April 17 and occupied the beach for a day. But the invaders were soon defeated by Castro's forces, as the promised air support from the U.S. Air Force was not authorized by President John F. Kennedy (1917–63), and Castro's secret service rounded up thousands of sympathizers and would-be conspirators, aborting the potential for the development of an urban resistance. The invasion embarrassed the United States.

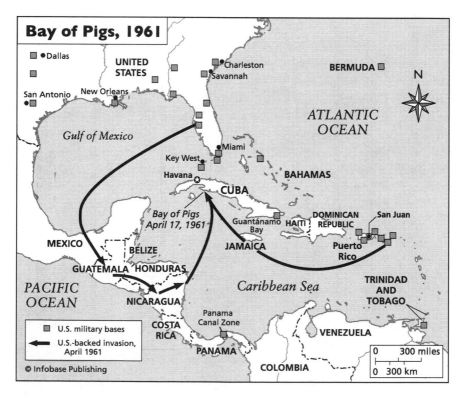

150

Photos of Castro leading the defense from a tank on the beachhead romanticized his image as a brave revolutionary and defender of Cuban and Latin American sovereignty. Confrontation was to be the centerpiece of Cuba-U.S. relations for the next five decades. The next battle was not far off.

The October Crisis

On October 14, 1962, an American U2 spy plane photographed nuclear missile installations in Cuba. For the next 13 days a strategic duel took place between Kennedy and Soviet Union prime minister Nikita Khrushchev (1894–1971). From October 16 to October 22, Kennedy and his advisers explored options for the removal of the missiles, including an invasion of the island. On October 22, Kennedy announced to the world that the missiles constituted aggressive conduct that would not be tolerated. In Cuba, Castro fortified the north coast of the island and mobilized the army. On October 23, the Soviet Union declared that U.S. interference in Cuban affairs violated the island's right to self-determination. On October 24, the United States blockaded Cuba with orders to sink any Soviet ships attempting to cross into Cuban waters; one Soviet ship bound for Cuba carried 20 nuclear warheads.

On October 26, Castro advised Khrushchev that a U.S. invasion of Cuba would trigger a thermonuclear war. If that were to happen, the Soviets should be the first to use nuclear weapons. The next day the Cubans shot down an American U2 spy plane flying over the island. Later the same day, the United States agreed not to invade the island and to remove warheads from Turkey if the Soviet Union disarmed and withdrew the Cuban missiles. On October 28, Khrushchev announced acceptance of the agreement.

The resolution of the October Crisis assured Castro that although the United States would continue a covert war against his regime, there would be no military invasion or expedition to the island. The crisis signaled to Cuban exiles the long-term survival of Castro's rule. However, the resolution angered Castro and the revolutionary government because the Soviets did not consult with them and reached an agreement with the United States without Cuban input. In the immediate aftermath, there was a cooling of relations between Havana and Moscow that would not completely heal until 1968.

Communism or Castroism?

Scholars have speculated about the factors that led to Castro's conversion to communism. Did Castro turn to communism and the Soviet

Union because of geopolitical strategic reasons and the unwillingness of the United States to support his revolution? Or did he turn to communism because of a deep commitment to Marxist ideology and mass struggle arrived at after a careful analysis of world conditions? There is also debate about whether his turn to communism was more a matter of convenience and self-preservation rather than ideological conviction and whether he has used the rhetoric of communism to justify a rule of nearly half a century. Regardless of how one answers those questions, for many decades the ruling party in Cuba has been the Communist Party, entrusted by the Constitution of 1976 to guide the state and organize and lead efforts to build socialism.

In 1961, the party was called the Partido Socialista Popular (Popular Socialist Party). In 1965 it became the Partido Comunista Cubano (Cuban Communist Party). In 1970, the party emerged as a key element in the revolution's efforts to consolidate and centralize power. In 1975, Castro declared that the Communist Party was the "soul of the Cuban Revolution." Membership increased from 50,000 in 1965 to 203,000 10 years later. By 2000 there were nearly 800,000 members. Senior officials within the party control key government and military posts. They are accountable to Castro, who is the party's first secretary; his brother Raul is the second secretary.

Another debated point is when Castro became a communist. During the struggle against Batista in the 1950s, Castro repeatedly denied that he was a communist. Once he was in power, he explained that he had to do so because Cubans were not ready to embrace communism before

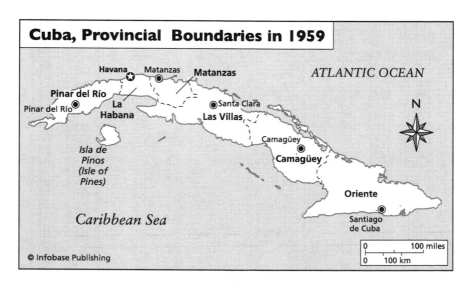

Cuba, Provincial Boundaries in 1959

ATLANTIC OCEAN

Havana Matanzas Matanzas

Pinar del Río

Pinar del Río La Habana Santa Clara

Las Villas

Isla de Pinos (Isle of Pines)

Camagüey

Camagüey

N

Oriente

Caribbean Sea

Santiago de Cuba

© Infobase Publishing

0   100 miles
0   100 km

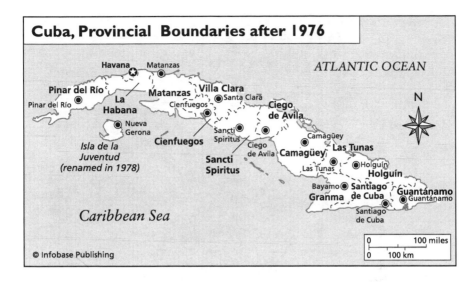

the revolution. In 1961, he proclaimed the revolution socialist, and in 1965, he appointed himself chairman of the central committee of the Cuban Communist Party. Castro's assertion that he was a communist of long-standing is disputed by some, who claim he made the statement of an early conversion to communism to ingratiate himself with the Soviet Union, whose leaders suspected he might have been more a nationalist than a Marxist.

Contesting Castro's Leadership

Victory and power for Castro meant the production of chronicles focusing exclusively on his fight against Batista, overshadowing the role played by other revolutionaries. In Cuba, some of these figures have been downplayed or removed from government texts. Outside the island, historians tend to omit them from accounts of the Cuban Revolution.

Castro was the best organized, the most charismatic, and the most efficient leader of the revolt against Batista. But there were a few leaders who might have challenged Castro's role and popularity had they survived the conflict, and there were some who did challenge Castro, leading to their arrest and imprisonment.

Camilo Cienfuegos (1932–59) was a tailor who joined Castro in Mexico and participated in the rebel landing in Cuba in 1956. He was a fearless fighter who distinguished himself in several battles, including the

THE ROMANCE OF CHE GUEVARA

Che Guevara, Cuba's best-known revolutionary other than Castro, was not from Cuba at all. Ernesto Guevara was born in 1928 in Argentina into a middle-class family with socialist ideas; days before her death in 1965, his mother wrote to him that she was an old woman "who hopes to see the world converted to socialism." In 1953, Guevara earned a medical degree before touring South America on a motorcycle. Witnessing poverty in countries such as Peru and Colombia, he offered his medical services for free. In 1954, he worked as an inspector in Guatemala in the government of President Jacobo Arbenz Guzmán (1913–71), which was overthrown with help from the

Rare photo of Che Guevara, the most romantic figure to emerge from the Cuban revolution (From *Album de la revolución cubana,* Habana, 1959, postcard 129. D. H. Figueredo's Collection)

battle of Santa Clara in 1958, where Batista's forces were finally defeated. He occupied Havana with Che Guevara before Castro's entry on January 8, 1959. Appointed chief of the rebel army, his devotion to Castro and the revolution made him popular with the masses. His objection to Castro's arrest of dissenting commander Huber Matos may have led to his disappearance on October 28, 1959, when his small airplane vanished during a night flight. His body was never found, and the mystery surrounding his death remains unsolved.

José Antonio Echeverría (1932–57), whose political objective was the personal removal of Batista from power, was the president of the Federation of University Students and founder of the Directorio Revolucionario, an urban guerrilla movement. Concerned over the publicity that Castro received after *New York Times* reporter Herbert

Central Intelligence Agency. The next year he traveled to Mexico, where he met Fidel Castro and joined the Cuban Revolution. Guevara was one of the survivors of the ill-fated Granma landing in December 1956. In 1958, he and a handful of guerrillas led an assault on an armored train carrying Batista troops. In 1959, he led the rebels into Havana. The Cuban people nicknamed him "Che," a common Argentine term of affection.

Guevara served in various administrative posts after Castro's victory, but he preferred movement and action. In 1965, he disappeared from Cuba. The rumor was that he had fallen from grace with Castro. In fact, the Argentine physician was involved in revolutionary efforts elsewhere, in the Congo in Africa, and then in Bolivia in South America. In Bolivia he led a small band of guerrillas, hoping his campaign would ignite continent-wide revolution. Bolivia's Communist Party did not support the enterprise, and Bolivian peasants did not rally to Guevara's side. His timing and site selection were bad; the Bolivian government had recently enacted rural land reform that mollified revolutionary sentiments in the Bolivian countryside. In fact, Bolivian peasants revealed his secret hiding place to authorities, and in 1967, he was captured by local troops advised by the Central Intelligence Agency. He was executed, and his hands were chopped off and reportedly sent to Castro as evidence. His body was buried in an unmarked grave. In 1997, his remains were exhumed and flown to Cuba, where he was buried in Santa Clara, the site of his victory over Batista's troops.

Encyclopedia of Cuba. Edited by Luis Martínez Fernández et al. Westport, Conn.: Greenwood Press, 2003, pp. 227–231.

Matthews published a series of sensational articles about him in 1957, Echeverría decided to escalate his revolutionary activities. He and members of the Directorio planned to assassinate Batista by storming the presidential palace and to rally Cubans to fight against the regime by taking over a radio station. The attack, which occurred on March 13, 1957, failed. Echeverría, with many of the conspirators, was killed while battling the police. His death created a vacuum that helped Castro solidify his position and leadership.

Frank País (1934–57) was a popular figure in the urban underground movement. In 1952, at the age of 18, he formed an organization to fight against Batista. In 1955, he joined the 26th of July Movement and provided food and weapons to Castro's forces in the Sierra Maestra. On November 30, 1956, he led a rebellion that successfully occupied government offices in Santiago for a few hours. He developed an intricate network that stretched throughout Cuba, coordinating sabotage and antigovernment actions. On July 30, 1957, he was killed by the police. His supporters turned to Castro for leadership and direction.

Huber Matos (1918–) took the first reinforcements from Santiago to the Sierra Maestra, where he participated in several battles. In 1959, Castro appointed him governor of the province of Camaguey. Fearing that the communists within the government were taking over the revolution, Matos resigned. He was accused of antirevolutionary activities and sentenced to 20 years' imprisonment; his followers were also arrested. Matos's arrest was a watershed. It demonstrated that Castro's vision for revolutionary change in Cuba could not be altered by dissent and that the revolutionary agenda would be implemented regardless of public opinion.

Eloy Gutiérrez Menoyo (1934–) was a participant in Echeverría's daring attack on the presidential palace. After the attack he escaped to the Escambray Mountains in central Cuba, where he founded a guerrilla movement. His political views clashed with Castro's growing socialist agenda, and after the triumph of the revolution, he planned an insurrection against Castro. Found guilty of antirevolutionary activities, he served 22 years in prison, where he was tortured and lost an eye. He was released in 1986 and went to live for a time in the United States. In 2003, he returned to Cuba and vowed to work for peaceful change.

Cienfuegos, Echevarría, and País are martyrs of the revolution with libraries and universities named in their honor. Gutiérrez Menoyo and Matos are not included in official histories of the revolution.

The Revolution's Accomplishments

Most of the accomplishments of the Cuban government occurred in the early years of the revolution. By 1960 the government identified 985,000 illiterates in a population of 6 million. A year later more than 105,000 students volunteered as teachers in the "Literacy Campaign." In 1962 Cuba reported a 96 percent literacy rate. During that era, more than 600 rural and more than 300 urban schools were built, and 4.5 million primary texts were published. By 1990 Cuban education was considered one of the best in the world, with an average of one teacher for every 42 residents and a half million university-trained professionals.

Universal medical care was challenged by the departure of more than 6,000 physicians who opposed the regime. In 1964 outpatient clinics were established throughout the island, reaching about 400 units by the 1990s. Centers for research were instituted with specializations in neurophysiology, cardiology, and radiology biology, among others. In the mid 1990s Cuba had more than 60,000 doctors, 9,000 dentists, and 75,000 nurses. As part of its foreign policy, Cuba sends doctors to serve in other countries such as Bolivia, Nicaragua, and Venezuela.

In 1959 the agrarian reform plan limited ownership to 996 acres of land, a move that accelerated the break in relations with the United States. In 1963 the second agrarian reform law limited ownership to 166 acres. The urban reform law set maximum rents for houses and apartments at 10 percent of the resident's income. In the 1970s volunteer brigades helped construct new homes throughout the island.

Culture War

In the 1960s there was an effort to create the "new Socialist man and woman" in Cuba. The new men and women of Cuba were to think first about what was good for the society rather than their own personal enrichment. To achieve that end, financial incentives such as additional pay and vacation time were eliminated and replaced by moral incentives. Workers who distinguished themselves as selfless and sacrificing were praised in the media and awarded pins and certificates. A plan by the government to eliminate money was debated. These efforts to reshape culture and society failed as worker production plummeted.

In 1961 Castro similarly encapsulated the revolution's approach toward artistic and political dissent with the phrase, "Within the revolution everything; outside the revolution nothing." Cuban writers and artists were forced to walk an intellectual tightrope between creative independence and the need to stay on the correct side of ongoing ideological debates. The revolution viewed art as a vehicle by which to strengthen loyalty in the citizenry, with Castro clarifying that the role of art was to make "men happier, better" (Lockwood, 207).

Restrictive periods for artistic expression were typified by the arrest of prominent writers, such as Heberto Padilla (1934–2000), a critic of the revolution, who was arrested in 1971. Padilla was forced to make a staged confession before the Unión de Escritores y Artistas de Cuba (Cuban Union of Writers and Artists), in which he accused his wife, Belkis Cuza Malé (1942–   ), and friends of making counterrevolutionary statements. This restrictive practice continued into the 1980s and 1990s with the censorship and arrest of dissident poets.

Glasnost, Perestroika, and the Special Period in Cuba

The same charisma that propelled Fidel Castro to triumph during the revolutionary struggle against the Batista dictatorship hindered the efficient management of the Cuban government once he was in power. Castro displayed a remarkable propensity for micromanaging the Cuban state, and his overwhelming authority and inability to delegate power occasionally paralyzed the revolution. Few were willing to make a decision without direct permission from Castro. This administrative style, shaped by Latin American *caudillismo,* where the strong ruler participates in every decision, was sometimes detrimental to the island's economy. Cuban bureaucrats and administrators yielded to the *comandante*'s every wish and dream, no matter how unrealistic or impractical.

Castro's schemes tended to be romantic and grandiose. In 1970, for example, he pushed for a 10-million-ton sugar harvest, a goal 3 million tons greater than the previous record of 7.2 million tons in 1953. To achieve this goal, virtually the entire population was mobilized to cut sugarcane in the countryside. Bus drivers and teachers, students and lawyers were sent to the cane fields regardless of their experience. This led to inefficiencies on a grand scale. While mobilizing the nation for the cane harvest, known as the *zafra,* other segments of the economy suffered. The earlier push to industrialize was ignored. Food shortages worsened, including a drop in the supply of beans, milk, and rice. The size of the cattle industry dropped from more than 7 million head in the 1960s to less than 5 million shortly after the harvest of 1970 (Martínez Fernández, 273). There were also failures in coffee production.

In the end, although the 1970 harvest yielded 8.5 million tons of sugar—the largest in the history of the island—the campaign for a 10-million-ton harvest failed. More importantly, the campaign marked a move away from Cuba's industrialization campaign and back to a reliance on sugar for foreign capital, which had been deemphasized in the immediate aftermath of the revolution because of its association with U.S. economic dominance.

In the 1970s and 1980s, the Cuban government found a new market for its sugar—the Soviet Union. As a result of the growing web of military and political connections between the two countries, the Soviet Union agreed to buy the bulk of Cuba's sugar at a subsidized price well above the world market price. Reliance on a foreign power was not a novelty, since for much of the 20th century Cuba had relied on the United States. Before the revolution, 74 percent of the island's exports went to the United States and 65 percent of the imports came from its northern neighbor (Martínez Fernández, 285). After the revolution, the percentages remained almost exactly the same, but the Soviet Union and the socialist bloc were now Cuba's principal trading partners. Nevertheless, food shortages were common on the island as the government attempted to distribute food evenly. Cuba also exported some foodstuffs to other socialist and emerging nations to generate foreign capital.

In return for the subsidies, Cuba became a stalwart defender of Soviet policies in the developing world. The height of this policy came in the mid-1970s, when Castro became the leader of the Non-Aligned Movement, despite Cuba's close ties to the Soviet Union. Cuba's efforts were discredited in the aftermath of the Soviet invasion of Afghanistan (1979–88), as the revolutionary government tried to defend and explain the Soviet Union's aggressive actions against a much smaller neighbor. Cuban commitment to the cause was not just words; Cuban blood was spilled defending socialist principles. In the 1970s, Cuban combat troops played a decisive role in defending Angola's Marxist government against U.S.-backed rebels supported by South African ground troops. Cuba was also instrumental in paving the way for Namibian independence, refusing to withdraw from Angola until the apartheid government of South Africa pulled out of Namibia, known then as the territory of South-West Africa. In this same period, Cuba sent technical advisers to assist socialist movements throughout Latin America, perhaps most notably to Nicaragua.

All of this began to change in 1985, when reformer Mikhail Gorbachev came to power in the Soviet Union. Gorbachev began to implement a series of policies known as glasnost and perestroika. Glasnost was the policy of seeking open engagement with the West in an effort to reduce tensions and improve the economy. Perestroika was an effort to encourage more open debate within Soviet society and, by example, inside the other communist nations. Gorbachev's stated goal was to reform communism without destroying it.

Castro immediately rejected these policies. The relationship between the two nations and the two men declined precipitously during Gorbachev's six-year tenure in power. In response to Gorbachev's reforms, Castro and the revolution initiated a new program called the Rectification Program aimed at minimizing the impact of Soviet measures on Cuba. While Gorbachev sought to open up the Soviet Union to market forces, the Cuban revolutionary government cut back on small farmers' markets and other free-enterprise initiatives. Almost anticipating a crisis in world socialism, the Cuban Revolution called for greater *conciencia* (conscience) on the part of workers. This was aimed at encouraging volunteerism among the workforce to boost production. Castro also sought to cut down on government bureaucracy, inefficiency, and theft.

Gorbachev was unable to control the forces he unleashed. Many of the 14 Republics of the Soviet Union, urged on by a more open climate, began to seek independence. As this occurred, the Soviet grip on Eastern Europe loosened, and soon there were calls for the complete dismantling of the socialist system. By 1991 the Soviet Union was no more, ripped apart by the reform efforts aimed at reinventing it. It was replaced by 14 different nations, the largest and most important of which was Russia. In short order, all the countries of Eastern Europe overthrew their communist governments.

Economic Crisis in Cuba

The collapse of the Soviet Union led to speculation about whether the Cuban revolutionary government could survive. Many in the Cuban exile community expected that Castro would be swept out of power. The downfall of the Soviet bloc plunged Cuba into economic crisis. Cuba's foreign trade dropped from $11.7 billion in 1990 to $2.7 billion in 1993 (Martínez-Fernández, 286). Soviet subsidies, estimated at between $4 and $5 billion a year, came to a screeching halt. The economic crisis this brought about was described by Castro as *"período especial en tiempos de paz"*—the "special period."

With the island's gross national product falling by 36 percent, the government took a series of emergency measures to ensure the survival of the population and the regime. The Cuban government encouraged foreign investment, especially in the tourist industry, where the number of hotel rooms grew from 13,000 in 1990 to 36,000 in 2000; allowed foreign currency, in particular the dollar, to circulate; and permitted self-employment. Some 200,000 Cubans seized the opportunity and set up businesses such as beauty parlors; taxi services; book stands; car, bicycle, and home appliance repair shops; and *paladares,* small restaurants in private homes. Prostitution, an old enemy the revolution suppressed in the early 1960s, resurfaced, and the Cuban government quietly accepted it. In the Cuba of the 1990s, prostitutes, called *jineteras* (horse riders), were young, attractive, and highly educated, offering sexual favors in exchange for dollars, entry into exclusive stores and clubs frequented by foreigners, and the potential of establishing a relation with a foreigner who might help them leave Cuba.

Decaying buildings in Old Havana during the Special Period (Photo by William Luis)

The measures taken by the government slowed down the economic decline. An ironic development was that the very Cuban exiles who wanted Castro out of power were supporting the regime by sending money to families and relatives on the island. For example, between 1989 and 1993, $1 billion was sent to Cuba. Remittances from Cuban exiles in the United States became the second-biggest source of foreign currency.

The tourism trade and the hunger for dollars served to reinvigorate the class system. Those with access to dollars, either because of employment in the tourist trade or because of relatives in the exile community, became a privileged group. A bellhop position at a tourist hotel was more coveted than a medical degree. Cubans with access to dollars could purchase goods, such as rum, coffee, and appliances, available only in the dollar stores. Cubans using pesos, the national currency, could not visit the dollar stores and were restricted to the limited supply in Cuban stores or what was assigned to them through the government rationing system. This class system was visible in a walk through neighborhoods in most of the major cities. Those with access to dollars were painting and repairing their homes, while the homes of their neighbors crumbled. For many, it was evident that the government's socialist policies were not working.

The economic measures could not address some of the most basic hardships caused by the collapse of Cuba's trading partners. There were outbreaks of disease, some affecting children, because of vitamin deficiencies in the Cuban diet. Blackouts, known as *apagones,* became a way of life. Electricity was cut off to homes for hours at a time to utilize scarce energy for factories and industry, although these were often forced to shut down as well. Gasoline became so scarce that many citizens were unable to use their cars, and bicycles became a common mode of transportation. The economic crisis was so severe that reproduction rates dropped, and abortion rates climbed.

These hardships fueled resentment. In August 1994, thousands of marginalized youths took to the streets of Havana, throwing rocks at the dollar stores and at a hotel favored by European tourists. As the police and paramilitary units confronted the protesters, a large group gathered at the *malecón,* the sea wall that hugs Havana's harbor, and chanted *"libertad, libertad"*—liberty, liberty. The secret service and the army arrested an unreported number of protesters, while the government cut telephone service and tried to ensure minimal international press coverage. Within days, Cuban human-rights leaders and dissidents were arrested, and the homes of suspected participants in the *maleconazo,* the *malecón* incident, were splattered with eggs, paint, even human waste by sympathizers of Castro's regime.

That the *maleconazo* did not evolve into a crisis for Castro's government demonstrated that in Cuba the mobilization of people as a tool of political protest was only successful when controlled, instigated, and monitored by the government. Without the government's participation, any attempt at mass protest was aborted by the secret service and the watchdog neighborhood organizations called Comités de la Defensa de la Revolución (Committees for the Defense of the Revolution).

The repression continued into the 21st century. In 2002, a group of reformers, calling their organization Proyecto Varela in memory of the Cuban priest and patriot Félix Varela, gathered 11,000 signatures asking for political reforms and free speech in Cuba. The reformers included Oswaldo Payá of the Christian Liberation Movement and Vladimiro Roca Antúnez, son of the former secretary general of the Cuban Communist Party. The island's 1976 constitution, substantially amended in 1992, permitted such petitions and their consideration by the Cuban government. The Cuban government rejected the petition, arguing that it was part of a plot by the United States to subvert and destroy the revolution. A year later, 50 prominent members of the Varela Project were arrested. Payá, a Nobel Peace Prize nominee and recipient of the Sakharov Prize by the European Union, was not arrested because of his notoriety. He continued to live in a house in Havana with the word *traidor* (traitor) painted on the front by a graffiti artist. By early 2007, with Fidel Castro in failing health, Payá was involved in creating what he called a "national dialogue" to consider political life after Castro and how to move the country to democracy and openness.

Castro and the Cuban revolutionary government have proven resilient over almost 50 years of political rule, despite strong U.S. opposition and frequent crises. It has employed a combination of repression, coercion, and persuasion to remain in power. The regime has also played on fears of a return by the Cuban exiles and economic and political domination by them. Tourism and other economic reforms, including the development of a pharmaceutical industry, as well as investment by Europe and Latin America, have created modest growth in the Cuban economy. As Cuba faces another transition, with Fidel Castro's death likely in the near future, there is a sense that the last battle of the Revolution of 1959 has not yet been fought.

9

FRAGMENTATION AND OCCUPATION: HAITI AND THE DOMINICAN REPUBLIC (1900–2000)

During the 19th century, the seeds of nationalism were planted in the anglophone and francophone Caribbean, where the inhabitants were growing aware of a political and cultural identity separate from France and England. Haiti was the pioneer in this political awakening, establishing its independence via revolution in 1804. In the Dominican Republic, which won independence from Haiti in 1844, Dominicans struggled with and defended their own independence from Spain.

U.S. Interventions

The United States considered the Caribbean its Mediterranean Sea (E. Williams 1984, 419). Just as Great Britain and France would not allow Americans to claim territory in the Mediterranean, the United States would not permit a European beachhead in the Caribbean. The United States assumed a paternal role in the region, claiming to protect the islands from themselves and from European intervention and ensuring that creditor nations, such as Germany, did not attempt to invade an island to claim payment on loans. (Such action nearly occurred twice in Haiti, in 1872 and 1897, when German battleships threatened to attack if the country did not repay loans to German banks or indemnify the German government for claims made on behalf of German nationals living in Haiti)

For the United States, enforcing the Monroe Doctrine, which claimed "America for the Americans," became a central foreign policy

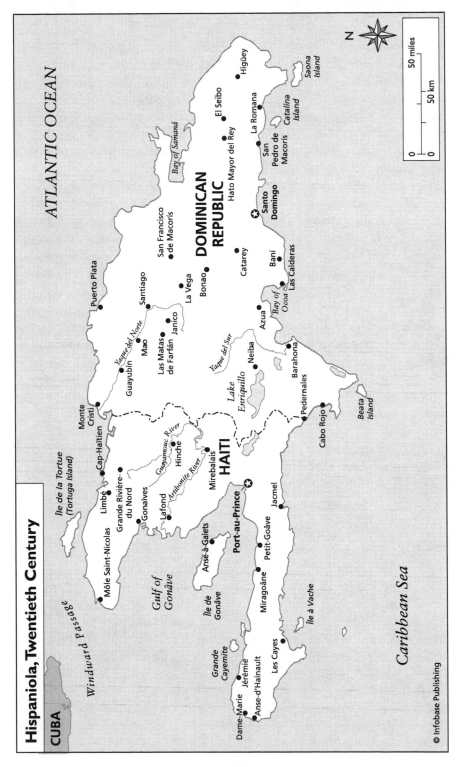

Hispaniola, Twentieth Century

CUBA

ATLANTIC OCEAN

Windward Passage

Île de la Tortue
(Tortuga Island)

Môle Saint-Nicolas

Limbé

Cap-Haïtien

Grande Rivière-
du Nord

Gonaïves

Lafond

Hinche

Guayamouc River

Artibonite River

Mirebalais

HAITI

Gulf of
Gonâve

Île de
Gonâve

Anse-à-Galets

Port-au-Prince

Petit-Goâve

Miragoâne

Île à Vache

Grande
Cayemite

Jérémie

Dame-Marie

Anse-d'Hainault

Les Cayes

Jacmel

Monte
Cristi

Guayubín

Mao

Las Matas
de Farfán

Janico

Yaque del Norte

Santiago

La Vega

Bonao

San Francisco
de Macorís

Puerto Plata

Bay of Samaná

DOMINICAN
REPUBLIC

Catarey

Baní

Azua

Bay of
Ocoa

Las Calderas

Yaque del Sur

Lake
Enriquillo

Neiba

Barahona

Pedernales

Cabo Rojo

Beata
Island

Santo
Domingo

Hato Mayor del Rey

San
Pedro de
Macorís

La Romana

El Seibo

Higüey

Catalina
Island

Saona
Island

Caribbean Sea

N

50 miles

50 km

© Infobase Publishing

165

aim. Theodore Roosevelt's interpretation of the doctrine in the early 1900s, known as the Roosevelt Corollary, further committed the United States to forcefully keeping foreign powers out of the region. However, rather than engage in open hostility with European nations, the United States favored prevention. One method for ensuring that the countries of the Caribbean met their foreign obligations was to control the customs houses. To prevent European intervention, the United States took control of the customs houses of Caribbean nations teetering on the precipice of economic default and forced them to pay their foreign debts before other economic obligations.

In 1905, the Dominican Republic was the first clinical test of this method, known as "receivership." Since the 1880s, the Dominican Republic had accumulated $32 million in loans from European nations. The administration of the customs house was burdened with corruption. Many customs officials were appointed because of their political connections and pocketed the tariffs and taxes assigned to products entering the country. The reduction in income this caused made it difficult for the country to make payments on its foreign loans. To ensure payment of the debt, the Dominican Republic agreed to let the United States administer the customs house and to use 55 percent of the tariffs to pay off creditors and the rest to be employed by the Dominican government for the public good. A similar arrangement was enforced in Haiti a decade later.

Unfolding Nationalism

The unfolding of nationalism played out across the Caribbean. The process of self-definition created fissures among and within the islands of the Caribbean and exposed an absence of unity and purpose that might be described as "fragmented nationalism," as scholar Franklin Knight calls it in his book *The Caribbean: The Genesis of Fragmented Nationalism* (Knight). Detached from their colonial mother countries, each island sought its own identity but was forced to come face-to-face with the realities of nationhood. Many of the islands emerged from dependent relations with their former colonial masters. They were left with issues about economic and political development that threatened to undermine their newly found sovereignties. Many of the island economies were dependent on one or two primary exports, and this made them ripe for exploitation by the United States or European powers. Members of the upper class in each society were often educated in the United States or Europe. They sought economic and political guidance from foreigners rather than fashioning solutions for the benefit of the local citizenry. They often acted in the best interests of foreign powers rather than the national interest. The result was a political cauldron ripe for chaos, rebellion, and revolution.

The Age of Fragmentation

Disunity in racial matters was acute. Through the slave system and its accompanying racial ideologies, the colonial empires taught whites that they were superior to individuals of mixed race. They created a pyramid of power, with white Europeans at the top, mixed-race individuals somewhere in the middle, and those of African ancestry at the bottom. Attempts by blacks to reduce disparities brought violent reaction from whites in power.

In Haiti, the gulf between blacks and mulattoes dated back to the colonial years. When a black president occupied office, the president favored those who were black. The reverse occurred when a mulatto assumed the presidency. In Jamaica, the generation of leaders that eventually led the island to self-rule in the 1940s consisted of mixed-ancestry aristocrats who were often described as "near white." When race and ethnicity were not at odds, conflicts emerged over perceived cultural values. In the Hispanic Caribbean, wealthy Europeans tended to view Europe as advanced and sophisticated, preferring the literature, arts, and fashion created in metropolises like Madrid and Barcelona. In Haiti, intellectuals and members of the upper class preferred Paris over Port-au-Prince and saw themselves as black Frenchmen, not Haitians.

A Model for Disunity

These attitudes were further intensified when people from one island looked at people from another. In writing about Cuba, the Dominican Republic, and Haiti, John Edwin Fagg said, "Haitians and Dominicans are traditionally hostile to one another, and Cubans are scarcely friends with either" (Fagg, 1). It was as if the antagonisms created by the wars frequently fought by the colonial powers in past centuries had been transferred to their former subjects. Monoculture further cultivated disunity as individual islands found themselves forced to trade primarily with former colonial powers, selling the one crop they cultivated, be it sugar or coffee. Even when possible, the Caribbean islands preferred to engage in commerce with Europe and the United States rather than with each other.

It was a model that encouraged colonial dependence and fostered nepotism. "Merchants depended first and foremost on kinship to secure loyalty and secrecy," observed historians Stanley and Barbara

Stein. From "[Europe] came young men often nephews, to their trade in America ... to marry into the ... family" (Stein and Stein, 19, 153). Family ties and preference, decades-old friendship, and social class bonds blocked the desire to seek solidarity with those who were different at home and with other Caribbean islands. These ills were fermented and encouraged by economics. Privileges of race, perceived cultural superiority, and social exclusivity were the rewards of wealth, and wealth was in the hands of the few, usually families who were either white or light-skinned.

Haiti's Occupation

From 1911 to 1915, there was general unrest and chaos in Haiti. In 1912, a president was blown up in the presidential palace. In 1913 another was poisoned, and three others were elected and then overthrown. The final crisis was the assassination on July 27, 1915, of President Vilbrun Guillaume Sam (?–1915), who was killed in retribution for summarily ordering the execution of 173 political rivals. President Sam sought safety and asylum in the French embassy, but an angry mob discovered his location, broke into the embassy, murdered him, and mutilated his body. Claiming concern for American property and citizens, the following day 3,000 U.S. Marines arrived in Port-au-Prince.

Even though U.S. officials claimed a need to protect American interests and a paternal desire to help Haiti, Washington contemplated occupation even before Sam's assassination. The U.S. Navy had recently drafted an undated document entitled "Plan for Landing and Occupying the City of Port-au-Prince," which outlined military action (Schmidt, 64). Concerned that Germany, already engaged in World War I (1914–18), might set up a base in Haiti, the United States wanted to secure the harbor at Môle Saint-Nicolas so that it could build a naval base there. Possession of the Haitian customs house was a third objective.

U.S. forces pressured Haiti's national assembly into electing Philippe Sudre Dartiguenave (1863–1926), who partially favored American interests, as president. A treaty was signed that gave the United States control of customs, supervised by an American financial adviser, and established a Haitian national guard. When members of the national assembly hesitated to sign the agreement, the United States threatened to withhold their salaries.

The United States controlled all of Haiti's government except for education and the judiciary. Haitians were not allowed to hold high office in government. The Senate was shut down, centering power in the president's office and with the U.S. Marines.

Péralte's Rebellion

Despite the nationalism of Haiti's upper class, their infatuation with French culture, and their disdain of American culture, they did not protest and did not fight against the U.S. occupation. Thus, Port-au-Prince was essentially quiet. The struggle against the occupation was fought in the countryside, spearheaded by private armies known as *cacos* and their leader, Charlemagne Péralte (1885–1919). In 1918, when the United States forced peasants to work building roads, the *cacos* rebelled. In response, the United States imposed a curfew in the cities, censored the press, disarmed all politicians, and dispatched the marines to the countryside.

The Caco War, as it became known, lasted a year. It was the first time American forces used airplanes to support the movement of ground troops. The conflict resulted in the deaths of more than 3,000 Haitians, while American forces lost 13 marines. The conflict allowed the United States, once again, to demonstrate its ability to control the destinies of the nations of the Caribbean, just as it had done in 1898. The United States portrayed Péralte as a peasant, but he had, in fact, served as a general in the Haitian army and was well educated. Péralte used guerrilla tactics to harass the Americans; his army, estimated in the thousands, once reached the outskirts of Port-au-Prince.

The Caco War ended with Péralte's death. U.S. commanders planted an agent within Péralte's forces and were able to surprise and kill the rebel. To prove that he was dead, the marines placed Péralte's corpse on a door with arms stretched out, as if he had been crucified. The photos taken of the deceased leader contributed to a legend that is still growing today.

In 1922, a Haitian shadow government was formed with two men running the country, an American high commissioner, Major General John Henry Russell (1872–1947), and Haitian president Louis Borno (1865–1942). General Russell held racist views representative of American insensitivity to race and Haitian culture. The marines, many from the North American South, displayed arrogance and appeared to consider Haitians inferior. Accusations of human rights violations contrasted sharply with U.S. reports about improved sanitation facilities and the construction of roads made possible by the military occupation.

HAITIAN WRITERS RESPOND TO THE OCCUPATION

The occupation prompted such an intellectual and creative reaction by Haitian writers that it served as a catalyst for the renaissance of Haitian letters. Many of the internationally renowned Haitian works of literature emerged during this period. The occupation stimulated writers to develop a distinct national identity and an affirmation of *négritude,* black consciousness. For decades, reaction against the occupation influenced and shaped the works of postoccupation writers and intellectuals.

The poet Edmond Laforest (1876–1915) committed suicide to protest the U.S. presence. Novelist Léon Laleau (1892–1979) published the novel *Le Choc,* which depicted the occupation, in 1932. Dr. Jean Price-Mars (1876–1969), who served as an adviser in the Haitian embassy in Washington, D.C., returned home to rally discouraged intellectuals. In 1928, he published *Ainsi parla l'oncle* (Thus spoke the uncle), in which he examined the events and attitudes that led to the occupation. In the book Price-Mars accused his countrymen of practicing collective *bovarisyme* (an allusion to the romantic delusions of the heroine of the 1856 novel *Madame Bovary,* by Gustave Flaubert) in pretending to be colored Frenchmen and Frenchwomen and denying their African heritage; he also accused Haitian aristocrats of neglecting the rest of the population, especially the black peasants.

In response to Price-Mars's call, younger writers turned to their origins and celebrated their blackness. The journal *Revue Indigène* (1927) was founded by Normil Sylvain (1900–29). It attempted to foster a national culture in Haiti and rejected U.S. influences as well as the imitation, then in vogue, of French literature by Haitian writers. One genre that proved popular was the peasant novel that portrayed sympathetically the struggles of the Haitian peasants; the most famous work to emerge was *Gouverneurs de la rosée* (Masters of the dew) (1944) by Jacques Roumain (1907–44).

Figueredo, D.H., ed. *Encyclopedia of Caribbean Literature.* Westport, Conn.: Greenwood Press, 2006, pp. 23–25.

When a new Haitian president, Sténio Vincent (1874–1959), was elected in 1930, he pressured the United States to end the occupation. In 1934, the marines were recalled from Haiti. The intervention was described by one scholar as universally unpopular and provoking violent resistance (Renda, 34).

Haiti

For much of the 20th century, Haiti was ruled by François Duvalier (1907–71), known as "Papa Doc." Duvalier attempted to bring stability to Haiti through the forcible imposition of a father-and-son dynasty, offering nearly three decades of apparent tranquility. It was tranquility, however, rooted in terror.

The son of a teacher and a baker, Duvalier attended the Lycée Pétion in Port-au-Prince, Haiti. In 1934 he graduated as a physician from medical school. During this period he seemed primarily concerned with literary activities and medical work. He took part in a medical campaign to wipe out yaws—a disease that afflicts the skin and bones and makes it difficult to walk—that brought him national attention. Since he appeared to have no political ambitions and was therefore viewed as incorruptible and honest, he was encouraged to aspire to the presidency. He did, winning the election in 1957.

Duvalier's hunger for power, however, proved insatiable, and he soon named himself president-for-life. He purged the armed forces of those who were disloyal to him. In 1959 he established a secret police, the hated Tonton Macoutes, which suppressed dissent. He banned labor unions and brought the Catholic Church under his control by expelling dissenting clergy and electing bishops.

Two characteristics of Duvalier's regime were his claim to be a Vodun priest, capable of omnipresence, and the practice of black fascism, based on his corrupt interpretations of *négritude,* black consciousness, promoted by Haitian Jean Price-Mars (1876–1969) and Martinican writer and poet Aimé Césaire (1913–). Duvalier maintained that the historic power of mulattoes in Haiti was based on ethnic and racial preferences and reflected Europeans' predilections for light-skinned blacks. Because of this, mulattoes were accustomed to and eager for power and had to be kept in check. His government was responsible for the deaths of 30,000 to 60,000 people, many of them mulattoes.

Before dying in 1971, Papa Doc Duvalier, as he was called, changed Haitian laws to allow the transfer of power to his son through the use of a fraudulent referendum where more than 2 million voters approved the succession, afraid that if they did not, they would suffer persecution.

In April 1971 Jean-Claude Duvalier (1951–), a teenager of 19, assumed control of Haiti after his father's death. Initially, Jean-Claude

DUVALIER AND VODUN

Duvalier employed "folk religion" as a means of controlling the Haitian people. In an article coauthored with Lorimer Denis and published in February 1944, Duvalier described Vodun "in light of national independence, as the supreme factor of Haitian unity, solidifying the African's past on 'le sol natal'—the native soil. Papa Doc's use of vodou in politics followed in the tradition of a long line of Haitian leaders, who exploited the religion for their own ends.... [His use] rested on three basic facts: the appropriation of the sacred force of the religion, the use of its magic to hurt and eventually destroy opponents and its profane use as a channel of political propaganda. Penetrating the religion in a systematic manner was, therefore, a guaranteed way of communicating to or receiving information from the people. This suggests that Papa Doc's exploitation of Haiti's folk religion rested not only on the desire to convert houngans (vodou priests) into members of his feared militia, the volontaires de la securité nationale (VSN), popularly known as the tontons macoutes, but also on his quest to establish the mechanisms for clear and direct lines of communication between the Haitian masses and their presidency. In fact, Papa Doc's leadership style was characterized by frequent personal interactions with members of the peasantry. It was not unusual, for instance, for persons from the countryside to be invited to meet with him in Port-au-Prince."

Lewis, R. Anthony. "Language, Culture and Power: Haiti Under the Duvaliers." *Caribbean Quarterly* 55, 4 (Dec. 2004): p. 1.

Duvalier reversed many of his father's dictatorial decrees, allowing for freedom of press, implementing educational reform, and sponsoring public projects. His wedding to an upper-class mulatto woman, at a cost of $3 million, and his preference for light-skinned blacks put him in conflict with the black middle class that had supported his father. Although he attempted to liberalize the government, repression and political terror were still its salient features, as opponents were arrested and tortured by army officers that the young dictator could not or did not wish to control. Unlike his father, who sentenced leaders of the opposition to death, Jean-Claude preferred to force them into exile.

U.S. president Jimmy Carter's emphasis on human rights probably contributed to the younger Duvalier's more lenient attitude. Carter (1924–) tied economic aid directly to human rights. Since half of Haiti's budget came from U.S. government grants, it was in Duvalier's best interests to show restraint. Jean-Claude loosened restrictions on the press. In 1983, he allowed Pope John Paul II to visit Haiti.

It was a strategy that backfired, as the press began to criticize the regime, and the pope used the visit to ask for political change. More than 500 Catholic societies were established to train the poor to organize into cohesive groups that could lobby for social benefits and challenge the government. When Duvalier censored the press once again, after arresting 100 opposition leaders, the Catholic Church resorted to using the pulpit, during Sunday mass, to inform the congregation of political developments on the island.

End of the Duvalier Dynasty

Several events accelerated the fall of the Duvalier regime. In 1980, 100 Haitians were stranded on a cay after attempting to reach the United States by boat. The government did nothing to rescue them, leaving the task to other Caribbean nations. Duvalier's lack of response was seen as evidence of his detachment from the poor and prompted protests throughout the nation. In 1984, during food riots, government troops shot and killed 40 protesters.

As Haiti's economy collapsed in the 1980s, students rallied against his regime. In 1985 more than 60,000 youths took to the streets of Port-au-Prince shouting: "We would rather die on our feet than live on our knees" (Bellegarde-Smith, 107). In the countryside, a peaceful rebellion was organized by peasant leaders. At the same time, the middle class urged officers in the army to overthrow the regime. They were all pushing for the end of the Duvalier era.

Early in 1986, the U.S. government withdrew its support of Duvalier and urged him to leave the country to avoid bloodshed. Lack of American support coupled with dissension in the army influenced Duvalier's decision to flee Haiti. On February 7, 1986, he flew to Paris, where he remains to this day. Now divorced, he has occasionally spoken of making a political comeback in Haiti by running for the presidency.

The Duvalier era scarred Haiti. In 1960 there were 200 millionaires in Haiti, while 90 percent of the population earned less than $120 a year; 1 percent of the richest Haitians owned 60 percent of the best land. Infant malnutrition rose from 21 percent in 1958 to 87 percent in 1980, and inflation hovered at 30 percent (Bellegarde-Smith, 109, 125).

During the combined years of Duvalier rule, from 1957 to 1986, between 20,000 and 50,000 Haitians were murdered, and one-fifth of the population fled the country (Bellegarde-Smith, 97). People lived in constant fear but muffled their protests. Some believed that François Duvalier effectively manipulated Vodun, had omniscient powers, and could hear everything they said. Silently, Haitians watched father and son as they stole nearly $1 billion from Haiti and lived like the rich French planters of the 18th century.

In 1987, a referendum for a new constitution was approved by more than a million voters. However, more than half the population did not participate in the electoral process, since many were still afraid of personal reprisals. Another factor was the inadequate voting procedures established by the government for the referendum. The new constitution recognized Creole, or Kreyòl, as Haiti's national language and decriminalized the practice of Vodunism. A civilian president, Leslie F. Manigat, was elected.

Expectations for reform and economic progress were dashed within the year when officers, upset by the civilian president's plans to change the military structure and curb its power, deposed Manigat and installed General Henri Namphy as ruler. Namphy was then deposed by another military man, General Prosper Avril. Once again, pressure from the United States as well as France and other nations restrained the military government. Elections were permitted in 1990, though in a climate of violence, as two would-be candidates were assassinated.

Jean-Bertrand Aristide

A former Silesian priest, Father Jean-Bertrand Aristide (1953–   ), first won the presidency in 1991 with 67.6 percent of the vote out of more than 3 million ballots cast. President Aristide delivered his inaugural speech in Creole, or Kreyòl. He promised to conduct a literacy campaign and raise the minimum wage. His agenda included placing high tariffs on such imports as sugar and rice from the United States and trying to identify, expropriate, and return to the country funds taken out of Haiti by the wealthy.

Aristide was soon opposed by many different factions, including Haiti's Communist Party, which wanted a communist in the presidency; the Catholic Church, which considered him too radical; and the military, many of whom were still loyal to Duvalier. The result was a coup d'état that sent the priest-politician first to Venezuela and then to the United States, where he campaigned for his return to power. In 1994, U.S. president Bill Clinton (1946–   ), perhaps concerned that political and economic uncertainties in Haiti would result in a massive boatlift, prepared an invasion of the island with more than 20,000 troops, with the intent of restoring Aristide to the presidency. The Haitian military agreed to a peaceful transition as long as Aristide stepped down from office two years later. Aristide honored the agreement and in 1996 left office, obeying the Haitian constitution, which does not allow a president to stay in office for two consecutive terms. Aristide's move endeared him to Haitian voters.

In the late 1990s he indicated his wish to run for the presidency once again. His return to office in 2000 was not as well received, though, as his campaign was tainted by violence and a voting process considered fraudulent by most Haitians. An observer wrote: "Several opposition candidates were murdered; the electoral court was browbeaten into awarding ten disputed Senate seats [and thus a majority] to Mr Aristide's party. Mr Aristide was then re-elected president in a poll boycotted by the opposition. Ironically, Mr Aristide would almost certainly have won a free vote. But he was turning into another Haitian despot, wanting absolute control of his destitute country. He relied on gangs to enforce his rule" ("Leaders: Whose Coup in Haiti?" *Economist*, 13).

During this second tenure in power Aristide was accused of allowing the drug trade to flow freely in Haiti and of recruiting thugs to serve him personally. By 2004 there was a popular move in the country to remove the president. A revolt erupted, and anti-Aristide rebels gained control of half the nation. Fearing a civil war, both the United States and France encouraged Aristide, like Duvalier almost a decade before, to flee into exile. The president did so on February 29, but from exile in central Africa he claimed he was kidnapped by U.S. military forces, charges denied by the American government.

The Dominican Republic

Just a year after occupying Haiti, the United States in 1916 began an eight-year occupation of the Dominican Republic. The reason was ostensibly the same as in Haiti: European powers were threatening to invade the Dominican Republic because of its inability to pay its foreign debt. As in Haiti, some Dominicans tried to resist the occupation. Some low-ranking officers, common soldiers, and peasants formed a resistance movement in the countryside. But the results were the same— overwhelming U.S. forces defeated the rebels. The use of machine guns and cannon proved as effective in the Dominican Republic as planes in Haiti. A battle that occurred in June 1916, a month after the marines' landing, illustrates the unevenness of the conflict. Rebels were routed at the town of La Barranquita, where they had chosen to make a stand. Out of 74 Dominican combatants, 26 were killed by the marines, who suffered only one casualty.

During the eight-year occupation, the United States imposed martial law on the island-nation. Occupation forces created many new ministries. They included the Department of Labor, which imposed minimum wages, and the Department of Health, which banned the practice of medicine by faith healers and demanded evidence of a university degree before certifying physicians. Roads were built to facilitate the movement of the armed forces, and a national police force was created to hunt down the bandits and rebels roaming the countryside. One of the police cadets was future dictator Rafael Leónidas Trujillo (1891–1961), who achieved recognition for his organizational skills.

With the end of World War I, Dominican nationalists launched a full-scale campaign to end U.S. occupation by forming La Unión Nacional Dominicana (the Dominican National Union). The organization waged a public relations campaign in Europe and Latin America to force an American withdrawal. In 1922 the Dominicans presented a plan for evacuation to the U.S. government. Its main point was the establishment of a provisional government to rule alongside a North American military governor until elections were held. After the election of a Dominican president, the United States would end the occupation. The plan was approved by both sides. In 1924 Horacio Vásquez (1860–1936) was elected president. In July of that year, U.S. troops left the Dominican Republic.

The rest of the 20th century in the Dominican Republic proved a period of supreme *caudillismo* as two men, Rafael L. Trujillo and Joaquín Balaguer, ruled from 1930 to 1996. Trujillo's reign (1930–61) was uninterrupted, although he used puppet presidents, such as his brother and Balaguer, to provide a civilian facade. Balaguer's rule was interrupted on several occasions, but he served as president from 1960 to 1962, 1966 to 1978, and 1986 to 1996.

Rafael Leónidas Trujillo, Dominican Dictator

In 1930 Rafael Trujillo was elected president with the support of the army, which he had commanded since 1925. On September 3, shortly after he took office, a hurricane nearly destroyed Santo Domingo. The disaster allowed Trujillo an opportunity to demonstrate his managerial skills. He cordoned off the capital and ensured that looting did not occur. Trujillo distributed food and water and within days was leading efforts to rebuild homes and neighborhoods. His resolve, decisiveness, and ability to get the work done, even if opposing views were silenced, endeared him to the armed forces and the middle class.

Trujillo's rule lasted 31 years (1930–61). Sometimes he ruled as president, and sometimes he ruled from behind a facade of civilian government. His government was characterized by economic progress and brutality. In 1931, Trujillo ordered a moratorium on the country's foreign debt payments, paying only the interest on the loans. In 1933 he balanced the national budget. In 1940, he regained control of the customs house from the United States, a psychological and economic boost to national sovereignty that earned him the title "restorer of the country's financial independence." Over the course of the 1940s, Trujillo bought branches of the First National City Bank to form the Dominican Republic's Bank of Reserves, paid off the national debt, and created the Dominican peso, replacing the U.S. dollar that had been used as the national currency since 1899. In 1955, his government purchased the Electric Company of Santo Domingo, owned by U.S. interests, and converted it into a Dominican corporation. Many of these financial gains were the result of World War II (1939–45), which created a market in the United States for rice and other agricultural products from the Dominican Republic.

Anti-Haitianism was a cornerstone of the Trujillo administration. The dictator used the cultural differences between Dominicans and Haitians to foster a strong sense of nationalism and identity among Dominicans. An intellectual upper class sprang up to foster and endorse Trujillo's vision of a Dominican culture steeped in the progressive ideas of Europe and Roman Catholicism as opposed to Haitian culture, which was depicted as backward, African, and mired in superstitions and Vodun. Traditional fears, based on past invasions of the Dominican Republic by Haiti, were used to fan the flames of fear. Anti-Haitianism was a useful distraction to conceal the almost total disregard of civil rights in the Trujillo years and the enormous amassing of private wealth by the Trujillo family.

In October 1937, Trujillo ordered the massacre of thousands of Haitians. The exact death toll is unknown, but estimates range from 4,000 to 20,000. Trujillo ordered his troops to use knives and machetes to kill anyone they suspected was Haitian. To determinate nationality, a simple test was employed. The word *pejeril* (parsley) was difficult for Creole (Kreyòl) speakers to say. If someone could not pronounce the word when challenged, that person was doomed.

The genocide lasted three days. The international press, concerned over the rise of Adolf Hitler (1889–1945), Francisco Franco (1892–1975), Benito Mussolini (1883–1945), and fascism in Europe, did not pay much attention to the Haitian massacre. Eventually, pressured by the United States, Cuba, and Mexico, Trujillo held mock trials for several officers. They were sentenced to 30 years in prison, did not serve any jail time, and agreed to pay the Haitian government $750,000 in damages, of which only $500,000 was paid.

By the end of his regime, some estimate that the Trujillo family owned between 50 and 60 percent of the arable land in the Dominican Republic. Between the government and their private businesses, they employed 75 percent of the workforce. In a nation with an average income of $200 per year, Trujillo amassed an estate estimated at $800 million. In addition to economic power, Trujillo solidified his regime by controlling the education system and the mass media. He was elaborately praised in public by his political allies. Official classroom texts referred to him by such nicknames as "the Sun" and "lightning." Trujillo statues and busts were placed throughout the country; the absence of a statue in a home could be construed as lack of support for the regime. Parks, streets, mountains, and towns were named in his honor. He even went so far as to rename the centuries-old city of Santo Domingo Ciudad Trujillo. The dictator established a one-party system to dominate politics in the Dominican Republic so that only candidates belonging to El Partido Dominicano (the Dominican Party) were eligible to seek elected office.

Torture and assassination of political opponents were the norm during the Trujillo era. Even those who sought asylum in other nations often became targets. In 1956, scholar Jesus de Galíndez (1915–56), who had written an exposé of how Trujillo accumulated his wealth illegally, was kidnapped by Trujillo's secret service in New York, flown to the Dominican Republic, and murdered there. Toward the end of the regime, Trujillo's henchmen murdered three sisters—Minerva (1926–60), Patria (1924–60), and Maria Teresa Mirabal (1936–60)—for their participation in the underground movement. The women were beaten to death, placed inside a car, and pushed off a cliff. In 1994, a fictionalized account of the lives of the Mirabal sisters was turned into a novel by Julia Alvarez entitled *In the Time of the Butterflies*. In 2001, the book was turned into a U.S. television film starring Salma Hayek and Edward James Olmos.

Ironically, the dictator himself came to his death in a car when he was shot by opponents on May 30, 1961. Even before his assassination,

Trujillo's days in power appeared to be numbered. By then, Trujillo was isolated by other Latin American leaders, who had grown tired of his dictatorial ways. In the closing days of his regime, the Organization of American States placed a trade embargo on the Dominican Republic after Trujillo attempted to assassinate Venezuelan president Romulo Betancourt (1908–81), a critic of his regime. The United States finally withdrew its support of the regime after a three-decade-long cozy relationship.

Death of Trujillo

The assassination of Rafael Trujillo in 1961 led to chaos in the Dominican Republic. After 31 years of living under a dictatorship that Eric Williams called "one of the most ruthless and efficient in the history of the entire world" (E. Williams 1984, 465), the Dominican people found themselves in a political vacuum. The dictator's son, Ramfis Trujillo (1929–69), took over the military. The puppet president, Joaquín Balaguer, placed in office by the tyrant, continued to rule the nation. Ramfis tracked down the members of the conspiracy who had plotted Trujillo's death and executed almost all of them.

Ramfis Trujillo, who had led the life of a playboy, did not have the ability to govern. Soon his uncles, Hector (1909–2002) and José Arismendi Trujillo (?–2000), attempted to run the government with him. In the meantime Balaguer, gaining confidence in his abilities to administer and acting for the first time without the tyrant's instructions, decided to grant an amnesty to all who had opposed Trujillo. The Trujillo brothers objected to this plan and attempted to remove Balaguer from office and arrest and murder members of the opposition.

The potential for another military dictatorship in the republic alarmed U.S. president John F. Kennedy (1917–63). He sent a battleship to the Dominican Republic and persuaded the brothers to relinquish power. On November 22, 1961, six months after the death of Trujillo, the name of the nation's capital reverted from Ciudad Trujillo to Santo Domingo, its colonial name. Vestiges of Trujillo's regime were removed as his statues were toppled from pedestals throughout the country. Balaguer remained in office as part of a civilian state council.

Juan Bosch, Poet and President

In 1962, the Dominican Republic held its first democratic election in a generation and elected Juan Bosch as president. If Balaguer represented the old Trujillo order, Bosch was symbolic of the progressive changes that leaders such as Fidel Castro were promoting throughout the Caribbean. A novelist, short-story writer, and essayist, Bosch was born in La Vega, Dominican Republic, on June 30, 1909. In 1937, protesting against the Trujillo dictatorship, Bosch left for Cuba. Two years later he founded the Partido Revolucionario Dominicano (PRD) (Dominican Revolutionary Party) in Cuba with the objective of over-throwing Trujillo and implementing a socialist agenda in the Dominican Republic. For the next two decades, Bosch and the party helped finance and plan several unsuccessful armed expeditions to oust Trujillo.

Upon winning the elections in 1962, Bosch's government imple-mented a progressive program. It limited the development of large land holdings by a single individual or corporation, approved equal pay for men and women, and instituted equal legal protection and benefits for legitimate and illegitimate children. The new regime soon made ene-mies. Its emphasis on freedom of speech—which permitted communist intellectuals to express their opinions and promote communism, and its preference for lay education versus parochial education—prompted the Catholic Church to describe Bosch as a communist. The new presi-dent approved a law limiting profits made by the sugar industry when exporting sugar (the limit was $5.83 per 100 pounds; any figure over that amount was to be handed over to the government), which angered businessmen. The military, whose power was curtailed by Bosch, began to plot against the president.

In 1963, seven months after taking office, Bosch was forced into exile, and a junta took over the government. Members of the PRD con-spired to restore the former president. In 1965 PRD militants occupied the presidential palace. As they planned Bosch's return from exile in Puerto Rico, the Dominican air force attacked the palace. The ensuing civil war, which lasted less than a year, resulted in the deaths of 2,000 Dominicans and the landing of U.S. Marines in Santo Domingo. In August 1965 a truce was signed, a provisional government was estab-lished, and elections were planned.

Balaguer was the winner in the 1966 election, receiving 57 percent of the vote after spending $13 million on his campaign; Bosch received 40 percent of the vote.

Joaquín Balaguer

Joaquín Balaguer was born in Villa Bisono, Dominican Republic, on September 1, 1906. At the age of 23, he earned a law degree from the Universidad Autónoma de Santo Domingo. He continued his studies in Paris, receiving a doctorate in law and in economics in 1934 from the Sorbonne.

In 1930, Balaguer helped Trujillo take power. He was assigned to the Dominican Republic's embassy in Spain in 1932 and then was made the Dominican Republic Council's secretary in Paris in 1934. This was the first of many posts he held during the Trujillo era, including minister of foreign relations, ambassadorships in several Latin American countries, and vice president of the republic. During this period he not only wrote speeches for Trujillo, but also penned several tomes on the literature and history of the Dominican Republic, the most famous of which were *Historia de la literatura dominicana* (History of the literature of the Dominican Republic) (1944), *Semblanzas literarias* (Literary portraits) (1948), and *El Cristo de la libertad* (The Christ of freedom) (1950).

During Balaguer's first two years as president, the United States, which wanted a conservative in power in the Caribbean to counterbalance Castro's influence, awarded Balaguer more than $130 million in funds. He used this money to build roads, bridges, housing projects, canals, dams, and tourist facilities. Foreign corporations were invited to mine gold and nickel.

The prosperity, however, was illusory. The funding came primarily from the United States, and the projects enriched the wealthy and Balaguer himself. As oil prices increased and sugar prices dropped in the 1970s, voters turned to Bosch's old party, the Partido Revolucionario Dominicano. In 1978, they elected a younger leader from the PRD, Antonio Guzmán (1911–82).

The decade of the 1980s was disastrous for the Dominican Republic. Sugar prices dropped to four cents a pound, and the nation's public debt reached $4 billion. Riots broke out in 1984 when the government raised oil prices in accordance with restrictions imposed by the International Monetary Fund. In 1986, Balaguer returned to power, embarking once again on public projects such as improving roads and building hydroelectric plants. He won elections again in 1990 and 1994, balancing the budget and curtailing inflation. The 1994 elections were highly suspect, and the defeated candidate, Francisco Peña Gómez (1937–98), called for a general strike to protest wide-ranging voter fraud. The United States brokered an agreement by which Balaguer would resign in two years rather than serve out his four-year term.

Balaguer died on July 14, 2002. As president, he was dictatorial and dishonest, often harassing electoral candidates, including Bosch, preventing voters from casting their votes, and delaying the count of the ballots. Yet he represented a transition from the 19th-century model of the rule of the strongman to the 20th-century model of rule by a politician willing to work within a democratic framework.

Successful Democracy in the Dominican Republic

The end of the era of *caudillismo* in the Dominican Republic came in 1996 when Balaguer, nearly 90 years old and ailing, left office. Two candidates dominated the ensuing presidential campaign, Peña Gómez and Leonel Fernández (1953–   ). Peña Gómez was a social democrat, and Fernández was a conservative with ties to the United States, where he was raised. The elections served as a platform for racism, as Peña Gómez was described as being of Haitian descent, was caricatured as a monkey, and was accused of wanting to unite the Dominican Republic with Haiti. The more perfidious component of the campaign was the assertion that the candidate's Haitian heritage clearly demonstrated his African roots, an ethnicity that many Dominicans view as inferior. The campaign played into the worst excesses of anti-Haitianism, a political and racial ideology that has prevailed in the Dominican Republic since the 19th century. Despite the racist campaign, Peña Gómez received 49 percent of the vote. The winner, however, with 51 percent of the vote, was Fernández.

President Fernández ended the isolationism cultivated by Balaguer and actively participated in such world forums as the Organization of American States. Internally, his policies kept inflation in the single digits, and the economy experienced a 7 percent growth rate. In 2000, as required by the constitution, Fernández stepped down, but he returned to power in 2004. By then the economy was crumbling, with a 50 percent inflation rate, bank failures due to $2.5 million in embezzlements, and 42 percent of the population living in poverty. Fernández implemented an austerity program that resulted in a reduction in public-sector jobs, tax increases, and better control over the national budget. These measures allowed him to secure a loan of $665 million from the International Monetary Fund. He then promoted tourism, which brought more than $2 billion annually into the country; courted Hollywood studios to film in the Dominican Republic; and developed a plan for a subway system.

His program was countered by criticism that Fernández was taking money from education to fund the construction of a subway, that he failed to curtail drug-related activities, and that he did nothing to combat corruption. The crime rate was another black eye for the Fernández administration. Records indicate that 1,086 murders were reported in

2001; by 2005 the number had risen to 2,382. A total of 9,300 murders were reported during this period (2001–05), with 790 of the victims being women (Pina, 1). The president responded by declaring a state of siege and ordering the army to patrol the streets of Santo Domingo.

The executive action could be seen as a reenactment of Trujillo's managing of Santo Domingo after a hurricane devastated the capital in 1930, when he ordered troops into the afflicted areas and replaced local government with military rule. But many in the Dominican Republic did not link the events. During Trujillo's tenure, there was no organized political party to oppose him, and Trujillo was a military man. Such was not the case in 2005 with Fernández.

It appears that in the 21st century, Hispaniola—the island that serves as home to the Dominican Republic and Haiti—is witnessing the growth of a fragile democracy in the Dominican Republic, but a democracy nonetheless, and a turbulent political process in Haiti as the Haitian people attempt to obey the constitution while establishing and maintaining a government elected by the people.

10

COMMONWEALTH, FEDERATION, AND AUTONOMY: PUERTO RICO, MARTINIQUE, GUADELOUPE, AND THE DUTCH CARIBBEAN (1900–2000)

As political leaders envisioned postcolonial governments, independence was not a common objective. It was true that the colonial powers oppressed the colonies, but imperial trade assured a source of income and a supply of products, even at minimal levels. Many of the leaders were also aware of geographical restrictions, such as the absence of powerful rivers to transport goods and long stretches of land for agriculture. A complete break with the colonial power could lead the new nation to dire economic situations. Thus, while some of the leaders in the smaller islands admired the spirit of independence, they sought a practical avenue that could ensure economic progress and tranquility for the citizens.

Puerto Rico Finding Itself

Under the terms of the Treaty of Paris, Spain ceded Puerto Rico to the United States. Defining Puerto Rico's political status with regard to the United States became the central theme of the new political relationship. It was a rocky relationship from the start. Military rule on the island ended in 1900 with the passage of the Foraker Act, which provided for a governor appointed by the U.S. president, an executive council, and a chamber of delegates. Puerto Ricans were allowed to elect a lower house consisting of 35 members, but most of the power rested with the governor and the executive council.

The Foraker Act produced great uncertainty because it did not grant Puerto Ricans independence, self-rule, or statehood. To remedy the situation, in 1917 U.S. president Woodrow Wilson (1856–1924) signed into law the Jones Act, which granted American citizenship to all Puerto Ricans. The new law gave the island more power over local matters and created a Puerto Rican Senate and House of Representatives; it also permitted Puerto Ricans to travel between the United States and Puerto Rico without documents. The act made Puerto Ricans subject to the military draft just as the United States was about to enter World War I. The U.S. president retained the right to appoint Puerto Rico's governor until 1947, when the law was amended to permit Puerto Ricans to elect their own governor.

Bestowing citizenship on Puerto Ricans added to their cultural conundrum. They were now citizens of a country whose mother tongue and culture were foreign to them. U.S. customs and traditions were based on Protestant religious values, unlike those of Puerto Rico, which followed Catholic-oriented Spanish traditions. Furthermore, the rest of Latin America did not know whether to view Puerto Ricans as Americans or as Latin Americans.

For the remainder of the 20th century, Puerto Ricans debated three political options to define their status: statehood, independence, or commonwealth, a combination of autonomy from and dependence on Washington. The apparent lack of interest by the United States in granting statehood to Puerto Rico, a policy supported by many Puerto Ricans in the early years of the relationship, contributed to the formation of an independence movement. Two leaders emerged embodying two different approaches: Pedro Albizu Campos and Luis Muñoz Marín. These two men dominated political life on the island throughout most of the 20th century.

Luis Muñoz Marín

The son of Luis Muñoz Rivera, and like his father given to writing poetry, Luis Muñoz Marín (1898–1980) toured the island in 1917. He saw how peasants were abused by owners and managers of sugar plantations and the coffee industry. At the time, he was a member of the Socialist Party. As he interviewed the peasants it became clear to him that while the island's upper class was struggling with political definitions and identities for the island, the working poor were concerned with the everyday struggles of making a living. Economic conditions were particularly

Governor Muñoz Marín, the first Puerto Rican elected to that office, supported the common-wealth status of the island. (Centro de Estudios Puertorriqueños)

hard for the rural poor, with 78 percent of cultivated land—more than 1 million acres—owned by foreign corporations and nearly 60 percent of agriculture devoted to the sugar industry. The industry did not provide year-round employment because the cane-cutting season lasts only a few months during the fall. With sugar prices established by the world market rather than the island, the laborers were paid about 50 cents for a

12-hour day. Beyond agriculture there was little industry, another barrier for economic growth for most people on the island.

As Muñoz Marín grew away from the Socialist Party, he joined the Liberal Party in 1931. The Liberal Party platform advocated limited government involvement in industry and public projects to create employment. Shortly thereafter he was elected to the Puerto Rican Senate. In 1938, he founded the Popular Democratic Party, advocating for the reduction of work hours. By this time, Muñoz Marín had decided that the important issue in Puerto Rico, where the cost of living was higher than in the United States, was not the political conflict between independence and colonialism, but economics (Cardona, 365). He began to campaign for economic changes on the island, such as promoting tax-free opportunities for American companies, and he traveled to New York to recruit companies. In 1948, Muñoz Marín became the first elected governor of Puerto Rico after that right was ceded to the island. As governor, he worked to establish a new political and economic relationship with the United States.

Muñoz Marín concluded that autonomy within the larger framework of the U.S. government was the best solution for the island. His concept of a commonwealth, which he and his political allies dubbed Estado Libre Asociado (Freely Associated State), allowed the island to administer its local government while still receiving federal assistance and protection from the United States. As members of a commonwealth, Puerto Ricans could travel back and forth to the United States to seek employment, which helped reduce local unemployment. On the macroeconomic side, Muñoz Marín was a supporter of what came to be known as Operation Bootstrap, an aggressive campaign to promote investment in Puerto Rico by U.S. corporations. It boosted the creation of industry over agriculture to improve the local economy and offered tax incentives to American corporations. Companies willing to invest in Puerto Rico were given 10-year tax breaks and low-interest government loans. The Puerto Rican government also agreed to provide worker training programs at its expense. The program succeeded in attracting 2,000 new factories and 100,000 jobs to the island. It also made the island a major consumer of U.S. products to the tune of $330 million a year during the 1950s.

Puerto Rico's Nationalist Movement

The proposed commonwealth was vigorously opposed by the nationalist movement. Under the leadership of attorney Pedro Albizu Campos (1891–1965), a Harvard University graduate, the nationalists demanded

Albizu Campos was the most ardent supporter of Puerto Rican independence in the 20th century. (Centro de Estudios Puertorriqueños)

independence. While Muñoz Marín was a traditional politician who worked within the system—using the benefits of family influence, name recognition, and connections with the island's upper class—Albizu Campos was a radical who championed a complete break with the United States.

Albizu Campos was a veteran who had served as an officer in the U.S. Army. Assigned to a black unit, Albizu Campos experienced discrimination within the army and in the cities and towns he visited in the southern United States. In 1930, he was elected president of the Nationalist Party and toured the island, telling audiences that Puerto Rico was a colony, a spoil of war for the North Americans. He urged Puerto Ricans to refrain from holding public office, focusing their energies instead on the island's independence. College students responded favorably to Albizu Campos's oratory skills and message; he also found support among the island's intellectuals and writers.

In 1935, a confrontation erupted between police and protesters at a pro-independence demonstration inspired by Albizu Campos on the Río Piedras campus of the University of Puerto Rico. The confrontation left four nationalists dead. It was the beginning of a violent phase of the independence movement that spread from San Juan to Washington. In February 1936, to avenge the four comrades killed in Río Piedras, two Puerto Rican nationalists killed an American colonel, Francis E. Riggs (?–1936), who was serving in Puerto Rico's police force. The assassins, Elias Beauchamp and Hiram Rosado, were arrested and killed by the police under suspicious circumstances. A month later, the Ponce Massacre occurred when Puerto Rican police fired on protesters, killing 19 and wounding more than 100. Perceived as the architect of the protests and marches, Albizu Campos was arrested and sentenced to prison in Georgia. With the independence leader behind bars and World War II on the verge of breaking out, a sort of truce emerged in the early 1940s.

In December 1947, Albizu Campos was released from prison. In his first statements to the press he vowed to continue his battle for independence. As the first gubernatorial election approached in 1948, the independence leader urged his compatriots not to vote for Muñoz Marín. Nevertheless, Muñoz Marín was elected.

The nationalist movement remained vibrant throughout the 1950s, although over time its popularity began to erode. Symbolic acts of rebellion, such as climbing over Puerto Rico's government house to remove the U.S. flag and replace it with the Puerto Rican flag, gave way to actions perceived by the American public as acts of terrorism.

In October 1950, nationalists in Puerto Rico attacked the police station in the town of Jayuya, killing one police officer and wounding several more. After cutting telephone lines and burning the town's post office, the nationalists declared Puerto Rico a free republic. The United States declared martial law, and the Puerto Rican National Guard surrounded the town. After air bombardment and artillery fire, the national guard defeated the rebels. A plot to assassinate Muñoz Marín was also uncovered during the same period. In 1954, four Puerto Rican nationalists attacked the U.S. House of Representatives. From the Ladies' Gallery, they shot some 30 rounds onto the floor of the chamber, wounding five congressmen.

On November 1, 1950, nationalist leaders Oscar Collazo and Griselio Torresola broke into the Blair House, the temporary home of U.S. president Harry S. Truman (1884–1972) and his family while reconstruction work was going on at the White House, with the intent of assassinating him. Truman and his family were not home at the time of the attack. A police officer was killed in the assault, and several more were wounded. Torresola was shot dead, and Collazo was wounded and arrested.

Commonwealth for Puerto Rico

For his involvement in some of these events, Albizu Campos was arrested again in 1951 and was found guilty of plotting against the U.S. government. As Albizu Campos began serving a 15-year sentence, Muñoz Marín was negotiating with the U.S. Labor Department for the temporary hiring of 50,000 to 100,000 Puerto Rican farmers to work in agriculture in the United States during the sugar industry's off-season, which lasted from July to January. This would ensure year-round employment for these laborers and realize one of the governor's objectives. A year later, 80 percent of Puerto Rican voters approved commonwealth status for the island, a vote that satisfied Muñoz Marín and was seen as a rejection of Albizu Campos and the independence movement.

The governor was reelected several times, serving from 1948 to 1964. He maintained that commonwealth was the best alternative for the island, an assertion often debated, with roughly half the population favoring statehood and the other half choosing commonwealth. There have been numerous plebiscites since 1967, and the vote has consistently been evenly split. The latest plebiscite, held in 1998, revealed that Puerto Ricans still remain torn on the question of status. In that election, when asked to choose between statehood, commonwealth, independence, or free association, just over 50 percent voted for "none of the above."

The latest wrinkle in the ambivalent relationship was the release of a report in December 2005 by the President's Task Force on Puerto Rico's Status. This report concluded that the U.S. Congress was not bound by the 1952 agreement establishing the commonwealth. It determined that the U.S. Constitution allows for only two possibilities regarding the permanent status of Puerto Rico: independence or statehood. The government of Puerto Rico is challenging the findings of the task force.

In 1964, Muñoz Marín pardoned an infirm Albizu Campos, who died a year later. Supporters thought of him as the conscience of Puerto Rico, "the last vestige of [the] patriots" of the 19th century (Iglesias, 224). In the 1980s and 1990s, Albizu Campos's dream of independence inspired the formation of a paramilitary group named Los Macheteros that was involved in terrorist activities in the United States and Puerto Rico, including bombing a restaurant in New York City and robbing several banks. In the meantime, the migration of Puerto Ricans to the United States continued. By the beginning of the 21st century, more than 3 million Puerto Ricans lived on the U.S. mainland, while another 4 million lived on the island.

Puerto Rico's Battle for Vieques

The island of Vieques, located off the coast of Puerto Rico, became a symbol of the battle between American colonialism and Puerto Rican sovereignty during the 1990s, although it was a contentious issue dating back to the establishment of a U.S. naval base there in the 1940s. During World War II (1939–45), Vieques offered the United States a position from which to monitor German submarine activities in the Caribbean Sea. The Vieques base was part of a series of U.S. military fortifications in the Caribbean to guard against potential attacks against the Panama Canal. After World War II the island was used as a U.S. Navy firing and practice range. Before the acquisition of 25,000 acres by the United States, the island was in economic decline. The economic backbone of the island was sugar. Competition from Jamaica and Cuba

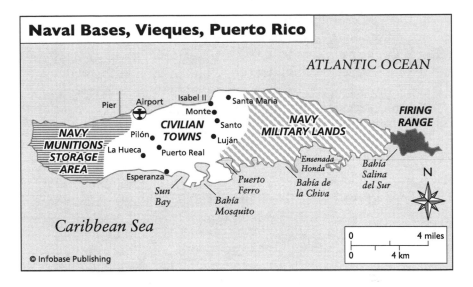

Naval Bases, Vieques, Puerto Rico

and a drop in the world price made the industry less profitable. Three of the island's four sugar mills were forced to close, and the amount of acreage planted in sugarcane was cut in half between 1935 and 1945. As a result many residents of Vieques—about 26 percent—resettled on the islands of St. Thomas and St. Croix, where they worked in the service industry and agriculture. The land acquired by the United States, which included several beaches, was owned primarily by absentee landlords. A Puerto Rican family and a corporation owned 88 percent of the acquired acreage, while the remaining land belonged to 200 owners. Once the United States took over the acreage, the laborers who occupied the land and worked as sugarcane cutters were displaced from the homes where they cultivated crops on small plots to feed their families.

In 1947, the United States devised a plan to convert the remaining civilian side of the island into part of the naval base, relocating residents to St. Croix. The plan was opposed by both Luis Muñoz Marín and Pedro Albizu Campos. The fears expressed by Albizu Campos that the U.S. presence on the tiny island would prove destructive to the people and the environment were realized during the 1950s. Alcoholism and prostitution reached epidemic proportions on the island. The presence of U.S. military personnel exacerbated tensions and often led to fights between locals and sailors.

Over time, the threat of an ecological and health nightmare mobilized the Puerto Rican people. The public realized there was a possibility "that lead and other contaminants [could] leak into the [island's] groundwater.

Furthermore, contamination from the [bombings] site could migrate to the ocean from storm-water runoff on the beaches. Nearly half the residents of Vieques eat fish once or twice a week, and a contaminated fish and shellfish population could create a public-health crisis throughout the island" (Goldberg, 7). When a mysterious animal called the "chupacabras" (goat sucker) appeared in Puerto Rico in the early 1990s, supposedly attacking small animals and draining their blood, many concluded that this vampirelike creature, yet to be found or photographed, was the creation of ecological experiments in Vieques.

In the 1960s, organized opposition against the base began to grow. Politicians, divided on the question of independence or commonwealth status for Puerto Rico, found unity in the fight to reclaim Vieques from the U.S. Navy. By the 1970s, activists often physically blocked the entrance to the base and created human chains near target-practice areas. By the 1980s and 1990s, there were hundreds of organized protests and blockades on the island by residents, protesters from Puerto Rico, and celebrities such as singer Ricky Martin and John F. Kennedy, Jr. In New York, Congressman José Serrano lobbied for a U.S. withdrawal from Vieques.

The Puerto Ricans were eventually victorious. In 2003, President George W. Bush agreed to end the use of the island for naval war games after 62 years. The United States began downsizing the base, indicating that the island base would be closed. It was a moment of Puerto Rican solidarity. Yet there were problems, again demonstrating the island's dependence on the United States. The naval base employed between 5,000 and 13,000 laborers, helping reduce the unemployment rate in towns such as Fajardo, a city on the main island from which workers were ferried to Vieques. As the military began to leave, restaurant owners in Vieques and Fajardo lamented the empty tables in their establishments. By some estimates, half of the businesses on the coast and on Vieques closed their doors.

The Puerto Rican government is currently working with the federal Environmental Protection Agency to clean up contamination caused by the U.S. Navy. There are also efforts under way to develop the island as a tourist and recreation site.

Some speculated that Washington only abandoned the base because developments in modern warfare technology and monitoring devices made Vieques irrelevant as a naval firing range. Nevertheless, the final departure of the U.S. Navy in May 2003 was cheered by Puerto Ricans who had mobilized for more than two decades. They proved that David could defeat Goliath.

The Virgin Islands

During World War I, the United States turned its attention to the Virgin Islands, fearing that the Germans would establish a submarine naval base on the territory. The United States purchased the Virgin Islands from Denmark in 1917, paying a sum of $25 million. Ten years later, the residents of the Virgin Islands were granted American citizenship by the U.S. Congress.

In a political structure similar to that of Puerto Rico, the Virgin Islands became a territory of the United States with a governor and local rule but complete dependence on the United States for military protection and international relations. The residents of the Virgin Islands cannot vote for an American president, a point of discontent for many local politicians, who have advocated for a referendum to clarify the island's political status. Such efforts have yet to receive wide support or attention in the United States. Thus, the issue remains unaddressed in the Virgin Islands and by the U.S. Congress.

Martinique

Frenchmen in France and in the Caribbean did not think much of Martinique, an attitude that was evident in 1902, when Mount Pelée erupted, wiping out the capital, Saint-Pierre, and causing the death of nearly 3,000 Martinicans. The high death toll was the result of slow bureaucratic response by administrators who failed to evacuate residents. The attitude of the colonial authorities showed that they were disconnected from day-to-day events on Martinique and were primarily concerned with the few white aristocrats living there, called *békés,* who had great political and economic influence.

When the French met a Martinican who showed promise, the tendency was to separate this individual from other Martinicans by sending him or her to France. The objective was to make the Martinican a replica of a French person, a black Frenchman or Frenchwoman. One such individual, named Aimé Césaire, challenged France and its relationship with Martinique.

Aimé Césaire

Aimé Césaire (1913–   ) was born in St. Pierre and grew up during a time, in the 1920s, when Martinique was experiencing political turmoil as organized workers protested against the *békés.* To reduce tensions, and the potential for rebellion, local officials promoted political integration with the national government of France. This was an idea explored intermittently since the 19th century.

The practice of political and cultural assimilation was intended to pave the way for islanders to work within the French political system and incorporate themselves into French culture. As part of the assimilation philosophy, French authorities rewarded intelligent students with scholarships to prestigious schools, or *lycées,* and then with academic scholarships to France, where the students attended colleges designed specifically for colonial subjects. These students became either teachers or administrators. Upon graduation they were sent back to their countries or were assigned to posts in other colonies. This was the anticipated path for Césaire, a brilliant student from a poor family who at an early age mastered French, English, and Latin.

In 1931, Césaire attended the Lycée Louis-le-Grand, a preparatory school in Paris for the École Normale Supérieure. By 1935, he had earned a teaching degree. In Paris, Césaire was influenced by Marxist ideology, the popularity of African art in Europe, and the Harlem Renaissance in the United States, where the creative work and thoughts of African-American men and women were presented to an appreciative white audience. Césaire socialized with two men who changed his life, Léopold Sédar Senghor (1906–2001), from Senegal, and Léon-Gontran Damas (1912–78), from French Guiana. These two young intellectuals introduced Césaire to African heritage and culture. He gained a new appreciation for a culture previously denied him; for despite French liberal attitudes, whatever was black was always deemed inferior. This was clearly expressed in the popular work the *Psychological Laws of the Evolution of People* (1894), written by the much admired psychologist Gustave Le Bon (1841–1931). LeBon maintained that people of color were naturally inferior to whites. Césaire, accustomed to this racist ideology, was awakened by the richness of African civilization and culture. The friendship among these men resulted in the creation of a short-lived journal, *L'etudiant noir* (The black student). Through his work, writing and editing this journal, Césaire began to affirm his African roots and to develop a black consciousness. In 1939, inspired by this new awareness, he wrote one of the most famous poems written in French, *Cahier d'un retour au pays natal* (Notebook of a return to the native land), in which he coined the term *négritude.*

Césaire returned to Martinique in 1939 and taught at the Lycée Schoelcher in Fort-de-France. With his wife, Suzanne Roussy Césaire (1913–50), and another teacher, René Ménil (1907–2004), he founded the journal *Tropiques,* which promoted a rejection of European values and criticized the Caribbean people as imitators of French culture rather than creators of their own culture. Around this time he became involved in local politics, advocating an anticolonial perspective.

In 1945, Césaire, supported by the Communist Party, was elected mayor of Fort-de-France, a post he maintained for five decades. He was also elected representative to the French National Assembly. In 1946, he supported changing Martinique's political status from a colony to an overseas French department rather than promoting Martinican independence.

Césaire sought an adaptation of the French system to Martinican culture and traditions rather than a blind process of assimilation. He wanted Martinicans to use the French system for their purposes rather than aping French culture and values. He viewed departmentalization as a way to achieve political equality with France. The people of Martinique applauded this move, but many non-Martinican intellectuals and activists saw it as another manifestation of colonialism. For Césaire the decision was a step toward "effective political and social progress" and "integration within France was . . . a victory over colonialism" (Pèrina, 131).

In 1956, Césaire rejected communist ideology. He published a document, *Lettre à Maurice Thorez* (Letter to Maurice Thorez), in which he explained his reason for resigning from the French Communist Party. He saw the party as using black people to achieve the political objectives of Communist leaders rather than helping black people fight against oppression. He then founded his own political party, the Parti Progressiste Martiniquais (Martinican Progressive Party).

During the 1950s and 1960s, Césaire's political philosophy was questioned by a new generation of Martinican activists. They included the writer Frantz Fanon (1925–61), who felt that Césaire betrayed the independence movement. But Césaire was aware of political developments in other parts of the Caribbean. He saw the dictatorships that arose in independent countries such as the Dominican Republic, the political chaos that followed the death of Trujillo in the Dominican Republic, and Castro's oppressive regime in Cuba. To him these were indications that independence did not necessarily lead to economic and personal freedom. Césaire felt that economic and political stability was more desirable than independence.

The Negritude Movement

The roots of *négritude* can be traced to Haiti. The awareness of a black consciousness first flourished there in the 19th century as a result of the Haitian Revolution and was reaffirmed in the writings of the Haitian intellectual Jean Price-Mars (1876–1969). In Paris in the 1930s, Césaire was influenced by the artists of the Harlem Renaissance in the United

States. Some of these artists, such as Jamaican-born Claude McKay (1889–1948), wrote about the fragmentation that existed within the black community as a result of skin color and oppression by whites.

Césaire began to criticize Europe in general and France in particular for its brutal colonization of Africa and Latin America. He condemned Europeans for promoting the belief that the white race was superior to all other races and dismissed the contention that Africa was primitive and without culture. Instead, he glorified the mystical bond between Africans and nature and celebrated Africans' physique, spirituality, family ties, and ancestral worship. Césaire rallied black people all over the world to embrace their African roots.

The *negritude* movement served as the expression of a Pan-African movement that sought to unite black people against the imperial oppression of Europe. It emphasized black reliance on their powers and intellect to create non-European political systems that sought solidarity and help from other black nations, predominantly in Africa. The concept influenced the political approaches of the Black Panther move-

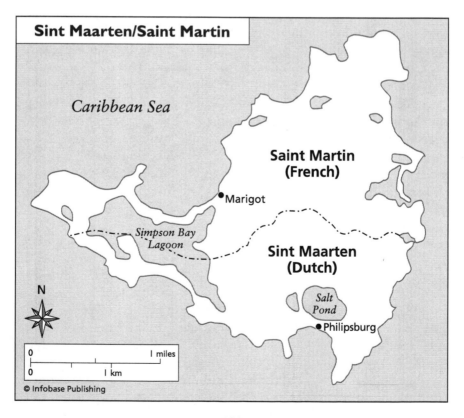

196

ment in the United States. It also affected the initial political activism of Frantz Fanon, who participated in the Algerian (1954–62) struggle against France and who believed that European white political power must be destroyed to achieve liberty for all blacks and people of color. In places like St. Martin, such cultural leaders as Lasana M. Sekou (1959—) embraced *négritude* in the 1980s as an affirmation that the St. Martinicans could determine their own political future without interference from European powers. Sekou rejected the colonial partition of his island whereby one side was French and the other Dutch: "The 'One People' are the people of the island's North and South, incorrectly called 'French side' and 'Dutch side' . . . [which are] colonial codes or designations [claiming] St. Martin for the Republic of France and the Kingdom of the Netherlands, instead of . . . the island's people" (Sekou, ix).

Still other intellectuals veered away from *négritude*. They claimed that the concept mythologized an Africa that never existed and negated the Caribbean's colonial experience. It also negated the region's multicultural universe, where people from France, India, and China and their descendants forged rich and complex cultural identities. There was also the fear that *négritude* could encourage an extreme form of black nationalism such as that practiced by Haitian dictator Francois Duvalier, who repressed people he did not consider black. It was suggested that *négritude* promoted, though not intentionally, a return to the philosophy of race purity espoused by white supremacists.

Martinique and Guadeloupe in France's Fold

While *négritude* celebrated black consciousness, there were also political and economic realities that needed to be addressed. This was the case in Guadeloupe, as it was in Martinique. The mainstays of the colonial economy—coffee and cocoa—were replaced by sugar and bananas, industries that were seriously damaged by hurricanes in 1921 and 1928. The result was a weak economic infrastructure that left Guadeloupe unable to support its population. Since its main trading partner was France, which purchased more than 60 percent of the island's goods, Guadeloupe, like Martinique, moved toward departmentalization. In 1946, Guadeloupe became an overseas department of France.

As part of France, or the French Union as it was called until 1958, the residents of Guadeloupe and Martinique were granted French citizenship, the colonial practice of forced labor was terminated, and the islands' budgets became part of France's national budget. The islanders were allowed to receive social security benefits. Medical services were set up to distribute drinking water and combat disease, and medical care was provided for infants. The two islands took possession of seats in France's National Assembly, the Council of the Republic, and the Assembly of the French Union. Voters on the two islands were granted the right to vote in France's presidential elections.

Local opposition to departmentalization grew in the 1960s and 1970s, though Césaire, who retired from politics in 1993, continued to maintain it was the right path for Martinique and Guadeloupe. However, a younger generation, feeling "part of France and Europe [but] apart because of [their] Caribbeanness," reserved final judgment: "Future decisions . . . will reveal if . . . dual membership was a thoughtful way to decolonize or, on the contrary, a new form of colonization" (Pèrina, 138).

Autonomy for the Dutch Caribbean

In 1937, the Dutch allowed the colonies of Aruba, Bonaire, Curaçao, Saba, Saint Eustatius, and St. Maarten to create a Staaten, a parliament, with a legislative body consisting of members—the numbers varying from island to island—whose election to the post was based on their economic and social class and educational levels, essentially middle-class or affluent candidates. The Staaten afforded the islands a modicum of self-rule. Between 1942 and 1954, steps were taken to allow the islands within the Dutch government to create a federation with a governor appointed by the queen and a legislative body of 22 members from the islands. While each island created its own laws and administrative units, the Dutch government provided defense and administered international relations.

Aruba lobbied to break away from the federation in the 1970s and succeeded in doing so in 1986. Some activists pressed for total independence in the early 1990s, but this option was rejected by the majority of the population. During this same period, Curaçao became the political center of the Dutch islands, serving as the government hub for the federation.

St. Maarten, with a successful tourist industry that brings 1.3 million visitors a year, began to contemplate independence in the late 1980s. By 2000, activists such as Lasana M. Sekou (1959–) were advocating a gradual break, starting with a withdrawal from the federation. The next step was to establish self-rule and eventually independence. This gradual approach was approved in a 1999–2000 referendum when more than 60 percent voted for autonomy and finally to become independent. Since this island is divided in half, with one side French and the other Dutch, opponents of independence have worried about which culture will emerge as dominant. The fractured colonial heritage leads some to wonder whether independence is a viable or desirable choice.

11

JAMAICA, TRINIDAD, AND GRENADA: UNCERTAIN GLORY (1900–2000)

As the era of British colonialism was approaching its end in the mid-20th century, Jamaica and Trinidad tended to attract the spotlight in the anglophone Caribbean. Jamaica was home to a charismatic and ingenious political family, the Manleys. This family—Edna Manley, her husband Norman, and their son Michael—helped shape the island's modern culture and developed the initial political agenda for self-rule in a postcolonial Jamaica. Edna Manley, an accomplished sculptor, edited a magazine, *Focus,* that brought to the English-speaking world the works of a generation of writers who were committed to social and political change on the island; some of the writers, such as novelist John Hearn (1926–95), achieved international recognition.

Trinidad was home to a scholarly personage with a gift for writing, namely Eric Williams. He introduced the English-speaking world to the history of the Caribbean from the perspective of a writer from the region. A graduate of Oxford University, he promoted a Caribbean identity rooted in the African experience while organizing a political movement in Trinidad that would eventually seek independence.

Loyal to England but Children of Jamaica

As the 19th century progressed, the people of Jamaica gradually came to see themselves as Jamaicans rather than British. The first indications of this trend were to be found in the literature of emerging poets who wrote odes celebrating their love for the island:

> I sing of the island I love,
> Jamaica, the land of my birth,

Of summer-lit heavens above,
An island the fairest on earth ...
Oh! Land that art dearest to me,
Though unworthy of thee is my song,
Wherever I wander, for thee
My love is abiding and strong.

The author of this poem, Tom Redcam (1870—1933), who is considered Jamaica's first poet, saw himself as loyal to Britain but also a child of Jamaica. In identifying with the natural beauty of the land, Jamaicans like Redcam and other West Indian writers were seeking their own identity separate from Britain. Beauty was no longer restricted to an English landscape. National pride no longer rested in identifying with Great Britain.

A further affirmation of being Jamaican and black, rather than British and white, appeared early in the 20th century in the figure of Marcus Garvey (1887–1940), who founded the Universal Negro Improvement Association (UNIA) in 1914. In 1916 he traveled to the United States, establishing UNIA's headquarters in Harlem. Three years later he created a shipping line, the Black Star Line. Its purpose was to transport blacks to Africa, which he viewed as the homeland, and to establish commerce between blacks in the United States and nations in Africa and the Caribbean. The experiment failed as a result of Garvey's poor managerial skills and dishonest business partners. Garvey was imprisoned in the United States due to financial mismanagement and was deported to Jamaica in 1927. Eight years later Garvey moved to England, where he died in 1940.

Garvey's advocacy for a homeland for all blacks, known as the "Back to Africa" movement, was internationally known. At one point his organization, UNIA, counted 2 million members in several countries, including Jamaica and the United States. Through his writings, speeches, and public appearances, he helped blacks in the United States and the Caribbean look away from Europe toward their roots in Africa. He took pride in being black, African, and Jamaican, and his pride was contagious.

First Steps toward Independence

In the 1930s, Jamaican workers began to affirm their individual rights and to protest against inequities on the island, where two-thirds of the land was owned by 900 families, mostly white, while 1 million Jamaicans held no property. The few black Jamaicans who owned land, usually about one acre, could barely harvest enough food to feed their families. Conditions in Jamaican cities were difficult: "In the 1930s, low wages, high unemployment, massive migration from the countryside to the major cities . . . created major social tensions" (West-Durán, 118). In 1938, several protests and rebellions occurred throughout the island, surprising British officials who erroneously regarded Jamaicans as complacent and often described the island as a model colony since the Morant Bay rebellion of 1865. The labor disputes that began in May 1938 on the sugar plantations of the West Indies Sugar Company left eight people dead and 171 wounded, with nearly 700 strikers arrested. Two leaders distinguished themselves during the disputes, Norman Manley (1893–1969) and Alexander Bustamante (1884–1977).

To address atrocious working conditions on the island—where salaries were arbitrarily set by companies with little collective bargaining, workers could be fired without cause, and work hours extended without additional pay—Norman Manley, a well-to-do attorney, established in 1938 the Peoples' National Party. The party promoted a socialist agenda that included free secondary education and medical clinics for all Jamaicans. In 1939, Manley's cousin, Alexander Bustamante, united Jamaica's unions, which represented agricultural and industry workers separately, under his own organization, the Bustamante Industrial Trade Union (BITU), beginning with a membership of 2,000 longshoremen and 4,000 agricultural workers (Hurwitz, 198). The island was heading for an economic showdown. Bustamante accused the governor of not informing the mother country of the dire nature of the situation. He advocated rebellion against the local government, although he continued to pledge loyalty to Great Britain. As World War II erupted, the Jamaican governor arrested Bustamante and accused him of planning to overthrow the government.

Norman Manley took over BITU and traveled throughout the island promoting membership. By 1942, BITU counted 20,000 members. The British government, fighting for survival against Germany, agreed to establish collective bargaining, tie salaries to a cost-of-living index, and passed the Colonial Development and Welfare Act to provide financial assistance to the needy. Upon his release from prison, Bustamante took charge of his own political party, the Jamaica Labor Party, which concentrated on labor issues. Both parties—the Peoples' National Party and the Jamaica Labor Party—began to pressure Great Britain for self-rule.

Jamaicans were granted universal suffrage in 1944, and a Jamaican constitution was approved. Bustamante and Manley became political rivals as both struggled to assume the leadership of the island's emerging national government. Bustamante was elected to the position of minister of communication in Jamaica's House of Parliament, defeating his cousin Manley. The position of minister of communication evolved into the chief minister in 1953.

In 1955, Manley won the seat of chief minister. Between 1944 and 1955, Manley changed strategies and veered away from his socialist base by courting the political support of the island's professionals and middle class. Criticized by the business sector for having too many contacts with leftist radicals, Manley dismissed from his party members who were identified as communists. His new moderate posture made him acceptable to conservative voters. Manley, like his political rival, Bustamante, continued to pressure Great Britain for independence.

West Indies Federation

Great Britain favored the creation of a West Indian Federation made up of all the British colonies in the Caribbean rather than independence for each group of islands. Caribbean businessmen discussed the idea of a federation after World War I. They favored it because it provided a measure of economic insurance to all the islands in the event of a drastic drop in world prices for commodities such as sugar or bananas. Union was seen as a sort of protection against the economic dangers of monoculture. By the 1930s, Great Britain concluded that the individual islands "had insufficient area, population, and wealth to create a viable economy. Some union of the various islands would tend to avoid duplication of offices and services and . . . would create a stronger and more unified administration" (Hurwitz, 209). The members of the federation were to be Antigua and Barbuda, Barbados, Dominica, Grenada, Jamaica, Montserrat, Saint Christopher-Nevis-Anguilla, Saint Lucia, Saint Vincent and the Grenadines, and Trinidad and Tobago.

Great Britain promoted the federation as the first step toward independence, and in that spirit the West Indian Federation was established on January 3, 1958. This was a formal reversal of British policy that for years worked to sow dissent among the islands to prevent them from forming a unified front against the empire. In the economic sphere, the British had discouraged direct trade between the islands, forcing it all to come through the mother country. These factors, plus a growing nationalism on each of the islands, doomed the federation to failure.

Neither Jamaica nor Trinidad, the largest islands in the British Caribbean, wanted to be a part of the federation, which left it stillborn from the start. Jamaica was experiencing an economic boom in the mining of bauxite, the growth of private industries, and tourism. In Trinidad, the production and sale of oil and gas reserves employed up to 20,000 workers. Since it seemed that these islands would carry the largest economic burden for the federation, Bustamante and Manley campaigned against the federation. They argued that it would have a detrimental impact on the Jamaican economy (Hurwitz, 213). As a result, Jamaica was the first to withdraw from the federation, followed by Trinidad. In 1962, just four years after its establishment, the federation was disbanded.

Challenges of Independence

In 1962, Jamaica and Trinidad achieved full independence. Bustamante became Jamaica's first independent prime minister and remained in control of the island and the union he founded until 1967. Manley remained in the opposition, contesting Bustamante's decisions. In doing this they helped fortify the two-party political system, which in turn discouraged the development of a dictatorship or oligarchy such as those that arose in Cuba, the Dominican Republic, and Haiti. In 1972, Manley's son, Michael (1924–97), was elected prime minister, a position he assumed again in 1989.

Michael Manley's election revealed that despite the establishment of a democratic system, Jamaican politics since independence was dominated by a few key families. Norman Manley and Bustamante were cousins who dominated the early years after independence. Michael Manley, Norman Manley's son, was a commanding figure in the 1970s and 1980s. He won his first election as prime minister in 1972 after defeating the incumbent, his cousin Hugh Shearer (1923–2004).

Jamaican politics is a stratified family affair where only the wealthy need apply. This disconnect between the upper class and the vast urban and rural poor population contributed to a growing culture of political violence. This violence, coupled with an enormous drug trade, fostered a politics of alienation often reflected in the protest music that is a staple of Jamaican culture.

The disparity is clearly seen in the fact that by the late 1960s, the wealth and power of Jamaica was in the hands of the few, an elitist group that was either white or "near white"—that is, of African and European descent. Because of this, college students in the 1960s began to espouse the ideology of professor and writer Walter Rodney (1942–80), who promoted a movement similar to the platform of the Black Panther Party in the United States. The movement advocated the equal distribution of political, economic, and social power among

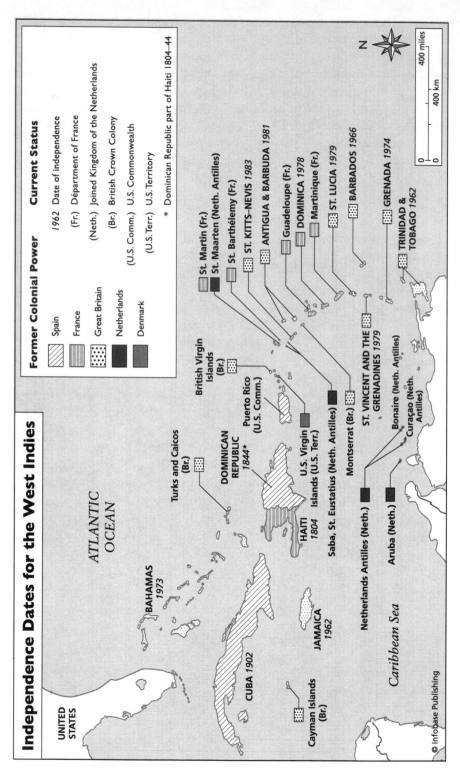

Independence Dates for the West Indies

Former Colonial Power

- Spain
- France
- Great Britain
- Netherlands
- Denmark

Current Status

- 1962   Date of independence
- (Fr.)   Départment of France
- (Neth.)   Joined Kingdom of the Netherlands
- (Br.)   British Crown Colony
- (U.S. Comm.)   U.S. Commonwealth
- (U.S. Terr.)   U.S. Territory

* Dominican Republic part of Haiti 1804–44

N

400 miles
400 km

UNITED STATES

ATLANTIC OCEAN

Caribbean Sea

BAHAMAS *1973*

CUBA *1902*

JAMAICA *1962*

Cayman Islands (Br.)

Turks and Caicos (Br.)

DOMINICAN REPUBLIC *1844**

HAITI *1804*

Puerto Rico (U.S. Comm.)

British Virgin Islands (Br.)

U.S. Virgin Islands (U.S. Terr.)

Saba, St. Eustatius (Neth. Antilles)

Montserrat (Br.)

St. Martin (Fr.)

St. Maarten (Neth. Antilles)

St. Barthélemy (Fr.)

ST. KITTS–NEVIS *1983*

ANTIGUA & BARBUDA *1981*

Guadeloupe (Fr.)

DOMINICA *1978*

Martinique (Fr.)

ST. LUCIA *1979*

BARBADOS *1966*

ST. VINCENT AND THE GRENADINES *1979*

GRENADA *1974*

TRINIDAD & TOBAGO *1962*

Netherlands Antilles (Neth.)

Aruba (Neth.)

Bonaire (Neth. Antilles)

Curaçao (Neth. Antilles)

© Infobase Publishing

204

blacks. Middle-class Jamaicans rejected Rodney's agenda, arguing that Jamaica did not suffer from the extreme racism that characterized the United States in the 19th and 20th centuries. Because of his politically inconvenient views, Rodney, a native of Guyana and a lecturer at the University of the West Indies on the island, was not allowed reentry into Jamaica in 1968, an action that brought about massive protests in Kingston led by students and the urban poor.

Conditions were further aggravated by contradictory developments in the economy. The middle class and those in the service industry benefited from the visits of 300,000 tourists staying at 11,000 hotels before 1970. The rural poor were affected by a decline in the sugar industry from 255,000 tons exported in 1965 to 180,000 tons in 1969. There was a distinct gap between the rich and poor: "In 1970 . . . 5 percent of the population received 27 percent of total income whereas 20 percent of the population received only 5 percent" (Kaplan, 232).

Michael Manley

Michael Manley took action to address the needs of Jamaicans, including those expressed by Rodney's supporters. In 1972, he established housing, health, and education programs for the poor and increased taxes on foreign mining corporations. He also cultivated a friendship with a Rastafarian leader, Claudius Henry, and began to use an ornamental cane that he received from Ethiopian emperor Haile Selassie (1892–1975). The Rastafarians, also called Rastas and Rastafaris, believed Selassie was God incarnate, that Africa was the place where all humanity originated, and that a person could reach his or her original state of being through meditation; they advocated a return to Africa, where they would live forever. The Rastafarians, who first appeared in the early 1930s, believed that the body is the true temple of God. Usually poor, many were squatters in Kingston and were discriminated against by most Jamaicans. In reaching out to the Rastas, Manley presented the image of a leader who was not an elitist.

Manley also applauded the Cuban Revolution. As he grew closer to Fidel Castro, the Jamaican Labour Party, under the leadership of Edward Seaga (1930–), criticized Manley's flirtations with socialism and campaigned against him in the 1980 elections. The Manley-Castro relationship raised the ire of Washington. His support of independence for Puerto Rico and his championing of Nelson Mandela (1918–) in South Africa at a time when the white-dominated nation was allied to the United States also troubled Washington. Manley complained that the United States put an "economic squeeze" on Jamaica in the months leading up to the election and helped Seaga defeat him in the race for prime minister. The campaign between the two men and their respective parties was marked by widespread urban violence that claimed hundreds of Jamaican lives.

Disturbances continued to plague Jamaica in the 1990s as a result of nearly 25 percent unemployment, high crime rates, social inequal-

THE RASTAFARIANS
OF JAMAICA

A s a relatively recent religion, Rastafarianism is often misunderstood by outsiders. One reason is that Rastafarians reject traditional Western religion and follow a set of beliefs that critics suggest is more improvisational than theological. Author Leslie Desmangles explains some of the behavior commonly misinterpreted:

> The Rastafari allude to several sources for keeping their hair untouched and natural. Some cite the biblical passage in which one who takes a holy 'vow of separation [separation from whites] no razor shall come upon his head' but should let 'his locks of hair hang the side of his head.' Still others would claim that locks and their unkempt appearance opposed the establishment. . . . The Rastafari believe that the killing of animals for human consumption does nothing more than promote death. . . . In contrast, a flower may continue to bloom even after it has been severed from its stem; a fruit will continue to ripen even after it has been cut from the tree. . . . The Rastafari follow a vegetarian diet that incorporates dairy products. They believe that a vegetarian diet is sacred. . . . According to the Rastafari, the most common reason for using [marijuana] is related to a biblical passage in which, during the sixth day of creation, God declared that he made the grasses and all vegetation for mankind's enjoyment. . . . The use of [marijuana] is a sacramental act that infuses within the body the sacred power of the spirit as it derives from nature. It also opens the mind . . . and allows for miraculous and unexpected revelations from the Almighty.

Desmangles, Leslie G., et al. "Religion in the Caribbean." In *Understanding the Contemporary Caribbean,* edited by Richard S. Hillman and Thomas J. D'Agostino. Boulder, Colo., and London: Lynne Rienner Publishers, 2003.

ity, and high inflation. A new political party, the National Democratic Movement, challenged the two established parties. Armed groups, representatives of the three parties, fought street battles. In the late 1990s these groups abandoned politics and affiliated themselves with drug traffickers.

Gangs of Jamaica

Criminal mobilization dominated Jamaican politics after 1980. Gangs were the political embodiment of the country's divisive political culture. For the most part, politics were debated peacefully among the upper class, but they were fought out on the streets between rival gangs with links to the major political parties. Through criminal activity Jamaican gangs ruled supreme in certain neighborhoods in Kingston. Their supremacy allowed them to distribute political favors and patronage, and it was common for politicians to turn to gangs for support. Such recognition augmented the gangs' reputations, making them the sole enforcers in many neighborhoods away from rich areas in Kingston. A cycle was created: The more criminal power a gang had, the more political influence it could yield in its territory; the more political recognition the gang received, the more its criminal influence increased.

Initially, poverty was the reason for the creation of the gangs. In 1991, average weekly salaries in Jamaica were about $30, and tourism was in decline. Economic desperation coupled with the lure of quick money and the island's central location between Colombia and New York made it an ideal transshipment location for cocaine bound for the United States. In 1998 nearly 40 percent of "mules"—people who hide cocaine within their bodies—arrested at U.S. airports were traveling from Jamaica. In 1999 about 4,000 Jamaicans on the island were arrested for drug trafficking.

The fact that so many of the gangs were admired by Jamaica's poor revealed a political failure. The government, attempting to rescue the crumbling economy in the late 1990s, stopped providing social services. The gangs stepped in to fill the void: "The local gang maintains its own system of law and order, complete with a holding cell fashioned from an old chicken coop and a street-corner court. It 'taxes' local businesses in return for protecting them, punishing those who refuse to pay with attacks on property and people. It provides a rudimentary welfare safety net by helping locals with school fees, lunch money, and employment—a function that the Jamaican government used to perform" (Rapley, 95).

In the late 1990s the government dispatched the military into crime-ridden neighborhoods. However, the Jamaican government was unprepared for a long-term, sustained effort, and the attempt to break the grip of gang power was abandoned. The emphasis switched to providing protection in affluent areas and zones frequented by tourists.

The rise of the gangs of Jamaica betrayed the frailty of the island's democratic process. At the same time, the government's unwillingness to assume dictatorial powers revealed a democratic commitment. This commitment to democracy, however, is tainted by corrupt politicians in league with gang leaders who accept the gangs because they help political parties win votes. This tacit acceptance was highlighted by the appearance in 1992 of then prime minister Edward Seaga at the funeral of a popular gang leader.

Scholar Alan West-Durán may best characterize the imperfect nature of Jamaican democracy in the following statement: "Jamaica celebrated its fortieth anniversary as an independent country in 2002, beset by many of the same ills of many poor countries. Despite . . . violence, patronage, and elements of coercion, the political system feature[d] flexibility and democratic negotiations; despite social upheaval, it has stayed clear of coups, military dictatorship, or bloody revolutions" (West-Durán, 124).

Trinidad

Through the 1930s, Trinidadians formed labor unions and political parties of which two became the best known, the British Empire Citizens' and Workers' Home Rule Party, founded by Tubal Uriah "Buzz"—T.U.B.—Butler (1897–1977), a preacher and labor unionist, and the Political Progress Group founded by Albert Gomes, a well-to-do writer. Prior to World War II in 1939, T.U.B. Butler organized a series of labor strikes to demand better working conditions and the end of racist practices within the labor administration, where workers who were white or light skinned were awarded administrative posts. Gomes was one of the first to realize the potential for African Trinidadians and East Indian Trinidadians to unite in a political struggle and sought their support, maintaining that above ethnic origin was the responsibility to serve Trinidad.

Without a clear political ideology, Albert Gomes identified with the poor of Trinidad and those on the margins of society. One of his earliest contributions was the promotion of the music of steel bands and calypso, both considered by the British as lewd and inferior, as a genuine art form. Serving as deputy mayor of Port of Spain, Trinidad's capital, and also in the legislative council during the 1940s, Gomes advocated for higher wages for workers. He also believed in the need of a federation for the islands and in 1958 was elected to the federation's parliament. Because he was wealthy—he owned a pharmacy, given to him by his father—and white, some Trinidadians suspected that Gomes was more aligned with the upper classes of the islands than the poor. By the late 1950s, Gomes's friend Eric Williams had eclipsed him.

The Rise of Eric Williams

From 1956 to 1971, Eric Williams (1911–81) dominated politics in Trinidad-Tobago through political maneuvering, intelligence, scholarship, and the ability to navigate turbulent relationships with the United States and Great Britain. At the same time he was widely loved by Trinidadians, who admired a politician who was a scholar and who in his writings placed the neglected deeds of black people of the Caribbean on a par with the deeds of white historical figures. In his rise to political power, Williams did not seek the support of labor unions, as leaders in other Caribbean nations had done. Instead, in 1956 Williams formed his own political party, the People's National Movement (PNM). Composed of middle-class professional men, the party opposed British colonialism and promoted agriculture and industrialization.

In 1956 Williams was elected chief minister of Trinidad-Tobago. He was soon engaged in a dispute with the United States over a naval base the British allowed the North Americans to set up at the beginning of World War II (1939–45). A pragmatic politician, Williams knew that since Trinidad was still a colony, he could not force the termination of the agreement between the British and the United States. However, he conducted an aggressive anti-American campaign, once leading more than 60,000 protesters to the American consulate. The result was that the United States agreed to pay the island $30 million, spread over five years. Although Williams was criticized for accepting the money, he used the funds to construct academic facilities at the University of the West Indies in St. Augustine, to build roads, to improve the railway system, and to improve the port facilities in Port of Spain (Palmer, 131–132). Williams's demands for the removal of the base pressured the United States to abandon it in 1967.

In 1962 Williams negotiated preparations for independence. He attracted international attention when he stated that colonial powers needed to repay former colonies for using and abusing their natural resources. He collaborated with the opposition party, the Democratic Labour Party (DLP), which represented the interests of the East Indian community, to find ways to incorporate them into the political process. One of the steps they took was to designate a commission to establish voting districts in East Indian neighborhoods and rural areas previously excluded from the political process. They worked to ensure greater voter registration and promote practices that encouraged greater participation by the opposition parties in the new government, especially East Indians, who felt excluded by Williams.

Throughout the rest of the 1960s, Williams endorsed capitalism, inviting foreign investment on the island. However, the unemployment of 45,000 Trinidadians and an increasing number of labor strikes—from nine in 1969 to more than 60 in 1970—revealed dissatisfaction with his leadership, especially among youths.

Claiming that the black elite, including Williams, were out of touch with the masses, the Black Power movement led massive protests in 1970. These protests came to be known as the Black Power Revolution. One rally, on March 4, 1970, attracted more than 10,000 protesters. On April 6, a police officer shot a young protester; the subsequent funeral was attended by 65,000 mourners. A state of emergency was declared, and Trinidadian authorities arrested more than 70 activists. Williams attempted to pass legislation to curb protests, but neither the people nor the politicians supported the initiative.

In the 1970s, straddling leftist ideals and capitalism, Williams controlled price increases in the local market, provided food subsidies to poorer sectors, increased old age pensions, and implemented a massive school construction program. These reforms were financed by an increase in oil revenues as world prices rose. Oil income rose from $33 million in 1972 to $1.58 billion in 1980 (McDonald, 195, 196).

As the island prospered economically, the East Indian community and multiethnic groups, including Chinese Trinidadians, expressed discontent with Williams and the PNM. They viewed the PNM as representing Afro-Trinidadian interests. Williams was aware of a falling-off in his personal popularity and in his political party, but declining health prevented him from fully addressing the challenge. After his death in 1981, the National Alliance for Reconstruction (NAR) defeated the People's National Movement. Arthur Napoleon Raymond—A. N. R.—Robinson (1926–   ), a former member of the PNM, was elected prime minister.

A Changing Society

In the 1980s, unemployment rates hovered between 17 and 20 percent, and 20 to 40 percent of the population lived in poverty. In 1990 an organization of black Muslims known as Jamaat Al Muslimeen stormed Parliament and the state television station, kidnapping Prime Minister A. N. R. Robinson. The confrontation between the kidnappers and the police ended in 30 deaths and more than 500 wounded. The hostages were released, and in an effort to maintain peace, the Muslim militants were granted amnesty. In 1995 Basdeo Panday (1933—   ) was elected prime minister; his cabinet consisted mostly of East Indians, reflecting the growth of Indo-Trinidadian political power.

This change was reflected in Trinidad's society: "Up to the 1960s, the Trinidadian economy centered around jobs that were divided up along racial lines: most Indo-Trinidadians lived in the countryside and labored on sugar estates or were farmers; most African-Trinidadians were in civil service, law, teaching, nursing, the police, and the army. . . . This changed . . . when protests and social changes brought much greater economic and social mobility to the Indo-Trinidadian community" (West-Durán, 196).

Perhaps the best-known member of the Indo-Trinidadian community is V. S. Naipaul (1932–   ), whose travel essays and novels on colonialism are acknowledged as some of the finest writings of the late 20th and early 21st centuries. Naipaul was awarded the Nobel Prize in literature in 2001. Naipaul, who now resides in England, is sometimes criticized for writing unsympathetically about colonial peoples.

St. Vincent and the Grenadines

In 1979, St. Vincent and the Grenadines gained independence from Great Britain after having been part of the West Indies Federation from 1958 to 1962. During the 1980s, there was labor unrest due to the displacement of hundreds of residents caused by the eruption of Mount Soufrière in 1979 and damages caused to the banana industry by a hurricane in 1982. By the end of the 20th century, though, tourism and the banana industry (the latter accounted for nearly $18 million in export receipts) were responsible for the employment of 67,000 workers in a population of 117,000. The queen of England is the symbolic monarch of St. Vincent and the Grenadines, but the actual power is in the hands of a democratically elected governor and parliament.

Grenada: Maurice Bishop and the People's Revolutionary Government

Admiration for the revolutionary tactics used in Cuba during the 1950s inspired the only successful armed revolution to take place in the anglophone Caribbean. In 1979 an attorney named Maurice Bishop (1944–83) led a coup d'état in Grenada against the rule of Prime Minister Eric Gairy (1920–97), a once-beloved political figure who had grown corrupt and despotic. Gairy amassed riches through ownership of restaurants, casinos, and nightclubs. In the 1970s, while the average Grenadian earned $50 a month, Gairy, as prime minister, was receiving a monthly tax-free check of $2,000 (Cotman, 10). Unemployment was at 50 percent, and education and health care were neglected, with only 36 percent of the health workers having any professional training. The General Hospital of Grenada lacked equipment and supplies, and dental clinics and rural health centers were virtually shut down. Like Haiti's Duvalier, who claimed he was a Vodun priest and who was given to conversing with spirits in the presence of foreign dignitaries, Gairy developed a predilection for the supernatural. He requested that the United Nations create a committee to study the presence of flying saucers in the Americas.

It was a bizarre evolution for a man who in the 1950s forged the rural poor and farm workers into a powerful labor union and created a political party, the Grenada United Labor Party (GULP), that took control of Grenada's ruling body in 1951 when Great Britain allowed the island virtual self-government. Gairy helped guide Grenada's transition to political independence in 1974. But Gairy, a man accustomed to employing strong-arm tactics to achieve his political and personal objectives, did not allow for criticism of his administration. He often denied employment in the civil service to opponents and resorted to violence through the use of a personal gang of thugs called the Mongoose Gang. In 1979, it was believed that Gairy authorized the use of violence against Maurice Bishop (1944–83), a rising political star, even authorizing assassination. It was this rumor that prompted Bishop to overthrow Gairy's regime.

Bishop's political movement was called the New Jewel Movement (NJM). In his first address to the Grenadian people in 1979, hours after the coup, Bishop announced the simplicity of his agenda: ". . . the revolution is for work, for food, for decent housing and health services, and for a bright future for our children and great-grand children" (Bishop, 78). NJM was formed in the 1970s with the primary objective of opposing Gairy. Under the guidance of Bishop and a young intellectual named Bernard Coard (1944–   ), the movement embraced Marxist-Leninist ideology.

Within its first two years in power, the new government, which called itself the People's Revolutionary Government (PRG), could point to a list of impressive accomplishments. They included making all schools free to all citizens, training teachers, providing free health care, and the free distribution of milk, butter, and rice to all pregnant women. The PRG experimented with creating processing plants to manufacture jam and jelly made from local products and created the National Institute of Handicraft to encourage the arts and recruit artists and intellectuals into the revolutionary process. The PRG built 32 houses in 1981 and 289 in 1982, providing grants or loans of $1.3 million to low-income earners (Steele, 388).

The revolution attracted the attention of Fidel Castro and other leaders. Castro dispatched doctors, teachers, and construction workers to the island. Venezuela donated petroleum products.

Military Buildup, Political Repression, and the Invasion of Grenada

There was a military buildup as well, an activity that was often denied in the early 1980s by supporters of Bishop and the PRG. By the end of 1980, Grenada had received thousands of Soviet rifles, hundreds of machine guns and pistols, and heavy artillery. These arms were accompanied by Cuba's promise to train the new Grenadian army, which was planned to increase from 600 to 10,000 soldiers. The potential military might and Bishop's growing friendship with Castro and the communist regime in Nicaragua concerned U.S. president Ronald Reagan (1911–2004). Reagan grew more alarmed as the Grenadians began work on a new international airport, constructed by volunteers from Cuba.

The PRG, eager to establish a communist state, refused to hold free elections and passed a series of laws designed to curb counterrevolutionary activities. These laws included the People's Laws Nos. 17 and 23, which permitted the government to arrest and hold without trial anyone suspected of planning subversive activities. The PRG implemented the reeducation of Rastafarians, who once supported Bishop. They were now forced to shave their heads and participate in government activities, which the government promoted as "voluntary." The PRG also censored the press, accusing publishers of representing capitalist interests.

A split occurred within the PRG, with Bernard Coard favoring a fast transformation into a communist government and Bishop preferring a slower process of reeducation and indoctrination to allow time for his compatriots to embrace revolutionary ideals and changes. The political differences between the two men could not be mended, with Coard expressing concern that Grenadians were supporting the revolution not because of dedication to revolutionary ideals but because of loyalty to Bishop.

On October 19, 1983, Coard's supporters arrested and executed Bishop, who was accused of betraying the revolution and fostering a personality cult, as well as a dozen of his personal followers and over 200 Grenadians who came to the government's headquarters to help Bishop upon learning of his detainment. It is reported that before dying Bishop said to his executioners, "I want to look my executioners in their

WAS CUBAN AID TO GRENADA CIVILIAN OR MILITARY IN NATURE?

Questions emerged after the war regarding Cuba's involvement in Grenada, with the United States affirming it was of a military nature, while the Cuban government maintained that it was technical assistance with minimum input from the military. Author Robert Millette supports the first view:

> Cuba provided nine Cuban military 'specialists' to be stationed permanently in the General Staff of the [revolutionary government] and twenty to be stationed permanently in the field with Grenadian units. In addition, more Cuban military personnel were to be assigned temporarily, six to General Staff and six or seven elsewhere in Grenada. Their mission was to assist Grenadian military men on the questions of ... combative and training of the troops ... and in the elaboration of the operative and mobilization plans for the defense of the country.... Cuban construction workers, other paramilitary personnel and regular militia forces ... outnumbered the total active strength of the Grenadians .... Fidel Castro stated ... 'of course, as workers, like all workers in Cuba, they have received military training.'

Millette, Robert E. The Grenada Revolution: Why It Failed. New York: Africana Research Publications, 1985, pp. 63, 65–66.

eyes" (Steele, 409). Immediately after his execution, Eugenia Charles, the prime minister of neighboring Dominica, asked the United States, on behalf of the Organization of Eastern Caribbean States (OECS), to intervene. On October 25, President Reagan authorized Operation Urgency. He cited the need to protect 500 U.S. medical students in Grenada and the request from the OCS to end anarchic conditions and restore order on the island.

Eugenia Charles, the Iron Lady of the Caribbean

Prime Minister Eugenia Charles (1919–2005) of Dominica was critical of Maurice Bishop for his failure to hold elections, the repressive policies he supported, and his admiration for the Cuban Revolution and communism. But when Coard executed Bishop and 200 of his supporters and then instituted a curfew that prevented family members from retrieving the remains of the dead, Charles discussed military options with the members of the Organization of the Eastern Caribbean. Since the OECS did not have the military might to intervene in Grenada, they suggested that she express their concerns to President Reagan.

Charles was elected prime minister in 1980, the first woman in the Caribbean to hold such office. Her agenda promoted capitalism and business as the best way to bring economic development to Dominica. She rejected the approach of authoritarian rule and central administration practiced in other Caribbean nations, such as Cuba. In 1982, she was a member of the Caribbean Basin Initiative, organized by Prime Minister Edward Seaga (1930–   ) of Jamaica and Prime Minister Tom Adams (1931–   ) of Barbados. She proposed that the United States allow Caribbean products into the country duty-free, and in return the Caribbean nations would give 10 percent tax credits to North American companies establishing businesses on the islands. The initiative requested $350 million for the eastern Caribbean before the collapse of the Grenada revolution, a request that was not granted.

The failure of the revolution allowed Charles to participate in the international arena, bringing attention to Dominica. She was criticized for her support of the American invasion of Grenada, which she described as a rescue mission rather than an invasion. Critics commented that Charles allowed Reagan to use her for his military designs on Grenada, but the friendship that evolved between Charles and Reagan resulted in a grant of $100 million to the island.

The struggle over Grenada and the roles played by Charles and Bishop illustrated the competing ideologies swirling through the

Caribbean in the period. Politicians like Charles embraced capitalism and favored economic cooperation with the United States, while revolutionaries like Bishop sought to break free of U.S. economic domination and saw communism as a vehicle to achieve that goal. Given the choice between the promise of personal economic gain and revolutionary self-sacrifice, the people of Grenada opted for the first. At least so it appeared when nearly all of the island's population, more than 100,000, lined the streets of Grenada to welcome the U.S. Marines.

The death of Eugenia Charles in 2005, Norman Manley in 1969, Michael Manley in 1997, and Eric Williams in 1981 marked the end of an era of strong personalities in the anglophone Caribbean who shaped the political movement for self-rule and administered the new nations after independence from Britain. As leaders, they exhibited authoritarian traits and were sometimes described by their opponents as dictators, but they refrained from creating dictatorships and were voted into and out of power by the people on numerous occasions. The political careers of these personages demonstrated that in the former British West Indies, the people preferred an imperfect political process rather than the long-term presence of military regimes or leaders who donned military garb to govern in the manner of a Duvalier in Haiti or Trujillo in the Dominican Republic.

12

THE 21ST CENTURY: IMMIGRATION AND UNCERTAINTIES

The journey out of the Hispanic Caribbean in the early 19th century was toward the mother country, *la madre patria*: Spain. It was a logical destination, since the islands were a cultural extension of the Iberian Peninsula, and life in Spain for *Caribeños* was made easier by a common language, a common heritage, and a common religion. It was standard practice for well-to-do parents to send their children to study in Spain. In fact, the book that inaugurated Puerto Rican literature, *Aguinaldo puertorriqueño* (1843), was written in Barcelona by Puerto Rican students homesick for the island. The one exception to this rule was the Dominican Republic, which for much of the 19th century battled Haitian invaders and was immersed in a series of civil wars that resulted in political chaos.

Later in the 19th century, when Cubans and Puerto Ricans began to contemplate a political break with Spain, *Caribeños* sought other destinations for educational advancement. Universities throughout South America, especially after the wars of independence of the 1810s and 1820s, became logical destinations. But the United States, particularly New York, became the destination of choice for the youths of Puerto Rico and Cuba. In the 1830s, the Cuban Félix Varela lived in Philadelphia before relocating to New York. A priest, Varela became known as the "Vicar of the Irish" during the cholera epidemic of the late 1830s, when 3,000 New Yorkers were afflicted and Varela nursed the sick and established makeshift hospitals in the poor Irish ghetto known as Five Points. In the meantime, a group of Cuban writers and intellectuals, like their Puerto Rican counterparts in Spain, produced an anthology of poetry that bemoaned their absence from Cuba, *El laud del desterrado* (1858).

Monument in St. Augustine to Father Félix Varela, who lived in Philadelphia, New York City, and St. Augustine and was admired for his work with the poor of those cities (Photo by Yvonne Massip)

The 1960s brought major changes to the makeup of the Hispanic Caribbean community in the United States. The first change occurred in 1959, with the triumph of the Cuban Revolution. The next change came as a result of the death of Dominican dictator Rafael Leónidas Trujillo in 1961.

Cubans in the United States

The first large Cuban migration to the United States occurred as a result of the Ten Years' War (1868–78), when more than 5,000 refugees fled to Florida and New York. One of the most ambitious immigrants was Vicente Martínez Ybor (1818–96), who established a tobacco factory in Key West just 90 miles from the Cuban coast (Appel, 43). In the late 1880s, Martínez Ybor relocated to Tampa, where he built a factory town in a swampy area that eventually came to bear his name—Ybor City. This Cuban exile community became a major funding source for Cuban independence fighters and was visited by José Martí as he sought money for the movement.

Martí traveled to Tampa from New York, where he lived and wrote for several newspapers, including the *New York Sun*. In Manhattan, Martí, the founder of the Partido Revolucionario Cubano (Cuban Revolutionary Party), associated with Puerto Rican patriots in exile, such as the brilliant writer and philosopher Eugenio María Hostos (1839–1903) and the poet Pachín Marín (1863–97). At this time, more than 2,000 Puerto Ricans and Cubans lived in New York. The hub of the community was the area around 14th Street, which was a vibrant neighborhood for people from Latin America and the Caribbean. One of the centers of the community was the Hotel Latino, where Spanish-speaking travelers frequently stayed and where those in search of Latin food frequently dined. These Cubans and Puerto Ricans viewed themselves as exiles with plans to return home, which, in fact, many did after the end of the Spanish-Cuban-American War and Spain's retreat from the Caribbean in 1898.

Many of the Tampa Cubans, however, did not return to Cuba because of the success of their ethnic enclave. Many Cubans became successful in the cigar-making industry and, with contributions from equally vibrant Italian and Spanish immigrant communities, turned Ybor City into a thriving community. Their offspring, who became known as *Tampeños,* nurtured a city that was culturally vibrant and dynamic. The immigrant communities of Tampa established separate cultural centers that served as home for traveling professional theater companies from Latin America and Spain; they also created mutual help societies that provided medical insurance, extended loans for home purchase and repairs, and even sponsored racially integrated sports teams. The dynamic environment spurred many to write of the community, and there are dozens of stories and novels, both fiction and memoirs, about life in Ybor City. Those writing about their experiences in Ybor City or using it as a setting in their work include Jose Yglesias, Ferdie Pacheco, Frank Urso, and William Durbin.

Cuban Immigration in the 1960s

In the 1950s, there was a small population of Cubans in the United States, about 10,000 in New York and a few hundred in New Jersey, as well as several thousand in Miami and Tampa. The new Cuban emigrants sought asylum from Batista's dictatorship but were also looking for economic opportunities. They worked in hotels and restaurants, in factories, and in the embroidery industry. In Miami, the exile community was virulent in its anti-Batista sentiments, and many were preparing for armed conflict in Cuba. Most of the Cubans in Dade County were associated with political organizations planning to oust Batista from power.

However, the exodus that characterizes the Cuban experience in the United States began quietly during the early hours of January 1, 1959. As Fidel Castro's army approached Havana, hundreds of Batista's allies ferried their money and luggage across the Florida Straits to Miami. Within a week, Pan American flights were transporting Cuban exiles to the United States. What began as a trickle grew into a diaspora, with 1.5 million Cubans in the Unites States by the late 1980s and another half million in countries such as Mexico, Spain, and Venezuela. The most dramatic episodes in the steady emigration from Cuba occurred during the Peter Pan Operation in the 1960s, the Mariel Boatlift of 1980, and the *balseros* (rafters) crisis of 1994.

Operación Pedro Pan

Operación Pedro Pan was the largest political exodus of unaccompanied children in the Americas. During this secret operation parents who feared communist indoctrination of their children sent their children out of the country. More than 14,000 children left Cuba without their parents. The movement, which lasted from 1960 to 1962, was spurred by a rumor that the Cuban government was planning to usurp parental authority and remove children from their families. The operation involved the Catholic Church in the United States as well as several Protestant and Jewish organizations. Parents targeted for arrest by the Cuban government or for anti-Castro activities sent their children off the island with the pretext that they were going abroad to study or for health reasons. In the United States, the children were placed in foster homes until they could be reunited with their parents. Reunification eventually occurred for most families, but the separation varied from several weeks to several years.

The Mariel Boatlift

The Mariel Boatlift took place from April 21 to September 26, 1980. During that time more than 125,000 Cuban refugees left the island. The exodus was the result of an incident in which several Cubans took refuge from the government at the Peruvian embassy. The embassy's refusal to surrender the would-be exiles to Cuba's secret service set the stage for confrontation. An angry Fidel Castro announced that anyone who wanted to seek asylum in the embassy was free to do so; in less than 24 hours, 10,800 Cubans flooded the diplomatic compound.

The negative publicity that Castro received as the world saw photos of angry Cubans yelling "Down with Castro" from the embassy prompted the dictator to invite Cubans in Miami to pick up their relatives. Hundreds of fishing boats and other small craft sailed from Key West to the port of Mariel, Cuba, in what became known as the Freedom Flotilla. The boats were overloaded, with many of the Cubans suffering from seasickness during the crossing. Upon reaching Key West, the new arrivals were placed in temporary camps—the Orange

Bowl in Miami served as a camp to wait for a relative to claim them with promises of financial support and housing.

To discredit the exiles, and the Cuban community in the United States, the Cuban government forced the relatives to take nearly 10,000 hard-core criminals and the mentally infirm. The resulting media coverage presented the latest wave of Cuban refugees as gangsters and drug addicts, as depicted in the 1983 cult film *Scarface*. The established Cuban exile community did not welcome the new emigrants with open arms because they were poorer and darker-skinned than earlier emigrant waves. They were also not as virulently anti-Castro, falling into the category of economic rather than political emigrants. Most demographic studies indicate that this emigrant group is as economically successful as their predecessors in the Cuban community, despite being subjected to racial and ethnic stereotyping on a grand scale.

Over the next two decades the Marielitos, as they were called, integrated into the Cuban community and the United States. The negative coverage of the exodus forced Cuban exiles to organize politically within the United States and to form a lobby in Washington, D.C. The most famous organization to emerge was the Cuban National Foundation, which campaigned successfully for the creation of an anti-Castro radio station, Radio Martí, within the Voice of America radio network. Radio Martí broadcasts uncensored news to Cuba, advocating for a diversity of opinion on the island and the eventual end of Castro's regime.

The *Balseros*

In 1994, during the months of August and September, 36,000 Cubans left the island on *balsas,* homemade rafts. The United States and Cuba agreed to control this dangerous exodus, and the Cuban government allowed for the annual migration of 20,000 Cubans a year for the next 10 years. The emigrants were selected through a lottery system after submitting letters of interest to the American Interests Section in Havana.

The crisis forced President Bill Clinton's administration to review immigration policy toward Cubans. The preferential treatment given to Cubans was a topic of frequent criticism by other groups, such as Haitians, who argued that they were discriminated against as a result of race. The U.S. policy of granting Cubans political asylum dates to the cold war and efforts to destabilize the revolutionary government. President Clinton (1946–) altered the policy by ordering that Cubans caught at sea were to be returned to the island, while those who made it to American shores would be granted political asylum in the United States.

MARIELITOS, UNWANTED CUBANS

The Marielitos were stereotyped as unwilling to work and too eager to depend financially on friends and relatives while also being critical of the way of life in the United States, especially the fast-paced lifestyle and materialism of Americans and Cuban-Americans. The first generation of Cuban-Americans felt that the Marielitos were not kindred spirits, which in fact was the case, since the latter reached maturity under a totalitarian regime that provided them with employment and few personal choices.

> ... the Marielitos found it difficult to shake the misfit label, and many faced discrimination. A Cuban-born social worker, the head of a City of Miami agency, was quoted three years after their arrival as saying that one-third of the Marielitos were 'trash.' A highly placed Dade County school official, also Cuban American, complained that the Mariel children '[came with] no concept of private property, nor that of authority as something to be respected out of admiration rather than fear.' [They were] ... caught between two powerful political forces—Castro's government and the exile community.

Levine, Robert M., and Moisés Asís. *Cuban Miami.* New Brunswick, N.J.: Rutgers University Press, 2000, pp. 51–52.

The Cuban-American community has made steady inroads into the political system of the United States. As of 2007 there were two Cuban-American U.S. senators, Mel Martínez of Florida and Robert Menendez of New Jersey. There were four Cuban-American members in the House of Representatives, all from Florida or New Jersey.

Puerto Ricans in the United States

The growth of the Spanish-speaking population on the East Coast during the first four decades of the 20th century was dominated by Puerto Ricans, partly the result of the 1917 Jones Act, which made Puerto Ricans citizens of the United States with the ability to travel back and forth between the island and the mainland without immigration restrictions. Transportation was easier because the Porto Rico Steamship

Company sailed four times a week from New York to San Juan and back for $50 for first-class passengers or $25 for second class. One market factor drawing Puerto Ricans to the United States was the need for farm laborers in small towns such as Vineland, New Jersey, where contractors arranged for groups of workers during planting season and harvest time. The advent of World War II (1939–45) increased the need not only for agricultural help but for industrial and service industry workers, too. As a result, Puerto Ricans made their way to cities like Camden and Newark, New Jersey, and Philadelphia. The big attraction, however, was New York, where by the end of the 1940s there were about 350,000 Puerto Ricans.

In the 1950s, the experience for many Puerto Ricans in New York was one of survival on the margins of society, living in poor neighborhoods and neglected tenements. It was a life marked by a daily struggle against discriminatory practices. They faced limited economic opportunities and an educational system that showed no interest in working with new emigrants, with only 1,000 teachers fluent in Spanish. In sheer frustration many Puerto Rican youths joined gangs. Gang warfare became a staple of New York urban life, and the Puerto Rican gangs struggled against other ethnic groups and sometimes against each other. This gang warfare came to national attention through its depiction in *West Side Story,* first as a Broadway play and then later as a motion picture.

The neighborhoods with the largest Puerto Rican populations were Harlem, the Upper West Side of New York, and East Harlem, known as Spanish Harlem. To curb gang violence there community leaders developed mutual-help organizations to redirect Puerto Rican youths away from gang life and to offer avenues for vocational training and educational opportunities. The work of these leaders placed them in contact with city politicians. In the early 1950s the mayor of New York formed a commission to study and monitor Puerto Rican affairs in Manhattan. By the mid-1950s Puerto Ricans were becoming a major cultural and ethnic presence in New York, with the likes of musician Tito Puente (1923–2000) gaining recognition for his virtuoso playing of *timbales,* drums, and the establishment of the Puerto Rican Day parade in 1958. *Nuyorican* literature evolved as another cultural expression of Puerto Rican identity. The word *Nuyorican* is a mixture of New York and Puerto Rican, which encapsulates the search for a new ethnic identity. This school of poetry and prose frequently uses both English and Spanish in writing and storytelling. Throughout the 1960s and 1970s *Nuyorican* poets and writers performed their works before live audiences at various

New York cafes. The influence of *Nuyorican* writers is still evident in the work of writers such as Esmeralda Santiago, who are in search of their ethnic identities.

Nuyoricans

A revolution of sorts occurred within the New York Puerto Rican community with the emergence in 1969 of a group known as the Young Lords. The Young Lords was initially composed of gang members. Inspired by the Black Panther movement and revolutionary figures like Che Guevara, they developed strategies to improve the lives of poor Puerto Ricans and other residents of *el barrio,* the Puerto Rican neighborhood. The Young Lords established breakfast centers for children so they would not go to school on an empty stomach, cleaned up streets and tenements, and once commandeered a medical mobile unit to give free testing for diabetes and other illnesses. They advocated independence for Puerto Rico and opposed the Vietnam War in the late 1960s. Perhaps the most significant and long-lasting contribution of the Young Lords was the ideology of self-empowerment that they promoted among Puerto Ricans. Poverty was not due simply to individual behavior but was the result of a discriminatory system and institutional racism that must be fought through community action and organization. The credo of the Young Lords helped instill pride in the Puerto Rican community.

A *Nuyorican* persona began to emerge as Puerto Ricans began to express more concern for political activism in New York than for political developments in Puerto Rico. The shift marked their evolution into Americans of Puerto Rican descent, still fiercely proud of their heritage but now more concerned with political and cultural developments on the mainland United States. This new generation did not travel to Puerto Rico as frequently as their parents. They lost some of their fluency in Spanish, often resorting to Spanglish, which is a combination of English and Spanish, and code switching as they spoke in one language, usually English, importing Spanish words and phrases.

Central political figures such as Herman Badillo (1929–) began to socialize with Democratic powerbrokers, advocating for economic and educational reforms for Puerto Ricans in New York and in the United States as a whole rather than on the island. In 1970 Badillo was elected to the U.S. Congress representing the South Bronx. At present, there are three Puerto Ricans serving in the House of Representatives—José Serrano and Nidia Velásquez, both of New York, and Luis Gutiérrez of Chicago.

JESÚS COLÓN (1901–1974), CHRONICLER OF NUYORICANS

By the 1940s, a vibrant Puerto Rican community was aware of the work of Puerto Rican activists and writers, men and women who were leading the way for a group of political figures that emerged a generation later. One of the most read and best loved was Jesús Colón. Today he is considered one of the founders of Nuyorican literature, a body of work written by Puerto Ricans who live predominantly in New York City and who address social issues in their writings.

Jesús Colón was a social commentator who chronicled the experience of Puerto Ricans in New York City from the 1930s to the early 1960s. (Centro de Estudios Puertorriqueños)

A noted Puerto Rican journalist and political activist, Jesús Colón ... started writing in Spanish for Hispanic periodicals in New York in the second decade of the twentieth century.... As he strived to develop his literary and journalistic career, he encountered racial prejudice, mainly because of his dark skin color.... After writing for many years in Spanish, in the late forties Colón became an English-language columnist for the Daily Worker, *the publication of the national office of the Communist Party.... His major themes [were] ... (1) the creation and development of a political consciousness, (2) the development of Puerto Rican nationalism, (3) advocacy for the working-class poor, and (4) the injustices of capitalist society in which racial and class discrimination are all too frequent and individual worth does not seem to exist.*

Kanellos, Nicolás. *Hispanic Literature of the United States: A Comprehensive Reference.* Westport, Conn.: Greenwood Press, 2003, pp. 88–89.

Dominican Immigration

Prior to 1961, immigration from the Dominican Republic was minuscule. In the early 1900s, there were small numbers of Dominicanos in Manhattan, essentially well-to-do students. Two of them became famous literary critics: the brothers Max (1885–1968) and Pedro Henríquez Ureña (1884–1946). Halfway through the century, there were pockets of Dominicans in New York, again seeking economic and educational opportunities. During this time, dictator Trujillo did not allow his compatriots to travel outside the nation, afraid of the bad publicity they would give the Dominican Republic.

A year after his assassination in 1961, about 1,000 Dominicans left the country; they were followed by 4,000 a year later. Fearing political instability in the Dominican Republic, the United States dispatched Ambassador John Bartlow Martin (1915–87) to look for ways of reducing tension on the island after the election of President Juan Bosch in 1963. Believing that increasing the exodus of Dominicans to the United States would result in more jobs on the island and therefore less political and economic friction, Martin recommended easing the process of granting visas to Dominicans. A year later, 10,000 Dominicans were granted visas. Despite stereotypical images that represented the Dominican émigrés as poor and uneducated, most emigrants were from the middle class and were college educated or experienced in a craft or trade. By 1970, almost 150,000 Dominicans were settled in the United States, with more than 65 percent choosing New York as their home; by 2000, that figure had increased to more than 700,000 Dominicans.

Dominicans in New York

In New York, the largest concentration of Dominicans settled in the Washington Heights area near the George Washington Bridge. By the late 1990s, there were about 200 bodegas (grocery stores) owned by Dominicans in New York as well as dozens of restaurants. Many emigrants maintained two jobs. Studies of the community during this period compared the Dominicans to Cubans in Miami.

Like their Cuban-American counterparts, Dominicans have worked hard to involve themselves in the political process of the United States. Throughout the 1990s and into the 21st century, Dominicans were elected to a number of municipal governing bodies throughout the northeastern United States, principally in New York, New Jersey, Massachusetts, and Rhode Island. In 2004, Dominicans, who are allowed to hold dual citizenship in both the Dominican Republic and the United States, voted in two presidential elections. The Dominican government established polling places in New York, Boston, and Providence, Rhode Island, to facilitate the voting. Organizations such as the Dominican American National Roundtable encourage political participation.

In 1994, the City University of New York established a research center dedicated to the study of the Dominican Republic and Dominicans in the United States. In October 2001, New Yorkers mourned the deaths of 260 Dominicans who died when an American Airlines jet crashed into a neighborhood in Queens, New York. Five years later the city of New York built a monument to the victims.

Haitians in the United States

During the 1950s, about 40,000 Haitians chose to emigrate to the Bahamas; 175,000 went to work in the Dominican Republic; several thousand went to Cuba; an unspecified number journeyed to Zaire; and more than 38,000 went to the United States. The Haitian immigration to the United States can be dated to the early 20th century, when about 500 upper-class families settled in the United States to avoid the turbulent occupation of Haiti by American forces (Laguerre, 23). Integrating into the Harlem society of the era, these families served as contacts for the next wave of emigrants, those escaping the Duvalier regimes.

Haitian immigration to the United States consisted of several phases. Those escaping the François Duvalier (1907–71) regime left the island in the late 1950s; it was an exodus composed of professionals and political opponents of the dictatorship. The second phase began after the transfer of power from Duvalier the father to Duvalier the son, Papa Doc to Baby Doc, in 1971. This wave of immigration was again made up of political dissidents but included a large number of itinerant laborers seeking better employment in places such as Florida and New York. By the early 1980s, there were 800,000 Haitians in the United States.

The massive flow of Haitian boat people, nearly 300,000, was the dominant characteristic of the wave that started in 1986 with the removal from power of Jean-Claude Duvalier (1951–   ). By the beginning of the 21st century, with 60 percent unemployment in Haiti, almost three out of 10 Haitians were seeking to flee the country.

Throughout the history of the emigration from Haiti, the gateways to the United States were Florida and New York, with nearly 50 percent residing in the Big Apple's metropolitan area. Both in Miami and in New York, the Haitian community encountered double racism, not just white racism but often conflicts with African Americans in urban areas who accused the Haitians of working for lower wages. Within the Haitian community, the youth struggled with issues of identity. Over time, as with the Puerto Rican community several generations earlier, young Haitian men and women began to identify more with life in the United States than in Haiti.

West Indians Elsewhere

Between the end of World War II and 1960, it is estimated that more than 170,000 West Indians, essentially from Barbados, Jamaica, and Trinidad, relocated to Great Britain in pursuit of employment and education. The bond of a common language and familiarity with British traditions encouraged the immigrations. The new arrivals were soon ghettoized outside London and quickly perceived by the British as second-class citizens. From the 1960s to the 1980s on, many West Indians chose to move to Canada, and by 1985, there were about 455,000 persons of Caribbean descent living in the country. The initial pattern of migration consisted of women who reached Canada with a contract, usually to work as domestics or to provide child care.

West Indians in Britain

The first mass migration from the West Indies to Great Britain began in the mid-1950s. Some West Indians traveled to Great Britain before the 1950s, but few intended to seek permanent residency. The best-known of these émigré pioneers was the poet and feminist Una Marson (1905–65), whose work with BBC radio resulted in the creation of *Caribbean Voices,* an outreach effort by the British to keep the islands within the imperial fold during World War II and to help defuse labor issues on the islands in the late 1940s. In this radio program, writers from the area read their works and promoted racial and civil harmony within the empire. It was the first British recognition of the existence of a Caribbean culture separate from that of Great Britain. Marson left for England in 1932, returning to Jamaica in 1946. Her presence in the mother country was made known through the radio program, encouraging intellectuals and would-be writers to seek passage across the Atlantic. This encouraged people looking for better economic opportunities to consider migration from Barbados, Jamaica, and Trinidad.

In 1948, the British Nationality Act gave residents of the anglophone Caribbean the right to claim citizenship in the United Kingdom, a status that ensured unrestricted entry into Britain. In 1955, 27,550 West Indians traveled to Great Britain. Most came from Jamaica, where vanishing agricultural opportunities spurred them to emigrate. During this period, 1 percent of the farms occupied 51 percent of farm acreage, indicating that the large plantation was still the agricultural model in common use. It was a model that left many without land or the possibility of acquiring it.

An average of 15,000 West Indians a year emigrated until 1961. At that time, the British, concerned with what they saw as a flood of black people inundating England, prompted Parliament to pass legislation limiting the number of jobs that could be made available for non-residents. However, since families were allowed to reunite, the movement from the West Indies continued until 1971, when migration to Canada and the United States became more attractive. In 1973, instead of West Indians traveling to Great Britain, nearly 3,000 West Indians either returned to the Caribbean or relocated to the United States. Nevertheless, by 1981 there were 519,000 West Indians living in the British Isles. Nearly 25 percent of them were 15 years old or younger, with the vast majority born in Great Britain.

Tensions surfaced between the white British and their black former subjects. There were several riots in London and cities such as Nottingham in the mid-1960s. In the late 1960s, three national committees were established to address racial conflicts, the Race Relations Board, the Community Relations Commission, and the Community Relations Committee. In 1976, the Race Relations Act was passed to enforce nondiscriminatory behavior in hiring and legal processes. Tensions continued, however, especially with the police targeting black youths. It was common for an officer to stop and arrest a black man in the ghettoes of Nottingham without evidence that any crime had been committed; it was the practice of what later became known in the United States as "racial profiling."

West Indians in Canada

By the 1980s, Canada was home to nearly a half million West Indians, nearly two-fifths of whom were Jamaicans. The preferred area for settlement was Toronto and its suburbs. Emigrants began to arrive in the 1960s when the Canadian government established a program to attract domestic workers from Jamaica. The first waves consisted of women, who then sent for their fiancés and husbands as well as their young children. Although many of the emigrants were well educated, professional positions were limited, and they had to find jobs as taxi drivers and in the service industry. They were occasionally targeted by racists. Acts of violence aimed at people of color took place in isolated locations, such as train stations and bus stops, late in the evening. The government responded in 1980 by creating several committees to study racial violence. In 1983, the government published the report *Equality Now,* which made recommendations to end institutional racism in education, employment, the legal system, and the media. In 1984, a trust of $5 million was established to combat racism, though no guidelines were announced for the implementation of the trust.

By 2001, there were nearly 50,000 Canadians of Trinidad-Tobagonian descent, the result of an emigration that started at the end of the 19th century. It is difficult to determine an exact figure, since Canada and the United States did not differentiate the country of origin during that period, instead placing all emigrants from the region in the general category of West Indians. From 1899 to 1924, it is estimated that 100,000 West Indians reached Canada.

Trinidad-Tobagonians in Canada sought employment in the mines of Nova Scotia, in shipyards, and as domestic servants. At the time, Canada limited permanent immigration to whites, particularly those from Europe. Because of this, Trinidad-Tobagonians were granted limited work permits and were expected to return home. During World War II, those who joined the armed forces were permitted to stay in Canada. The end of racial quotas in 1967 allowed for an increase in the movement from Trinidad-Tobago, and it is believed that about 40,000 arrived between 1967 and 1991. Toronto became the center of emigrant life in Canada. It is the most diverse city in Canada, with populations from China, India, Pakistan, the Philippines, and Russia as well as from the Caribbean and Latin America.

Haitians in France and in Canada

In 1945, France was troubled by a labor shortage caused by the death toll of World War II. For this reason, the National Immigration Office was assigned the task of coordinating the entry of emigrant workers. That office reported that 30,171 workers arrived in France in 1946. In 1956, that figure jumped to 65,428 arrivals. These workers originated mostly from Africa, Italy, and Spain. In 1963, the Bureau for Migration from the Overseas Department was created to attract workers from Guadeloupe and Martinique. Since these workers were French citizens, they were not considered emigrants. A decade after the establishment of the bureau, there were a total of 115,465 persons from Guadalupe and Martinique in France. These workers found employment as domestics, municipal workers, and hospital aides.

Unlike the migrants from Guadeloupe and Martinique, Haitians did not choose France as a destination: "In spite of France's liberal asylum policies, and the high regard that many Haitians have for French culture, comparatively few Haitians migrate to that country, and for the most part, those who do are usually professionals. . . . Of . . . 350,000 Haitians . . . who left Haiti during the 1950–75 period, only about 4,000 had immigrated to France" (Miller, 51). Canada was the destination for nearly 25,000 Haitians fleeing the dictatorship of the Duvaliers. Highly educated, many of these Haitians found employment in professional fields in Quebec. However, about 2,000 Haitians worked in the service industry and were often the victims of discriminatory practices. For example, in 1983 a group of Haitian taxi drivers reported that they were underpaid and brought a lawsuit, which they won, against their employers.

The 21st Century: Uncertain Future

A study conducted in 2004 by the Central Intelligence Agency on Latin America and the Caribbean in the 21st century, entitled *Latin America 2020: Discussion of Long-Term Scenarios,* concluded that the region was going to be less significant in global affairs in the new century than in the past and with little influence in the world (Oppenheimer, 9). Gone are the narcissistic planters with powerful lobbies in England and France. Soon to pass from the scene is Fidel Castro, along with his revolutionary rhetoric and insurrectionist fervor that lit a fire across several continents. So what then of the Caribbean in the new millennium?

If history tells us anything, the importance of the region cannot be measured simply by its size. The region has had a major impact on world events over the last three centuries. The Haitian Revolution of the late 18th and early 19th century was a unique event: the only successful slave revolution in modern history. It sent a strong and clear message that the slave system would not stand. It fundamentally challenged the racist ideologies of the period and contributed to the ongoing debate about race and what scholars call the defining of the "other"—a phenomenon common in all societies.

In the 20th century, the Cuban Revolution presented a fundamental ideological and political challenge to the United States, and the implications of that revolution were felt across the world. Even today, although the revolution has been largely discredited, its influence can be seen in the leftward shift of political movements across Latin America. Castro remains a greatly admired figure in Latin America, not because Latin

Americans wish to adopt the Cuban model of government, but because for five decades he has stood up to the United States. In that regard, he remains a symbol of the larger struggle of Latin America for political and economic sovereignty.

This brief overview cannot even begin to do justice to the Caribbean's enormous cultural contributions to the world. Reggae, calypso, son (a music and dance genre) rumba, salsa, merengue, and Afro-Cuban jazz just begin to touch the surface of the region's contribution to world music. V. S. Naipaul, José Martí, Eric Williams, Miguel Barnet, Alejo Carpentier, Kamau Brathwaite and their counterparts in the Caribbean diaspora such as Junot Díaz, Cristina Garcia, Oscar Hijuelos, and the performers of Nuyorican poetry and literature, among many others, are part of important literary movements across the globe.

The Caribbean has a way of surprising the world. This is not likely to change in the 21st century. Part of that ability to surprise lies in the region's turbulent history. The modern Caribbean was born in conflict—the conflict of the conquest—and was nurtured on more conflict: the slave system, colonialism, and revolution. Within the islands is a composite of many of the different cultures, colors, and ethnicities of the world struggling to coexist within a relatively small area. It is a struggle that faces us all in this age of globalization, where all of us will be forced into contact with other cultures in ways both upsetting and beautiful, challenging and rewarding. The Caribbean still has many revelations for the rest of the world at the dawn of the 21st century.

Political Change

Political changes seem imminent, particularly in Cuba, Puerto Rico, and St. Martin. In Jamaica, a high incidence of violent crimes and lawlessness poses a fundamental challenge to the structure of the political system that merits careful scrutiny.

Cuba

In Cuba, the situation was tenuous at the beginning of 2007. In August 2006, Castro was absent from power due to illness. There was speculation that he was dying of cancer, but no one knew for sure because his condition was a state secret. This was a cause for celebration in Miami, particularly in the area around La Calle Ocho (Eighth Street, the center of Little Havana), where Cuban exiles waved flags and shouted "Viva Cuba Libre." They were joyful that for the first time in 46 years Castro was forced to hand over power to his younger brother Raul and was not in complete charge of the island.

Castro's end appears to be near, although those predicting his death must do so with great humility, given the many times in the past that rumors of his death have been greatly exaggerated. As his 80th birthday was celebrated on the island, those who opposed Castro dreamed of a Cuba without him, while his supporters worried about life in Cuba without him. At his birthday celebrations in Havana in December 2006, he failed to attend a ceremony held for him at a theater and did not take his seat at a reviewing stand in Havana to watch the Cuban military march before him. The soldiers, still forming a military procession evocative of the Stalin era, marched before Raul Castro instead. The elder Castro was also absent from ceremonies marking the 54th anniversary of the attack on the Moncada barracks in July 2007 and celebrations on August 13, 2007, marking his 81st birthday.

The potential for violence in Cuba is clear. Will the political factions within the Cuban revolutionary government, held together by Castro's commanding presence, come apart and begin to fight each other? Will the United States, faced with the increasing likelihood of a failed Iraq policy, seek to arm dissidents within Cuba in an effort to achieve "victory" somewhere in the world? What of a future role in Cuba for the exile community? Will Cuba erupt into a bloodbath of vengeance as it did in 1933, when another Cuban dictator, Gerardo Machado, fell from power?

A number of political scenarios are being debated regarding the future of Cuba. One possibility, not seen as likely by political commentators in the United States and not favored by Cuban exiles, is a continuation of the status quo—Cuba with another Castro in charge, the prolongation of political repression, and the continuation of hostility between the United States and Cuba. Another possibility is that Raul Castro will seek to imitate China, encouraging a gradual acceptance of capitalism while ruling with a strong hand. Still another scenario posits that Raul Castro will seek to rule as a dictator like his brother and that the people of Cuba, perhaps with outside assistance, will rebel and oust him after a bloody civil war.

Puerto Rico

Meanwhile, in Puerto Rico, the matter of whether to be an independent nation, a state, or a commonwealth of the United States continues to dominate debate on the island. In the 1960s, the triumph of the Cuban Revolution encouraged Puerto Rican nationalists to believe independence was possible: If Cuba could challenge the United States, so could

Puerto Rico. This hope lingered into the 1970s and 1980s as Fidel Castro, Jamaica's Michael Manley, and Grenada's Maurice Bishop indicated their support for the movement. In the meantime, several Puerto Rican governors who favored statehood were elected. Yet whenever the matter is put to a vote, Puerto Ricans are evenly divided on the issue. This ambivalence served to preserve the current commonwealth status, which has been upheld in plebiscites taken in 1967, 1993, and 1998.

In the 21st century, opponents of statehood maintain that such a political change would impair the island's ability to offer "special tax incentives to attract industry and investment [and would impose a] federal tax structure [while] downsizing local government and, therefore, [creating] higher unemployment" (Acevedo-Vilá, 77). By the year 2000, only 5 percent of the population favored independence. The objection is that Puerto Ricans now enjoy the benefits of being American citizens and are unwilling to let those benefits go. The third option is to enhance the island's commonwealth status by allowing Puerto Rico to chart its own foreign relations, including drafting its own homeland security laws and establishing its own immigration policy. The debate will go on as Puerto Rico and the United States continue to jostle and redefine the ambivalent nature of their political relationship. Changes to the commonwealth compact seem to be the most likely outcome, rather than a definitive union with or a break from the United States.

St. Martin/Sint Maarten

In St. Martin/Sint Maarten, political reformers refuse to use the Dutch spelling of the island's name, using the English version instead: St. Martin. The political objective of the nationalists is to reach independence via three steps. The first step would be to cease being a county or district of bigger islands. This would mean that the French side of St. Martin would no longer report to Guadeloupe (which occurred in July 2007) and the Dutch side would no longer report to Curaçao. The second step would be to become a department or province of the European colonial powers in charge of the island: France and the Netherlands. The third step would be to follow departmentalization with self-rule. Eventually it is anticipated that self-rule will yield to independence, as occurred in the British West Indies.

One obstacle is the question of which side of the island will emerge dominant after independence: the Dutch side or the French? Supporters of self-rule and eventual independence often answer that those designations are reflective of a colonial mentality, and there is only one St. Martin and one people, the St. Martinians. A clear sense dominates St. Martin in the first decade of the new century: Something is happening politically that cannot be stopped.

A strategy emerged at the beginning of the 21st century to change the perception of the island from another cruise line destination to a vital cultural center. With that objective, an annual book fair was funded by the St. Martin's Chamber of Commerce and local corporations so that authors of the African and Caribbean diaspora, located throughout the world, will visit the island to promote Caribbean literature. In return they will spread the word about cultural developments in St. Martin upon their return home.

Jamaica

In Jamaica, observers argue that the increase of gang violence may fundamentally alter the politics of the island. In 2005 and 2006 gang violence was aimed at the business community and the police, sectors traditionally seen as representative of Jamaica's ruling society. In two locations, Spanish Town and Mandeville, gangsters openly challenged local authority in 2005. But more disturbing to government officials is the fact that residents of those towns literally applauded the violent actions taken by the gangs. In Spanish Town, gang members attacked several business owners who defended their stores against robbers. In Mandeville, gang members and other residents, objecting to police action against them, burned cars along a major thoroughfare and vandalized the courthouse.

The violence and the support for it worries some politicians: "The rapidity of popular mobilizations . . . in [Mandeville] and Spanish Town . . . all suggest the paper-thin acceptance of the legitimacy and the depth of the disconnection. . . . The Jamaican state, and the social bloc that operates within its circles, remains in power, but mounting evidence suggests that its hold is increasingly tenuous" (Meeks, 3). It was no accident that most gangsters in Jamaica hung portraits of Che Guevara and Nelson Mandela in their headquarters. It is as if these gang leaders want Jamaicans to understand that gang activities are not just about drug trafficking and violence, but are also a potential excursion into the political arena.

Tourism

Whatever political changes take place, all the nations of the Caribbean will need a source of income. For many islands, sugar was the source of

Woman selling guava rum in St. Martin. For the smaller islands tourism provides half of the annual gross national product. (Photo by D. H. Figueredo)

income during the 19th and early 20th centuries. In the 2000s, tourism is the new sugar.

In the past 20 years, from the mid 1980s to 2005, the number of tourists visiting the islands has increased from nearly 9 million to more than 2 billion; in the Bahamas alone in 1986, nearly 2 million tourists flew to the island, while in 2005 the figure was close to 5 million. For most of the islands this has led to employment opportunities for thousands in the service industry. On the smaller islands, tourism makes up half of the gross national product.

Tourism has affected the ecology of many of the islands as airports, hotels, and condominiums were erected to satisfy the needs of tourists. Typically, tourists are North American families with disposable income who contribute roughly $3,000 to the local economy during a one-week stay. The shopping districts in places like St. Martin and St. Thomas often exist to meet the needs of the more than 100,000 annual visitors who arrive on cruise ships to tour the island for a day.

The tourist industry, like the plantations of the 19th century, was built to serve foreigners. In catering to the whims of the visitors, the industry has incorporated underground features such as drugs and prostitution. The former typically occurs outside the realm of the law. The latter, described as "sex work," is often included in formal arrangements made by some components of the tourist industry. On some islands, for example, sex workers are permitted aboard cruise ships to rendezvous with clients. The most common practice is for sex providers to be associated with a bar, restaurant, or beach resort. But there are also organized sex tours (Kempadoo, 54) and sex-oriented resorts for both the straight and gay populations. The result is that in some islands, as many as 40,000 women work as prostitutes (Facio, 138); it is also estimated that on some of the islands up to 38 percent of males in the tourist industry augment their earnings as gay prostitutes. An even darker side to the tourist boom is the child sex trade, a growing trend in the Caribbean and parts of Asia. In the Caribbean it is estimated that more than a half million child prostitutes between the ages of 5 and 17 are trafficked throughout the islands.

The sex industry contributes to the AIDS epidemic in the Caribbean. In 2002 it was reported that 500,000 people were diagnosed with the deadly disease; many contracted the illness through work in the sex trade (Wilkinson, 1).

The tourist industry encourages a stereotypical rendering of the islands as beaches and trees and women in bikinis and of the residents

A quiet street in St. Martin after the tourists have returned to the cruise lines (Photo by D. H. Figueredo)

as people of color selling their wares on sidewalks or inside picturesque huts. These images conceal some pressing social issues created by tourism. Since the industry caters to wealthy foreigners, much wealthier than most of the local population, it creates shopping and dining environments that the islanders cannot afford. On a typical evening in the French city of Marigot on Saint Martin, few black or brown faces are seen among the diners in the exclusive restaurants downtown. Their pocketbooks simply cannot afford a $200 dinner at this tourist mecca. The result of this dichotomy, played out across the Caribbean, is what has come to be known as "tourism apartheid," a system in which islanders cannot enjoy the riches of their own homeland and are perpetually called on to serve the wealthy, typically visitors from the United States, Canada, and Europe.

And, as in colonial times, fortunes in the islands are subject to the fortunes of the visitors. Events in the United States and Europe affect the tourist industry. After the attacks on the United States of September 11, 2001, and the subsequent wars in Afghanistan and Iraq, tourism declined in the region by about 1 million visitors. Oil price increases in 2006 impacted tourism on the smaller islands, such as Bonaire, where the industry experienced about a 10 percent decline.

Yet tourism remains one of the most important sources of income for the Caribbean. The creation of such multinational organizations as the Caribbean Tourism Organization and the Caribbean Hotel Association ensure lobbying efforts on behalf of the islands in the United States and Europe and extensive television advertising in those nations. Tourism is clearly a main component of the Caribbean economies of the 21st century.

Remittances

Another source of external revenue that benefits the Caribbean is remittances—money sent home by emigrants, refugees, and exiles living in Canada, Europe, and the United States. Caribbean emigrants in the United States provide about one-third of the remittances. A 2002 study found that nearly 30 percent of families in the Dominican Republic received funds from abroad, totaling $1.8 billion (Sana and Massey, 517). In 2003, nearly $4 billion was sent to Cuba, Haiti, and Jamaica (Lapointe, 1). The financial contributions from expatriates/exiles/emigrants fostered a movement to keep them involved in the political life of their respective countries. As an example, the Dominican Republic allows for dual citizenship with the United States and allows Dominicans living in the United States to vote in national elections. A politically involved community living abroad increases the likelihood that remittances will continue.

Remittances to Selected Caribbean Countries (in millions of $US)			
Country	2001	2002	2003
Cuba	930	1,265	1,194
Dominican Republic	1,807	2,206	2,217
Haiti	810	931	977
Jamaica	967	1,288	1,425
Trinidad-Tobago	not available	59	88

Adapted from: Lapointe, Michelle. "Diasporas in Caribbean Development: Rapporteur's Report." Report of the Inter-American Dialogue and World Bank, August 2004.

Those living abroad are often among the biggest political fundraisers, a trend not lost on Caribbean politicians. In the past, politicians from Puerto Rico were flown into New York or heavily Puerto Rican communities, such as Perth Amboy, New Jersey, to bolster local candidates. Now presidential candidates from the Dominican Republic regularly campaign for votes in the United States. The webs of transnationalism are the subject of a growing area of research and scholarship; the impact of this trend on ethnic communities in the United States and the countries of the Caribbean merits careful watching.

The impact of remittances is a subject of some debate. Remittances help the families who remain in the Caribbean increase their savings and provide them with better access to doctors and health services as well as schooling in private institutions. The remittances contribute to the economic stability of some families and to a reduction in poverty and social inequality. However, some observers believe that remittances do very little to alleviate the social conditions in the receiving countries. That debate will continue, but the trend is clear: Remittances will remain a major and growing source of income in the Caribbean as the 21st century unfolds.

The Future

It is obvious that independence has not brought self-sufficiency and that the islands of the Caribbean still depend to varying degrees on their former mother countries. Considering the lack of resources, the limited space on the islands, and the political fragmentation, it does not appear that the Caribbean will be able to stand completely on its own early in the century. This leads to a fundamental question about their future. Are the islands destined to serve as little Gardens of Eden for well-to-do tourists in resorts purposely isolated from the native populations? In some sense, perhaps, the Caribbean is still a chain of fortresses, as in colonial times. In this case, they are fortresses where foreigners tan, drink, and eat while the local residents serve them. Perhaps the *encomiendas* of the past have been reinvented and repackaged for the 21st century.

APPENDIX 1

TABLES

Area and Population of Islands of the Caribbean, 2005		
Island	Area (square km)	Population
Anguilla	102	13,677
Antigua	280	68,722
Aruba	193	71,566
Bahamas	13,940	301,790
Barbados	431	279,250
Barbuda	161	2,000
British Virgin Islands	153	22,643
Cayman Islands	262	44,270
Cuba	110,860	11,346,670
Dominican Republic	48,730	8,950,034
Grenada	344	89,502
Guadeloupe	1,780	448,713
Haiti	27,750	8,121,622
Jamaica	10,991	2,731,832
Martinique	1,100	432,900
Montserrat	102	9,341
Puerto Rico	9,104	3,916,632
St. Kitts-Nevis	261	38,958
St. Lucia	616	166,312
St. Vincent and Grenadines	389	117,534
Trinidad-Tobago	5,128	1,088,644
Turks and Caicos	430	20,556
U.S. Virgin Islands (St. Croix, St. Thomas, St. John)	352	108,708

Theodora Web site. "Countries of the World." Available online. URL: www. theodora. com/wfb/abc_world_fact_book.html. Accessed on May 30, 2006.

Population in the Spanish Caribbean, 1750

Island	Population including slaves
Cuba	75,000
Hispaniola	35,000
Jamaica	1,300
Puerto Rico	3,039

Population in the British West Indies, 1670–1680

Island	Year	Population including slaves
Antigua	1678	4,480
Barbados	1684	68,743
Jamaica	1673	17,272
Montserrat	1684	3,674
Nevis	1684	7,370
St. Kitts	1684	3,333

Population in the French Caribbean, 1660–1680

Island	Year	Population including slaves
Guadeloupe	1670	8,696
Martinique	1664	15,401
Saint-Domingue	1681	6,648

Adapted from: Rogoziński, Jan. *A Brief History of the Caribbean: From the Arawak and the Carib to the Present.* New York: A Meridian Book, Penguin, 1992, pp. 45, 69, 75, 76, 87.

18th Century: Spain at War

1701–15	War of Spanish Succession
1718–20	War against France and England
1727–29	War against France and England
1733–38	War against Austria
1739–41	War of Jenkins' Ear
1740–48	War of Austrian Succession
1756–63	Seven Years' War
1779–86	Participation in the American Revolutionary War
1796–1800	War against England

Adapted from: Prago, Alberto. *The Revolutions in Spanish America: The Independence Movements of 1808–1825.* New York: MacMillan, 1970, pp. 235–236.

Haitian Rulers during the 19th Century

Jean-Jacques Dessalines	Governor-General	January 1, 1804–September 22, 1804
Jacques I (Dessalines)	Emperor	September 22, 1804–October 17, 1806
Henry Christophe	President	February 17, 1807–March 26, 1811
Henri I	King	March 26, 1811–October 8, 1820
Alexandre Pétion	President	March 9, 1807–March 29, 1818
Jean-Pierre Boyer	President	March 30, 1818–March 13, 1843
Executive Council	Provisional government	March 14, 1843–December 30, 1843
Rivière Hérard	President	December 31, 1843–May 3, 1844
Philippe Guerrier	President	May 3, 1844–April 15, 1845

Haitian Rulers *(continued)*		
Jean-Louis Pierrot	President	April 16, 1845– March 1, 1846
Jean-Baptiste Riché	President	March 1, 1846– February 27, 1847
Faustin Soulouque	President	March 1, 1847– August 25, 1849
Faustin I (Soulouque)	Emperor	August 25, 1849– January 13, 1859
Fabre Geffrard	President	January 13, 1859– March 13, 1867
Sylvain Salnave	President	June 14, 1867– December 19, 1869
Executive Council	Provisional government	December 27, 1869– March 19, 1870
Nissage-Saget (Jean-Nicolas Nissage-Saget)	President	March 19, 1870– May 12, 1874
Michel Domingue	President	June 11, 1874– April 15, 1876
Pierre-Théoma Boisrond-Canal	President	July 17, 1876– July 17, 1879
Lysius-Félicité Salomon	President	October 23, 1879– August 10, 1888
Executive Council	Provisional government	August 18, 1888– December 15, 1888
François Denys Légitime	President	December 16, 1888– August 22, 1889
Executive Council	Provisional government	August 27, 1889– October 9, 1889
Florvil Hyppolite	President	October 9, 1889– March 24, 1896
Tirésias Simon Sam	President	March 31, 1896– May 12, 1902

Schutt-Ainé, Patricia, and the staff of Libraire Au Service de la Culture. *Haiti: A Basic Reference Book; General Information on Haiti.* Miami and Port-au-Prince: Librairie Au Service de la Culture, 1994, pp. 70–71.

Presidents of the Dominican Republic, 1844–1861

Pedro Santana	November 13, 1844–August 4, 1848
Council of Secretaries of State	August 4–September 8, 1848
Manuel Jimenes	September 8, 1848–May 29, 1849
Pedro Santana (supreme chief of the republic)	May 30–September 23, 1849
Buenaventura Báez	September 24, 1849–February 15, 1853
Pedro Santana	February 15, 1853–May 26, 1856
Manuel de Regla Mota	May 26–October 8, 1856
Buenaventura Báez	October 8, 1856–June 13, 1858
José Desiderio Valverde	June 13–July 28, 1858
Pedro Santana	July 28, 1858–March 18, 1861

Spanish Governors-General of Santo Domingo, 1861–1865

Pedro Santana	March 18, 1861–July 20, 1862
Felipe Ribero	July 20, 1862–October 22, 1863
Carlos de Vargas	October 22, 1863–March 30, 1864
José de la Gándara	October 22, 1863–March 30, 1864

Heads of State of the Dominican Republic, 1863–1865

José Antonio Salcedo	September 14, 1863–October 10, 1864
Gaspar Polanco	October 10, 1864–January 23, 1865
Benigno Filomeno de Rojas	January 24–March 24, 1865

Adapted from: "List of Presidents of the Dominican Republic." Available online: http://www.answers.com/topic/list-of-presidents-of-the-dominican-republic. Accessed on July 5, 2006.

Haitian Presidents before and during U.S. Occupation		
Presidents	Years	Outcome
Tirésias Simon Sam	March 31, 1896– May 12, 1902	Resigned
Executive Council	May 13, 1902– December 21, 1902	Disbanded
Nord Alexis	December 21, 1902– December 2, 1908	Ousted
Antoine Simon	December 17, 1908– August 2, 1911	Ousted
Cincinnatus Leconte	August 14, 1911– August 8, 1912	Murdered
Tancrède Auguste	August 12, 1912– May 2, 1913	Died in office
Michel Oreste	May 4, 1913– January 27, 1914	Ousted
Oreste Zamor	February 8, 1914– October 29, 1914	Ousted
Davilmar Théodore	November 7, 1914– February 22, 1915	Ousted
Vilbrun Guillaume Sam	March 4, 1915– July 27, 1915	Murdered
Sudre Dartiguenave	August 12, 1915– May 15, 1922	End of term
Louis Borno	May 15, 1922– May 15, 1930	End of term
Louis Eugène Roy	May 15, 1930– November 18, 1930	End of term
Sténio Vincent	November 18, 1930– May 15, 1941	Resigned

Adapted from: Schutt-Ainé, Patricia, et al. *Haiti: A Basic Reference Book*. Miami: Librairie Au Service de la Culture, 1994, pp. 71–72.

Chief Ministers of Jamaica

William Alexander Bustamante	May 5, 1953–February 2, 1955
Norman Washington Manley	February 2, 1955–July 4, 1959

Prime Ministers of Jamaica

William Alexander Bustamante	April 29, 1962–February 23, 1967
Donald Burns Sangster	February 23–April 11, 1967
Hugh Shearer	April 11, 1967–March 2, 1972
Michael Manley	March 2, 1972–November 1, 1980
Edward Seaga	November 1, 1980–February 10, 1989
Michael Manley	February 10, 1989–March 30, 1992
P. J. Patterson	March 30, 1992–March 30, 2006
Portia Simpson-Miller	March 30, 2006–present

Adapted from various sources, including: "Jamaica." Available online: http://www.worldstatesmen.org/Jamaica.htm. Accessed on December 1st, 2006.

Dominican Republic Presidents after Trujillo

Presidents	Dates
Joaquín Balaguer	August 3, 1960–January 16, 1962
Rafael Filiberto Bonnelly	January 18, 1962–February 27, 1963
Juan Bosch	February 27, 1963–September 25, 1963
Triumvirate	September 26, 1963–April 25, 1965
Antonio Imbert Barrera	May 7, 1965–August 30, 1965
Héctor García Godoy	September 3, 1965–July 1, 1966
Joaquín Balaguer	July 1, 1966–August 16, 1978
Antonio Guzmán Fernández	August 16, 1978–July 4, 1982
Jacobo Majluta Azar	July 4, 1982–August 16, 1982
Salvador Jorge Blanco	August 16, 1982–August 16, 1986

Dominican Republic Presidents after Trujillo *(continued)*	
Presidents	Dates
Joaquín Balaguer	August 16, 1986–August 16, 1996
Leonel Fernández Reyna	August 16, 1996–August 16, 2000
Hipólito Mejía	August 16, 2000–August 16, 2004
Leonel Fernández Reyna	August 16, 2004–present

Adapted from Ruíz Burgos, Victor Eddy. *Los gobiernos de la República Dominicana.* Santo Domingo: Biblioteca Nacional, 1993.

Governors of Puerto Rico, 1949–Present		
Governor	Dates	Political Party
Luis Muñoz Marín	January 2, 1949–January 2, 1965	Popular Democratic
Roberto Sánchez Vilella	January 2, 1965–January 2, 1969	Popular Democratic
Luis A. Ferré	January 2, 1969–January 2, 1973	New Progressive
Rafael Hernández Colón	January 2, 1973–January 2, 1977	Popular Democratic
Carlos Romero Barceló	January 2, 1977–January 2, 1985	New Progressive
Rafael Hernández Colón	January 2, 1985–January 2, 1993	Popular Democratic
Pedro Rosselló González	January 2, 1993–January 2, 2001	New Progressive
Sila M. Calderón	January 2, 2001–January 2, 2005	Popular Democratic
Aníbal Acevedo Vilá	January 2, 2005–present	Popular Democratic

Presidents of Cuba, 1902–Present

Presidents	Dates	Political Party
Tomás Estrada Palma	May 20, 1902–September 28, 1906	Moderate
William Howard Taft	September 29, 1906–October 2nd, 1906	Provisional U.S. Governor
Charles E. Magoon	October 2nd, 1906–January 28, 1909	Provisional U.S. Governor
José Miguel Gómez	January 28, 1909–May 20, 1913	Liberal
Mario García Menocal	May 20, 1913– May 20, 1921	Conservative
Alfredo Zayas y Alfonso	May 20, 1921– May 20, 1925	Cuban Popular Party
Gerardo Machado y Morales	May 20, 1925–August 12, 1933	Liberal
Alberto Herrera	August 12, 1933	Military Provisional on Machado's behalf
Carlos Manuel de Céspedes y Quesada	August 12, 1933–September 4, 1933	Coalition of revolutionary parties
The Pentarchy (Ramón Grau San Martín, Sergio Carbó Morera, Porfirio Franca, José Miguel Irisarri, Guillermo Portela)	September 4, 1933–September 10, 1933	Several parties
Ramón Grau San Martín	September 10, 1933–January 15, 1934	Cuban Revolutionary Party
Carlos Hevia	January 15, 1934–January 18, 1934	Cuban Revolutionary Party
Manuel Márquez Sterling	January 18, 1934	No affiliation; provisional

Presidents of Cuba, 1902–Present *(continued)*

Presidents	Dates	Political Party
Carlos Mendieta Montefur	January 18, 1934– December 11, 1935	National Union
José Antonio Barnet y Vinajeras	December 11, 1935– May 20, 1936	National Union
Miguel Mariano Gómez	May 20, 1936– December 24, 1936	Republican Action Party
Federico Laredo Brú	December 24, 1936– October 10, 1940	National Union
Fulgencio Batista	October 10, 1940– October 10, 1944	Coalition of several political parties; no particular affiliation
Ramón Grau San Martín	October 10, 1944– October 10, 1948	Cuban Revolutionary Party
Carlos Prío Socarrás	October 10, 1948– March 10, 1952	Cuban Revolutionary Party
Fulgencio Batista	March 10, 1952– April 6, 1954	Military
Andrés Domingo y Morales	April 6, 1954– February 24, 1955	On Batista's behalf
Fulgencio Batista	February 24, 1955– January 1, 1959	Military
Anselmo Alliegro	January 1, 1959	Provisional
Carlos Manuel Piedra	January 1–2, 1959	Provisional
Manuel Urrutia Lleó	January 1, 1959– July 16, 1959	Revolutionary government
Osvaldo Dorticós Torrado	July 16, 1959– February 14, 1976	Communist Party
Fidel Castro	July 14, 1976– present	Communist Party

Presidents of Haiti, 1941–Present	
Presidents	**Dates**
Élie Lescot	1941–1946
Franck Lavaud (Chairman of the Military Executive Committee)	1946
Dumarsais Estimé	1946–1950
Franck Lavaud (Chairman of the Junta of Government)	1950
Paul-Eugène Magloire	1950–1956
Joseph Nemours Pierre-Louis*	1956–1957
Franck Sylvain*	1957
Executive Government Council*	1957
Antonio Thrasybule Kébreau (Chairman of the Military Council)	1957
François Duvalier	1957–1971
Jean-Claude Duvalier	1971–1986
Henri Namphy (Chairman of the National Council of Government)	1986–1988
Leslie-François Manigat	1988
Henri Namphy (Head of the Military Government)	1989–1989
Prosper Avril	1989–1990
Ertha Pascal-Trouillot*	1990–1991
Jean-Bertrand Aristide	1991
Joseph Nérette*	1991–1992
Marc Bazin (Acting Prime Minister)	1992–1993
Jean-Bertrand Aristide	1993–1994
Émile Jonassaint*	1994
Jean-Bertrand Aristide	1994–1996
René Garcia Préval	1996–2000
Jean-Bertrand Aristide	2000–2004
Boniface Alexandre*	2004–2006
René Garcia Préval	2006–present
* provisional president	

Caribbean Immigration to the United States: Two Decades

Country	1960–1970	1970–1980
Antigua	Not available	36,501
Barbados	9,689	20,948
Cuba	265,052	402,023
Dominican Republic	94,872	148,016
Dominica	Not available	6,100
Haiti	38,468	68,916
Grenada	Not available	7,765
Jamaica	73,351	141,995
Trinidad	24,965	61,726

Adapted from: Pator, Robert, ed. *Migration and Development in the Caribbean: The Unexplored Connection.* Boulder, Colo., and London: Westview Press, 1985, p. 8.

Appendix 2

Basic Facts About the Caribbean

Official Name

The Caribbean is also known as the Antilles and the West Indies. It consists of three subgroups, the Greater Antilles, the Lesser Antilles, and the Bahamas.

Greater Antilles

The names of the countries that officially make up the Greater Antilles are Cuba, Dominican Republic, Haiti, Jamaica, and Puerto Rico.

Lesser Antilles

The Lesser Antilles consists of three subgroups, the Leeward Islands, the Windward Islands, and the Leeward Antilles.

Leeward Islands: The U.S. Virgin Islands (consisting of St. Thomas, St. John, and St. Croix), the British Virgin Islands (consisting of Tortola, Virgin Gorda, Anegada, Jost Van Dyke), Anguilla, Antigua, Barbuda, Dominica, Guadeloupe (Basse-Terre, Grande-Terre, La Désirade, Les Saintes, Marie-Galante, St. Martin*), Montserrat, Nevis, Redonda, Saba, Saint Barthélemey,* Saint Kitts, and Sint Eustatius.

Windward Islands: Barbados, Grenada, Grenadines, Martinique, Saint Lucia, Saint Vincent, and Trinidad and Tobago.

Leeward Antilles: Aruba, Curaçao, and Bonaire.

*Note: As of February 2007, St. Martin and Saint Barthélemy are no longer part of Guadeloupe and are administered as separate overseas departments of France.

Geography

Area

	Size	Highest Point (ft)
Caribbean	229,173 sq km	Pico Duarte 3,175 m (1,058) (Dominican Republic)
Anguilla	102 sq km	Crocus Hill 65 m (21)
Antigua and Barbuda	443 sq km	Boggy Peak 402 m (132)
Bahamas	10,070 sq km	Mount Alvernia 63 m (21)
Barbados	431 sq km	Mount Hillaby 336 m (112)
British Virgin Islands (consisting of Tortola, Virgin Gorda, Anegada, Jost Van Dyke)	153 sq km	Mount Sage 521 m (173)
Cuba	110,860 sq km	Pico Turquino 2,005 m (668)
Dominica	754 sq km	Morne Diablatins 1,447 m (486)
Dominican Republic	48,380 sq km	Pico Duarte 3,175 m (1,055)
Grenada	344 sq km	Mount Saint Catherine 840 m (280)
Guadeloupe (Basse-Terre, Grande-Terre, La Désirade, Les Saintes, Marie-Galante, St. Martin)	1,628 sq km	Soufrière 1,484 m (494)
Haiti	27,560 sq km	Chaîne de la Selle 2,680 m (873)
Jamaica	10,831 sq km	Blue Mountain Peak 2,256 m (752)
Martinique	1,060 sq km	Montagne Pelee 1,397 m (465)
Montserrat	102 sq km	English's Crater 930 m (310)
Netherland Antilles (Aruba, Bonaire, Curaçao, St. Maarten, Saba, and St. Eustatius)	960 sq km	Mount Scenery 862 m (281)
Puerto Rico	8,870 sq km	Cerro de Punta 1,339 m (446)

(table continues)

(continued)

	Size	Highest Point (ft)
Saint Kitts and Nevis	261 sq km	Mount Liamuiga 1,156 m (385)
Saint Lucia	606 sq km	Mount Gimie 950 m (316)
Saint Vincent and the Grenadines	389 sq km	La Soufrière 1,234 m (411)
Trinidad and Tobago	5,128 sq km	El Cerro del Aripo 940 m (313)
U.S. Virgin Islands (St. Thomas, St. John, and St. Croix)	346 sq km	Crown Mountain 475 m (158)

Boundaries

To the north of the Caribbean lies the United States; the Gulf of Mexico, Mexico, and Central America are to the west of the islands; to the south are the Caribbean Sea and South America; and to the east is the Atlantic Ocean.

Topography

Consisting of more than 700 landmasses of various sizes and stretching 2,500 miles across from west to east, the topography of the Caribbean varies from island to island or from island group to island group. Islands like Barbados and Antigua are flat, while such islands as Dominica and Grenada present steep cliffs. Cuba and the Dominican Republic have long valleys with mountains and hills that yield majestic views. The islands are near each other, making island hopping, in the past and in the present, relatively easy. Also, with the exception of Cuba and the Dominican Republic, which are the largest islands in the Caribbean, the islands tend to be small. It is feasible, for example, to drive the length and width of St. Martin/Sint Maarten in one day. All the islands are surrounded by sandy beaches, and the beaches are adorned by a variety of picturesque palm trees.

The soil lends itself to easy cultivation of such products as sugarcane, cotton, tobacco, bananas, and cocoa, and the abundance of rain from May to November, varying from 30 inches to 200 inches of rainfall, can allow for a rich harvest. The temperature ranges from 70 to 90°F, with the trade winds refreshing the islands even during the height of summer in July and August. However, this apparent paradise is often threatened by hurricanes, since the Caribbean experiences an average of 18 hurricanes a year.

Government

	Date of Independence	System of Government	Date of Constitution	Capital
Anguilla		Overseas territory of the United Kindgom	1982	The Valley
Antigua and Barbuda	November 1, 1981	Constitutional parliamentary democracy	November 1, 1981	Saint John
Bahamas	July 10, 1973	Constitutional parliamentary democracy	July 10, 1973	Nassau
Barbados	November 30, 1966	Parliamentary democracy	November 30, 1966	Bridgetown
British Virgin Islands (Tortola, Virgin Gorda, Anegada, Jost Van Dyke)		Overseas territory of the United Kingdom	June 1, 1977, amended in 2000	Road Town
Cuba	May 20, 1902	Communist state	February 24 1976; amended July 1992 and June 2002	Havana
Dominica	November 3, 1978	Parliamentary democracy	November 3, 1978	Roseau
Dominican Republic	February 27, 1844	Representative democracy	November 28, 1966; amended July 25, 2002	Santo Domingo
Grenada	February 7, 1974	Parliamentary democracy	December 19, 1973	Saint George
Guadeloupe (Basse-Terre, Grande-Terre, La Désirade, Les Saintes, Marie-Galante, St. Martin)		Overseas department of France	October 4, 1958 (French Constitution)	Basse-Terre

(table continues)

257

	Date of Independence	System of Government	Date of Constitution	Capital
Haiti	January 1, 1804	Elected government	Several constitutions enacted, last modified constitution adopted in March 1987	Port-au-Prince
Jamaica	August 6, 1962	Constitutional parliamentary democracy	August 6, 1962	Kingston
Martinique		Overseas department of France	October 4, 1958 (French Constitution)	Fort-de-France
Montserrat		Overseas territory of the United Kingdom	December 19, 1989	Plymouth
Netherland Antilles (Aruba, Bonaire, Curaçao, St. Maarten, Saba, and St. Eustatius)		Autonomous within the Kingdom of the Netherlands	December 29, 1954	Willemstad, Curaçao
Puerto Rico		U.S. commonwealth	Ratified March 3, 1952, approved by U.S. Congress July 3, 1952, effective July 25, 1952	San Juan
Saint Kitts and Nevis	September 19, 1983	Parliamentary democracy	September 19, 1983	Basseterre
Saint Lucia	February 22, 1979	Parliamentary democracy	February 22, 1979	Castries
Saint Vincent and the Grenadines	October 27, 1979	Parliamentary democracy	October 27, 1979	Kingstown
Trinidad and Tobago	August 31, 1962	Parliamentary democracy	August 1, 1976	Port-of-Spain

	Date of Independence	System of Government	Date of Constitution	Capital
U.S. Virgin Islands (St. Thomas, St. John, St. Croix)		Unincorporated territory of the United States	Revised Organic Act of July 22, 1954	Charlotte Amalie

Politics

There are numerous political parties spread throughout the region. The best-known are the Communist Party of Cuba, the Jamaican Labor Party, Martinique Progressive Party, the Dominican Republic's Dominican Revolutionary Party, and Trinidad's People National Movement.

Population

	Population	Official Language	Dominant Religion*
Caribbean	more than 37,000,000 (2006)	Dutch, English, French, Creole, Spanish	Roman Catholic, 90 percent in Hispanic and French islands; Protestant, over 80 percent in the British West Indies
Anguilla	13,677 (2006)	English	Protestant, 80 percent
Antigua and Barbuda	68,722 (2006)	English	Anglican/Protestant
Bahamas	303,611 (2006)	English	Protestant, 64 percent; Anglican 15 percent; Roman Catholic, 12 percent
Barbados	279,254 (2006)	English	Protestant, 67 percent; Roman Catholic, 4 percent
British Virgin Islands (Tortola, Virgin Gorda, Anegada, Jost Van Dyke)	22,016 (2006)	English	Protestant, 87 percent; Roman Catholic, 10 percent

(table continues)

	Population	Official Language	Dominant Religion*
Cuba	11,346,670 (2006)	Spanish	Roman Catholic, 85 percent pre–1959
Dominica	69,029 (2006)	English	Roman Catholic, 77 percent; Protestant 15 percent
Dominican Republic	8,950,034 (2006)	Spanish	Roman Catholic, 95 percent
Grenada	89,502 (2006)	English	Roman Catholic, 53 percent; Anglican, 13 percent; Protestant, 33 percent
Guadeloupe (Basse-Terre, Grande-Terre, La Désirade, Les Saintes, Marie-Galante, St. Martin)	448,713 (2006)	French	Roman Catholic, 95 percent; Hindu and diverse African belief systems, 4 percent; Protestant 1 percent
Haiti	8,121,622 (2006)	French, Creole	Roman Catholic, 80 percent; Protestant, 16 percent; Vodun, 50 percent, including Catholic worshippers
Jamaica	2,731,832 (2006)	English	Protestant, 61 percent; Roman Catholic, 4 percent; other spiritual practices (Rastafarianism, Pocomania), 34 percent
Martinique	432,900 (2006)	French	Roman Catholic, 85 percent; Protestant, 10 percent
Montserrat	9,341 (2006)	English	Anglican/Protestant
Netherland Antilles (Aruba, Bonaire, Curaçao, St. Maarten, Saba, St. Eustatius)	291,000 (2006)	Dutch	Roman Catholic, 72 percent; Protestant, 14 percent
Puerto Rico	3,912,055 (2006)	Spanish	Roman Catholic, 85 percent; Protestant, 15 percent

	Population	Official Language	Dominant Religion*
Saint Kitts and Nevis	38,858 (2006)	English	Roman Catholic, Anglican, Protestant, no estimates
Saint Lucia	166,312 (2006)	English	Roman Catholic, 67 percent; Protestant, 20 percent
Saint Vincent and the Grenadines	177,534 (2006)	English	Anglican, 47 percent; Protestant 20 percent; Roman Catholic, 13 percent
Trinidad and Tobago	1,088,644 (2006)	English	Roman Catholic, 26 percent; Hindu, 22 percent; Protestant, 29 percent; Muslims, 6 percent
U.S. Virgin Islands (St. Thomas, St. John, and St. Croix)	108,708 (2006)	English	Protestant, 60 percent; Roman Catholic, 34 percent

*Besides Catholicism and Protestantism, there are several religions of African origin practiced throughout the Caribbean, although figures are not reported by the local governments. They include Pocomonia and Rastafarianism in Jamaica, Santeria in Cuba, and Vodunism in Haiti.

Ethnic Groups

Highly mixed, the dominant groups are of African, Chinese, European, East Indian, Carib, and Taino descent, with intermarriage a common experience. Thus, there are Caribbeans of African and Chinese descent, and there are Caribbeans of European, African, and Chinese descent. About 75 percent of the Caribbean population reflects these intermarriages, that is, African mixed with either European, Chinese, or Carib. It is estimated that 22 percent of Caribbeans are white, and the remaining percentage reflective of Chinese and East Indian ancestors. The majority of the white population lives in the Hispanic Caribbean, with Cuba accounting for 50 percent of the people of European descent.

Such ethnic diversity produces a diversity of languages spoken in the Caribbean: Chinese, Dutch, English, French, Hindi, Creole, Papiamentu, and Spanish.

Economy

	GDP	Agriculture	Industry	Services	Currency
Caribbean	Over $265 billion (2204–2006, est.)	Bananas, beans, citrus, cocoa, coffee, mangoes, plantains, rice, sugar, tobacco; fish, poultry	Sugar, rum, petroleum processing	Tourism, pharmaceutical, light industry assembling of parts produced elsewhere in the world	Various
Anguilla	$108.9 million (2004, est.)	Tobacco		Tourism	East Caribbean dollar
Antigua and Barbuda	$750 million (2002 est.)	Cotton, bananas, coconuts, cucumbers, mangoes, sugar, vegetables		Tourism	East Caribbean dollar
Bahamas	$6.476 billion (2006 est.)	Citrus, vegetables, poultry	Cement, salt, rum, aragonite	Tourism, banking, pharmaceuticals, oil transshipment	Bahamian dollar
Barbados	$5.108 billion (2006 est.)	Sugarcane, vegetables, cotton	Sugar	Tourism, light manufacturing	Barbadian dollar
British Virgin Islands (Tortola, Virgin Gorda, Anegada, Jost Van Dyke)	$853.4 million (2004 est.)	Fruits, vegetables; livestock, poultry, fish		Tourism, light manufacturing, construction	U.S. dollar
Cuba	$44.54 billion (2006 est.)	Sugar, tobacco, citrus, coffee, rice, potatoes, beans, livestock	Sugar processing and refining, petroleum, tobacco	Pharmaceuticals, tourism	Cuban peso and convertible peso

	GDP	Agriculture	Industry	Services	Currency
Dominica	$384 million (2003 est.)	Bananas, citrus, mangoes, root crops, coconuts, cocoa	Soap, coconut oil, copra, furniture, cement blocks, shoes	Tourism	East Caribbean dollar
Dominican Republic	$73.74 billion (2006 est.)	Sugar, coffee, cotton, cocoa, tobacco, rice, beans, potatoes, corn, bananas, cattle, pigs, dairy products, beef, eggs	Sugar processing and refining, tobacco	Tourism	Dominican peso
Grenada	$440 million (2002 est.)	Bananas, cocoa, nutmeg, mace, citrus, avocados, root crops, sugarcane, corn, vegetables	Food and beverages, textiles, construction	Tourism, light assembly operations	East Caribbean dollar
Guadeloupe (Basse-Terre, Grande-Terre, La Désirade, Les Saintes, Marie-Galante, St. Martin)	$3.513 billion (2003 est.)	Bananas, sugarcane, tropical fruits and vegetables, cattle, pigs, goats	Construction, cement, rum, sugar	Tourism	Euro
Haiti	$14.56 billion (2006 est.)	Coffee, mangoes, sugarcane, rice, corn, sorghum, wood	Sugar refining, flour milling	Light assembly based on imported parts	Gourde
Jamaica	$12.71 billion (2006 est.)	Sugarcane, bananas, coffee, citrus, yams, ackees, vegetables, poultry, goats, milk; crustaceans, mollusks	Bauxite/alumina, rum	Tourism, telecommunications	Jamaican dollar
Martinique	$6.117 billion (2003 est.)	Pineapples, avocados, bananas, flowers, vegetables, sugarcane	Rum, construction, cement, oil refining, sugar, tourism	Tourism	Euro

(table continues)

	GDP	Agriculture	Industry	Services	Currency
Montserrat	$29 million (2002 est.)	Cabbages, carrots, cucumbers, tomatoes, onions, peppers, livestock products	Rum	Tourism, electronic appliances	East Caribbean dollar
Netherland Antilles (Aruba, Bonaire, Curaçao, St. Maarten, Saba, St. Eustatius)	$2.8 billion (2004 est.)	Aloes, sorghum, peanuts, vegetables, tropical fruit	Petroleum refining, light manufacturing	Tourism, petroleum transshipment facilities	Netherlands Antillean guilder
Puerto Rico	$74.89 billion (2006 est.)	Sugarcane, coffee, pineapples, plantains, bananas, livestock products, chickens	Electronics, apparel, food products	Tourism, pharmaceuticals	U.S. dollar
Saint Kitts and Nevis	$339 million (2002 est.)	Sugarcane, rice, yams, vegetables, bananas, fish	Sugar processing, cotton, salt, copra	Tourism	East Caribbean dollar
Saint Lucia	$866 million (2002 est.)	Bananas, coconuts, vegetables, citrus, root crops, cocoa	Clothing, beverages, corrugated cardboard boxes, lime processing, coconut processing	Tourism, assembly of electronic components	East Caribbean dollar
Saint Vincent and the Grenadines	$342 million (2002 est.)	Bananas, coconuts, sweet potatoes, spices, cattle, sheep, pigs, goats, fish	Food processing, cement, furniture		East Caribbean dollar
Trinidad and Tobago	$20.99 billion (2006 est.)	Cocoa, rice, citrus, coffee, vegetables, poultry	Food processing, cement, beverage, cotton textiles, petroleum, chemicals	Tourism	Trinidad and Tobago dollar

	GDP	Agriculture	Industry	Services	Currency
U.S. Virgin Islands (St. Thomas, St. John, St. Croix)	$1.577 billion (2004 est.)	Fruit, vegetables, sorghum, Senepol cattle	Petroleum refining, rum distilling, construction	Tourism, pharmaceuticals	U.S. dollar

APPENDIX 3

CHRONOLOGY

Pre-Columbian Inhabitants

Circa 500 B.C.E.	Tainos arrive in the Caribbean
Circa 100 C.E.	Caribs reach the islands

Two Worlds in Collision: The Spanish Conquest

1451	Christopher Columbus born in Genoa, Italy
1453	Ottoman Empire blocks route to Asia, forcing Europeans to find new routes
1469	Isabella of Castile and Ferdinand of Aragon marry, begin unifying Spain
1492	Isabella and Ferdinand agree to support Columbus's plans to reach Asia by sailing west
	Columbus reaches Caribbean on October 12
1493	second voyage of Columbus
1494	Treaty of Tordesillas draws an imaginary line at 46° 37', assigns new lands west of the line to Spain, new lands east of the line to Portugal
1498	third voyage of Columbus
1499	*encomienda* system introduced in the Caribbean: indigenous population is forced to work for the colonizers
1500	Columbus sent back to Spain in chains
1502	Santo Domingo the first European-chartered city in the Americas
	Nicolás de Ovando, first governor in the Caribbean, arrives in Hispaniola
1502–1504	fourth and final voyage of Columbus
1502	Hispaniola colonized

1503	la Casa de Contratación (House of Contracts) created to oversee business transactions in New World
1505	first African slaves shipped to Caribbean
1506	Columbus dies in Spain
1508	Puerto Rico colonized
1509	Jamaica colonized
1511	Cuba colonized
1511–1512	Chieftain Hatuey burned at the stake
1515	Spanish king names Bartolomé de Las Casas "The Protector of the Indians"
1518	slaves shipped directly from Africa to the Caribbean
1520–1530	sugarcane planting and cutting begins in Puerto Rico and Jamaica
1533	Taino chief Enriquillo granted pardon by Emperor Charles V (King Charles I of Spain)
1535	Viceroyalties created to govern Spanish possessions in the Americas
1550	*encomienda* system abolished
1552	Bartolomé de Las Casas publishes *Brevísima relación de la destrucción de las Indias* (*Brief Account of the Destruction of the Indies*)

Colonization and Rebellion

1560s	Jean Nicot introduces tobacco to Parisian society, names the leaf *Nicotiana Tabacum*
1564	Spanish admiral massacres 200 Frenchmen near present-day Saint Augustine
1580	Spain institutes the *asiento,* a formal licensing agreement for importing slaves
1585–1586	Francis Drake loots Santo Domingo
1585–1598	King Philip II of Spain and colonial governors build fortresses to protect Caribbean cities; some of the construction continued for another century and a half
1600s	tobacco cultivation spreads in Cuba
1624	British colonize Bermudas
1627–1635	French settle St. Kitts, take possession of Guadeloupe

1631	Dutch take over southern part of Sint Maarten
1640s	sugarcane plantations become important sources of income for colonists
1648	Spanish leave Sint Maarten to Dutch
1655	British invade Jamaica
	French gain possession of St. Croix
1660s	Barbados exports about 28 million pounds of sugar a year
1675	rebellion in Barbados
1685	Black Code enacted in France
1692	slave revolt in Barbados
1697	France acquires Saint-Domingue, which becomes French side of Hispaniola
1717	Real Factoría de Tabacos established to purchase all tobacco produced in Cuba
1723	tobacco growers in Cuba rebel against Spanish monopoly of tobacco industry; many tobacco growers relocate to Vuelta Abajo (present-day Pinar del Río)
1739	governor of Jamaica signs a truce with the Maroons
1739	the War of Jenkins' Ear
1740	James Oglethorpe, governor of Georgia, attacks St. Augustine, Florida
1742	Spanish soldiers attack the governor of Georgia, James Oglethorpe, but are defeated
1743	birth of Toussaint Louverture
1750s	Saint-Domingue produces 61,000 tons of sugar a year
1758	Maroon leader Mackandal captured, burned at the stake in Haiti
1759	Great Britain captures the island of Guadeloupe
1762	Great Britain captures the island of Martinique, invades Havana
1763	British take Grenada from France
	British occupation of Cuba ends with the signing of the Treaty of Paris
1776	the American Revolution
1779	Bernardo de Gálvez, Spanish governor of Louisiana, leads expeditions against the British along the Mississippi River and in Florida

1779–1780	British and French battle each other in the Caribbean Sea
1782	British defeat the French in the Battle of the Saints off the island of Dominica
	Spanish and French abandon designs for invasion of Jamaica
1783	independence of the North American colonies creates new market for Caribbean goods
1787	*The Interesting Narratives of the Life of Olaudah Equiano, or Gustavus Vassa, The African, written by himself,* by Olaudah Equiano, is published
	Society for Effecting the Abolition of the Slave Trade founded in England
1788	Societé des Amis des Noirs founded in Paris
1789	French Revolution begins in Paris
	salt becomes the major industry of St. Martin
1790	rebellion in Haiti led by Vincent Ogé; Ogé is captured, executed by French planters
1791	in Paris the French king is removed from power
	governors of Guadeloupe and Martinique declare support for monarchy
	Haitian Revolution
	slaves in Guadeloupe rebel
	Toussaint Louverture defeats the French, Spanish, and British
1792	king and queen of France are executed
1793	second war between the British and the Maroons in Jamaica
1794	French National Assembly in Paris abolishes slavery
	British troops invade Guadeloupe, Martinique, and St. Lucia
	French commander Victor Hugues forces the British out of Guadeloupe
1795	Spain gives Hispaniola to France under the Treaty of Basilia
	Fedon's Rebellion in Grenada
	slavery abandoned in St. Martin
1801	Toussaint Louverture invades the Spanish side of Hispaniola and abolishes slavery all over the island

1802	France reestablishes slavery
	Napoléon Bonaparte sends troops to remove Louverture from power and reestablish slavery
	Louverture is arrested and sent to Europe
1803	Jean-Jacques Dessalines defeats the French and proclaims Saint-Domingue a free republic, naming the new nation Haiti
	Toussaint Louverture dies in prison in France
1804	Haiti declares independence
	Jean-Jacques Dessalines proclaims himself Emperor Jacques I of Haiti
	United States bans trade with Haiti
1806	Jean-Jacques Dessalines is assassinated in Haiti
	Republic of Haiti is divided; Henry Christophe declares himself king of Northern Haiti (from 1811) and Alexander Pétion rules in the south (from 1806)
1807	British laws end the slave trade
1808	Napoléon Bonaparte invades Spain
1810–1811	slave rebellion in Cuba
1811	Venezuela declares its independence from Spain
1813	Spanish defeat the French invaders; the first Spanish Constitution
1816	Easter Rebellion in Barbados
1818	Alexandre Pétion dies
	Jean-Pierre Boyer becomes president of south of Haiti
1819	Colombia declares independence from Spain
1820	Jean-Pierre Boyer unites Haiti, annexes Spanish side of island of Hispaniola
1821	Peru declares independence from Spain
	Guatemala, Nicaragua, Honduras, Costa Rica, and El Salvador declare independence, establish the United Provinces of Central America in 1822
1822	Ecuador and Mexico declare independence from Spain
	slavery abolished in the Dominican Republic
1822–1844	Haiti occupies Spanish side of Hispaniola
1823	Anti-Slavery Society founded in Great Britain

1824	Simón Bolívar defeats Spanish forces in South America
1825	Barbados passes Consolidation Law increasing rights of slaves
1826	*Jicoténcal,* first Latin-American novel written and published in the United States
1831	slave insurrection in Jamaica; 300 insurrectionists hanged
1832	Emancipation Act ends slavery in all British possessions
1833	memoir of Mary Prince, *The History of Mary Prince, a West Indian Slave, Related by Herself,* is published
1838	pro-independence society La Trinitaria founded in Santo Domingo
1839	the *Amistad* incident
	antislavery novel *Francisco: el ingenio o las delicias del campo,* by Anselmo Suárez y Romero, published in Cuba
1844	Manifestación de la Parte Este, claiming independence from Haiti, signed in the Dominican Republic
1845	first East Indian laborers arrive in Trinidad
1848	slavery abolished in St. Martin
1860	abolitionist society Sociedad Abolicionista Español founded in Spain
1861	Dominican president invites Spain to annex the republic; the annexation plunges the country into civil war
1862	President Abraham Lincoln recognizes Haiti as sovereign nation
1865	Morant Bay Rebellion in Jamaica
	Spain withdraws from Dominican Republic
1867	antislavery drama *La cuarterona,* by Alejandro Tapia y Rivera, is staged in Puerto Rico; antislavery manifesto *Proyecto para la abolición de la esclavitud en Puerto Rico* is published
1873	Puerto Rico abolishes slavery
1886	Spanish government bans slavery in Cuba

Puerto Rico, Cuba, and the Spanish-Cuban-American War

1848	*libreta* system instituted in Puerto Rico
1851	General Narciso López makes a second unsuccessful attempt to seize Cuba; is captured and executed
1868	rebellion in Puerto Rico, known as El Grito de Lares
	rebellion in Cuba, known as El Grito de Yara
1873	Puerto Rico abolishes slavery
1877	General Arsenio Martínez Campos sent to Cuba; Martínez Campos captures president of the Cuban republic at arms, Tomás Estrada Palma; begins truce negotiations
1878	truce signed in Cuba between Spanish forces and Cuban insurgents
	Puerto Rico allowed certain level of self-rule
1881	Cuban doctor Carlos J. Finlay presents findings that yellow fever is transmitted by mosquitoes
1886	Spanish government bans slavery in Cuba
1891	José Martí raises funds among Cuban cigar workers in Florida
1892	Partido Revolucionario Cubano (Cuban Revolutionary Party) founded
1895	José Martí authorizes war against Spanish in Cuba; Martí is killed on May 19
1897	William Randolph Hearst publicizes the case of jailed Cuban patriot Evangelina Cisneros
	Puerto Rico granted autonomy by the Spanish
1898	U.S. battleship *Maine* explodes in Havana harbor; United States declares war on Spain; Treaty of Paris gives the United States control of Cuba, the Philippines, and Puerto Rico
1901	Cuban Constitution approved; Platt Amendment allows for American military intervention when deemed necessary by Americans; United States establishes naval base in Guantanamo, Cuba
1902	Tomás Estrada Palma elected first president of Cuba; U.S. occupation ends

The 20th Century

1900	the Foraker Act institutes U.S.-run government in Puerto Rico
	U.S. doctor Walter Reed proves that yellow fever is transmitted by mosquitoes
1905	Dominican Republic agrees to let United States administer Customs House
1912	"the race war" in Cuba; U.S. Marines fighting alongside Cuban soldiers, under the command of white Cuban officers, massacre nearly 3,000 men, mostly Afro-Cubans
1914	Universal Negro Improvement Association (UNIA) founded in Jamaica
1915	Haitian president Vilbrun Guillaume Sam assassinated; Haiti occupied by U.S. Marines
1916	United States occupies the Dominican Republic
1917	the Jones Act gives American citizenship to Puerto Ricans
1918	the Caco War in Haiti
1919	Marcus Garvey creates Black Star shipping line
1922	United States and Dominican Republic agree to plan for evacuation of American forces from the Dominican Republic
1924	Horacio Vásquez elected president of Dominican Republic; U.S. troops withdraw, ending occupation
1930	Pedro Albizu Campos elected president of Nationalist Party in Puerto Rico
	Rafael Trujillo elected president of the Dominican Republic
1931	Luis Muñoz Marín elected to Puerto Rican Senate
1933	urban warfare campaign in Cuba against dictator Gerardo Machado; Machado forced to leave office
	Carlos Manuel de Céspedes y Quesada becomes president of Cuba
	Carlos Manuel de Céspedes y Quesada overthrown by Fulgencio Batista
1935	confrontation between police and protesters on Río Piedras campus of the University of Puerto Rico results in the deaths of four nationalists

1936	February: Puerto Rican nationalists kill an American colonel in Puerto Rico
	March: the Ponce Massacre in Puerto Rico leaves 19 dead, more than 100 wounded; perceived as the architect of the protests and marches, Pedro Albizu Campos is arrested and sentenced to prison
1937	Netherlands allows Aruba, Bonaire, Curaçao, Saba, Saint Eustatius, and Sint Maarten to create a Staaten, or parliament
	October: Rafael Trujillo orders the genocide of thousands of Haitians in the Dominican Republic
1938	labor disputes in Jamaica lead to riots
	Luis Muñoz Marín founds the Popular Democratic Party in Puerto Rico
	May: labor disputes in Jamaica leave eight people dead, 171 wounded; nearly 700 strikers are arrested
1939	Alexander Bustamante unites Jamaica's unions in the Bustamante Industrial Trade Union (BITU)
	Martinican Aimé Césaire coins the term *négritude* in the poem *Cahier d'un retour au pays natal*
1940	in Dominican Republic, Rafael Trujillo regains control from the United States of the Customs House
	new constitution drafted in Cuba; former army sergeant Fulgencio Batista is elected president
1940s	Jamaican leaders lobby Britain for self-rule
	United States establishes naval base in Vieques, off the coast of Puerto Rico
1944	Fulgencio Batista retires from the presidency in Cuba
	universal suffrage is granted to Jamaicans; a Jamaican Constitution is approved; Alexander Bustamante is elected minister of communication in Jamaica
1945	Aimé Césaire is elected mayor of Fort-de-France, Martinique, and representative to the French National Assembly
1946	Martinique and Guadeloupe become overseas departments of France

1947	Puerto Ricans are allowed to vote for their own governor rather than having one appointed by Washington
1948	Luis Muñoz Marín is elected the first Puerto Rican governor of the island
1950	following nationalist attacks, the United States declares martial law in Puerto Rico
	November 1: Puerto Rican nationalists attack the home where U.S. President Truman is staying in an attempt to assassinate him
1951	Grenada is virtually given self-government by Great Britain by allowing the island to manage its domestic affairs and local politics
1952	March 10: Fulgencio Batista ousts democratically elected president Carlos Prío Socarrá
1953	July 26: Fidel Castro leads an attack on the Moncada Fortress in Santiago; most of the participants are killed
1954	Puerto Rican nationalists wound five congressmen in an attack on the U.S. Capitol
1955	Fidel Castro granted amnesty, travels to Mexico
	Norman Manley elected chief minister in Jamaica
	Eric Williams elected chief minister of Trinidad and Tobago
1956	Fidel Castro returns to Cuba
1957	François Duvalier elected president of Haiti
1958	West Indian Federation unites anglophone islands of the Caribbean (Jamaica, Trinidad and Tobago, Cayman Islands, Bahamas, Antigua and Barbuda, St. Kitts-Nevis-Anguilla, Montserrat, Dominica, St. Lucia, St. Vincent and the Grenadines, Grenada, Barbados)
1959	Fidel Castro marches into Havana
	François Duvalier establishes Tonton Macoutes, secret police, to suppress dissent
1959–1965	200,000 Cubans seek asylum in the United States
1960	Rafael Trujillo orders murder of the Mirabal sisters—Minerva, Patria, Maria Teresa—who become legendary for courage, martyrdom

1961	Rafael Trujillo assassinated in the Dominican Republic; brief regime led by dictator's son Ramfis Trujillo; civil council formed under Joaquin Balaguer
	the Bay of Pigs incident in Cuba
1962	Jamaica and Trinidad independent
	West Indian Federation disbanded
	Juan Bosch wins presidency in Dominican Republic
	the October Crisis in Cuba
	Operación Pedro Pan begins in Cuba
1963	Juan Bosch ousted by junta in Dominican Republic
1964	Pedro Albizu Campos pardoned in Puerto Rico
1965	Che Guevara disappears from Cuba
	civil war in Dominican Republic; U.S. Marines intervene
1967	Che Guevara captured and executed by Bolivian forces
1968	Walter Rodney denied entry into Jamaica
1970	Black Power Revolution in Trinidad
1971	François Duvalier dies; his son Jean-Claude assumes control in Haiti
1972	Michael Manley elected prime minister in Jamaica
1974	Grenada independent from Great Britain
1976	Communist Party, led by Fidel Castro, runs government in Cuba
1979	Maurice Bishop overthrows Eric Gairy in Grenada
1980	New Jewel Movement implements reforms in housing, education, and health care in Grenada
	Mariel Boatlift brings thousands of Cubans to United States
1983	Maurice Bishop assassinated in Grenada; U.S. government authorizes invasion of island
	Pope John Paul II allowed to visit Haiti; press, others criticize Duvalier regime
	in Canada the government publishes the report *Equality Now,* which makes recommendations to end institutional racism in education, employ-

ment, the legal system, and the media; a year later a trust of $5 million is established to combat racism targeted at West Indians.

in Quebec, a group of Haitian taxi drivers reports that they are underpaid and bring a successful lawsuit against their employers

1984	riots in cities in Dominican Republic
1986	United States asks Jean-Claude Duvalier to resign in Haiti; Duvalier seeks asylum in France
1990	Father Jean-Bertrand Aristide elected president of Haiti; Aristide is ousted, seeks asylum in United States
1990	Jamaat Al Muslimeen members kidnap prime minister A. N. R. Robinson of Trinidad
1991	downfall of Soviet bloc plunges Cuba into economic crisis known as the Special Period
1994	Aristide returns to the presidency of Haiti
	youth riots in Havana
	balseros (rafters) flee Cuba for United States
1995	Basdeo Panday elected prime minister in Trinidad
1996	Joaquín Balaguer retires from presidency of Dominican Republic
1998	in a referendum in Puerto Rico, 46.4 percent of the voters reject statehood while 50.2 percent reject all presented options: statehood, independence, and commonwealth

The 21st Century: Immigration and Uncertainties

2000	Jean-Bertrand Aristide elected president in Haiti amid claims of fraud
2000s	tourists visiting the Caribbean islands increase from 9 million in the 1980s to more than 2 billion in 2005
2002	reform requests of Proyecto Varela rejected by Cuban government
2003	U.S. Navy withdraws base from island of Vieques, off the coast of Puerto Rico
2004	at U.S. urging, Jean-Bertrand Aristide resigns as president of Haiti and travels to Africa
2006–2007	Fidel Castro's illness causes uncertainty in Cuba

2007   St. Martin and Saint Barthélemy break from Gua-
                daloupe, administered directly by France as sepa-
                rate overseas departments
                Hurricane Dean results in 12 deaths across the
                Caribbean and destroys nearly the entire banana
                crop in Dominica, Martinique, and Guadeloupe
                and 70 percent of the sugarcane plantations on
                Martinique; also extensively damages St. Lucia
                and Jamaica

APPENDIX 4

BIBLIOGRAPHY

Acevedo, Ramón Luis. *Pachín Marín: poeta en libertad*. San Juan: Instituto de Cultura Puertorriqueña, Cuadernos de Cultura, No. 4, 2001.

Acevedo-Vila, Aníbal. "Rethinking the Future of the U.S.–Puerto Rico Relationship: Towards the 21st Century." In *Taking Sides: Clashing Views on Latin American Issues*. Dubuque, Iowa: McGraw Hill, 2007.

Acosta, Ivonne. *El grito de Vieques y otros ensayos históricos (1990–1999)*. San Juan, P.R.: Editorial Cultural, 2002.

Albizu Campos, Pedro. *Pedro Albizu Campos: obras escogidas*. Edited by J. Benjamin Torres. San Juan, P.R.: Editorial Jelofe, distribuido por Ediciones Puerto Rico, 1975, 1981.

Algarín, Miguel, and Holman, Bob. *Aloud: Voices from the Nuyorican Poets Café*. New York: H. Holt, 1994.

Appel, John C. "The Unionization of Florida Cigarmakers and the Coming of the War with Spain." *Hispanic American Historical Review* Feb. 1956: 36–49.

Appiah, Kwame Anthony, and Gates, Henry Louis, Jr., eds. *Africana: The Encyclopedia of the African and African American Experience*. New York: Basic Civitas Books, 1999.

Argote-Freyre, Frank. *Fulgencio Batista: From Revolutionary to Strongman*. New Brunswick, N.J.: Rutgers University Press, 2006.

Arpini, Adriana. *Eugenio María de Hostos, un hacedor de la libertad*. Mendoza, Argentina: Editorial de la Universidad Nacional de Cuyo, 2002.

Báez, Víctor, ed. *La Gran Enciclopedia de Puerto Rico*. San Juan: Puerto Rico en la Mano and La Gran Enciclopedia de Puerto Rico, 1981.

Banks, Kenneth J. *Chasing Empire across the Sea: Communications and the State in the French Atlantic. 1713–1763*. Montreal and Ithaca, N.Y.: McGill-Queen's University Press, 2002.

Barnes, Albert. *An Inquiry into the Scriptural Views of Slavery.* New York: Negro Universities Press, 1857, 1969.

Bellegarde-Smith, Patrick. *Haiti: The Breached Citadel.* Boulder, Colo.: Westview Press, 1990.

Berrian, Albert H., and Long, Richard A., eds. *Négritude: Essays and Studies.* Hampton, Va.: Hampton Institute Press, 1967.

Bishop, Maurice. *Forward Ever! Three Years of the Grenadian Revolution: Speeches of Maurice Bishop.* Sydney and New York: Pathfinder Press, 1982.

Boodhoo, Ken I. *The Elusive Eric Williams.* Kingston, Jamaica: I. Randle, 2001.

Burton, David H. *Theodore Roosevelt: Confident Imperialist.* Philadelphia: University of Philadelphia Press, 1968.

Bush, Barbara. *Slave Women in Caribbean Society, 1650–1838.* Kingston, Jamaica and Bloomington, Ind.: Heinemman Publishers and Indiana University Press, 1990.

Butts, Ellen, and Schwartz, Joyce R. *Fidel Castro.* Minneapolis: Lerner Publications Co., 2005.

Cabeza de Vaca, Álvar Núñez. *The Account: Álvar Núñez Cabeza de Vaca's Relación.* Houston, Tex.: Arte Público Press, 1993.

Cabezas, Amelia. "Between Love and Money: Sex Tourism and Citizenship in Cuba and the Dominican Republic." *Signs: Journal of Women in Culture and Society.* 29, no. 4 (Summer 2004). Available online: URL: www.caribbeannetnews.com/cgi-script/csArticles/articles/000045/004588.html. Accessed on December 9, 2006.

Cancel, Mario R. *Segundo Ruíz Belvis: el procer y el ser humano (una aproximación crítica a su vida).* Bayamón, Editorial Universidad de América; San Juan: Centro de Estudios Avanzados de Puerto Rico y el Caribe; Hormigueros, Municipio de Hormigueros, 1994.

Cardona, Luis Antonio. *A History of the Puerto Ricans in the United States of America.* Bethesda, Md.: Carreta Press, 1995.

Carpentier, Alejo. *El reino de este mundo.* Mexico City: Edíción y Distribución Ibero Americana de Publicaciones, 1949.

———. *El siglo de las luces.* Barcelona: Bruguera, 1979.

Casablanca, Marie-Jean. *L'émigration corse á Porto Rico.* Paris: Le Signet, 1993.

Césaire, Aimé. *Cahier d'un retour au pays natal.* Paris: Présence Africaine, 1951.

Césaire, Aimé. *Notebook of a Return to My Native Land/Cahier d'un retour au pays natal.* Translated by Mireille Rosello with Annie Pritchard. Newcastle upon Tyne: Bloodaxe Books, 1995.

Céspedes, Carlos Manuel de. *Pasión por Cuba y por la iglesia: aproximación biográfica al P. Félix Varela.* Madrid: Biblioteca de Autores Cristianos, 1998.

Chasteen, John Charles. *Born in Blood and Fire.* New York and London: W. W. Norton & Company, 2001.

Chronicle of the French Revolution, 1788—1799. London: Chronicle Publications; New York: Prentice Hall, 1989.

Coleman, Loren, and Clark, Jerome. *Cryptozoology A to Z.* New York: Fireside, 1999.

Collier, Simon. *From Cortes to Castro: An Introduction to the History of Latin America, 1492–1973.* New York: Macmillan Publishing, 1974.

Comisión Económica Para América Latina y el Caribe. *La crisis urbana en America Latina y el Caribe: Reflexiones sobre alternativas de solución.* Santiago, Chile: Naciones Unidas, 1989.

Connolly, Sean. *Castro.* London: Hodder & Stoughton, 2002.

Corretjer, Juan Antonio. "The Day Puerto Rico Became a Nation." In *The Puerto Ricans: A Documentary History,* edited by Kal Wagenheim and Olga Wagenheim. Princeton, N.J.: Marcus Weiners, 1994, 2002.

Cortés, Eladio, and Barrea-Marlys, Mirta. *Encyclopedia of Latin America Theater.* Westport, Conn., and London: Greenwood Press, 2003.

Cotman, John Walton. *The Gorrion Tree: Cuba and the Grenada Revolution.* New York: P. Lang, 1993.

Crasweller, Robert D. *The Caribbean Community: Changing Societies and U.S. Policy.* New York and Washington: Praeger Publishers, 1972.

———. *Trujillo: The Life and Times of a Caribbean Dictator.* New York: Macmillan, 1966.

Cuevas Zequeira, Sergio. *Manuel de Zequeira y Arango y los albores de la cultura cubana.* Habana, Cuba: Tipografía Moderna de A. Dombecker, 1923.

Cundall, Frank. *Historic Jamaica.* London: The Institute of Jamaica, 1915.

Dana, Richard. "Havana, 1859." In *The Reader's Companion to Cuba,* edited by Alan Ryan, 1–26. San Diego, New York and London: Harcourt Brace Co, 1997.

Dash, J. Michael. *Culture and Customs of Haiti.* Westport, Conn.: Greenwood Press, 2001.

Dayan, Joan. *Haiti, History, and the Gods.* Berkeley, Los Angeles and London: University of California Press, 1995.

Dent, David W. *The Legacy of the Monroe Doctrine: A Reference Guide to U.S. Involvement in Latin America and the Caribbean.* Westport, Conn.: Greenwood Press, 1999.

Diederich, Bernard. *Papa Doc: Haiti and Its Dictator.* New York: Harmondsworth, Penguin, 1972.

Domínguez, Jaime de Jesús. *Historia dominicana.* Santo Domingo, República Dominicana: ABC Editorial, 2001.

Dominican Migration: Transnational Perspectives. Edited by Ernesto Sagas and Sintia Molina. Gainesville: University of Florida, 2004.

Dubois, Laurent. *A Colony of Citizens: Revolution and Slave Emancipation in the French Caribbean, 1787–1804.* Chapel Hill, N.C.: published for the Omohundro Institute of Early American History and Culture, Williamsburg, Va., by the University of North Carolina Press, 2004.

Dupuy, R. Ernest, et al. *The American Revolution: A Global War.* New York: David McKay Company, 1977.

Enciclopedia Ilustrada de la Republica Dominicana. Santo Domingo, Republica Dominicana: Eduprogreso, S.A., 2003.

Equiano, Olaudah. *The Interesting Narratives of the Life of Olaudah Equiano, or Gustavus Vassa, The African, written by himself, 1789.* London: Dawson of Pall Mall, 1969.

Ethnicities: Children of Immigrants in America. Edited by Ruben G. Rumbaut and Alejandro Portes. Berkeley: University of California Press, 2001.

Facio, Alda. "Trafficking in Women and Children for the Sex Trade: Reflections from a Latin American Human Rights Feminist." *Canadian Woman Studies* 22, 3/4 (Spring/Summer 2003): 136.

Fagg, John Edwin. *Cuba, Haiti & the Dominican Republic.* Englewood Cliffs, N.J.: Prentice Hall, 1965.

Falola, Toyin. *Key Events in African History. A Reference Guide.* Westport, Conn.: Greenwood Press, 2002.

Fanon, Frantz. *Toward the African Revolution.* Translated by Haakon Chevalier. New York: Grove Press, 1969.

Fernandez, Ronald, et al., eds. *Puerto Rico: Past and Present; an Encyclopedia.* Westport, Conn.: Greenwood, 1998.

Fernández Méndez, Eugenio. *Luis Muñoz Rivera, hombre visible.* San Juan, P.R.: P. Biblioteca de Autores Puertorriqueños, 1982.

Ferrao, Luis Angel. *Pedro Albizu Campos y el nacionalismo puertorriqueño.* San Juan, P.R.: Editorial Cultural, 1990.

Ferrer Canales, José. *Martí y Hostos.* Río Piedras: Instituto de Estudios Hostosianos, Universidad de Puerto Rico, San Juan: Centro de Estudios Avanzados de Puerto Rico y el Caribe, 1990.

Foner, Nancy. *Jamaica Farewell: Jamaican Migrants in London.* Berkeley and Los Angeles: University of California Press, 1978.

Foner, Philip S. *A History of Cuba and its Relations with the United States.* Vol. 1. New York: International Publishers, 1962.

Franklin, Jane. *The Cuban Revolution and the United States. A Chronological History.* Melbourne, Australia, and New York: Ocean Press/Center for Cuban Studies. 1992.

Fuente, Alejandro de la. *A Nation for All: Race, Inequality, and Politics in Twentieth-Century Cuba.* Chapel Hill: University of North Carolina Press, 2001.

Fuentes, Carlos. *The Buried Mirror: Reflections on Spain and the New World.* New York: Houghton Mifflin, 1992.

Galván, Manuel de Jesús. *Enriquillo: leyenda histórica dominicana, 1503–1533.* Santo Domingo: Ediciones de la Fundación Corripio, 1990.

Gerónimo, Joaquín. *En el nombre de Bosch.* Santo Domingo, República Dominicana: Editora Alfa Omega, 2001.

Goldberg, Mark. "Primeval Minefield." *The American Prospect* 15, 11 (Nov. 24, 2003).

González López, Emilio. *Historia de la civilización Española.* New York: Las Americas Publishing, 1970.

Grenier, Guillermo J. and Lisandro Perez. *The Legacy of Exile: Cubans in the United States.* Boston: Allyn and Bacon, 2003.

Hakluyt, Richard. In *Readings in Caribbean History and Economics,* edited by Roberta Marx Nelson. New York: Gordon and Breach Science Publishers, 1981.

Harney, Stefano. *Nationalism and Identity: Culture and the Imagination in a Caribbean Diaspora.* Kingston, Jamaica: University of the West Indies, 1996.

Hart, Stephen, and Young, Richard. *Contemporary Latin American Cultural Studies.* London: Arnold, 2003.

Haviser, Jay B. *Amerindian Cultural Geography on Curaçao.* Leiden, Netherlands: Rijksuniversiteit te Leiden, 1987.

———. *In Search of St. Martin's Ancient Peoples: Prehistoric Archaeology.* Philipsburg, St. Martin: House of Nehesi, 1995.

Hernández, Ramona, et al. *Dominican New Yorkers: A Socioeconomic Profile.* New York: CUNY Dominican Studies Institute, Dominican Research Monograph Series, 1995.

Hernández González, Heriberto. *Félix Varela: retorno y presencia.* Habana, Cuba: Imagen Contemporánea, 1997.

Iglesias, César Andreu. "The Conscience of the People." In *The Puerto Ricans: A Documentary History,* edited by Kal Wagenheim and Olga Jiménez de Wagenheim. New York: Praeger Publishers, 1973.

James, C. R. L. *The Black Jacobins: Toussaint L'Ouverture and the San Domingo Revolution.* New York: Vintage Books, 1963, 1989.

January, Brendan. *Fidel Castro: Cuban Revolutionary.* New York: Franklin Watts, 2003.

Jarrett-Macauley, Delia. *The Life of Una Marson: 1905 to 65.* Manchester and New York: University Press, 1998.

Kaplan, Irving, et al. *Area Handbook for Jamaica.* Washington, D.C.: U.S. Government Printing Office, 1975.

Kempadoo, Kamala. "Freelancers, Temporary Wives, and Beach-Boys: Researching Sex Work in the Caribbean." *Feminist Review* (London) 67, no. 1 (Spring 2001): 39–62.

King, John, ed. *The Cambridge Companion to Modern Latin American Culture.* Cambridge and New York: Cambridge University Press, 2004.

Klein, Herbert S. *African Slavery in Latin America and the Caribbean.* Oxford and New York: Oxford University Press, 1986.

Knight, Franklin W. *The Caribbean, the Genesis of a Fragmented Nationalism.* New York: Oxford University Press, 1978.

Knight, Franklin W. *The Caribbean, the Genesis of a Fragmented Nationalism.* 2nd ed. New York: Oxford University Press, 1990.

Koslow, Philip. *Centuries of Greatness: The West African Kingdoms, 1750–1900.* New York and Philadelphia: Chelsea House Publishers, 1995.

Kullen, Allan S., comp. *The Peopling of America: A Timeline of Events That Helped Shape Our Nation.* Beltsville, Md.: Americans All, 1992.

Laguerre, Michel S. *American Odyssey: Haitians in New York City.* Ithaca, N.Y., and London: Cornell University Press, 1984.

Lai, Walton. "Chinese Indentured Labor Migrations to the British West Indies in the 19th Century." In *Caribbean Asians: Chinese, Indian, and Japanese Experiences in Trinidad and the Dominican Republic,* edited by Roger Sanjek. Flushing, N.Y.: Asian/American Center at Queens College, CUNY, 1990.

Lal, Deepak. *In Praise of Empires: Globalization and Order.* New York: Palgrave Macmillan, 2004.

Lapointe, Michelle. "Diasporas in Caribbean Development: Rapporteur's Report." Report of the Inter-American Dialogue and World Bank, August 2004.

Latinos: Remaking America. Edited by Marcelo M. Suarez-Orozco and Mariela M. Paez. Berkeley: University of California Press, 2002.

"Leaders: Whose Coup in Haiti? *The Economist* (London) 370, no. 8365 (March 6, 2004): 13.

Leonard, Thomas M. *Fidel Castro: A Biography.* Westport, Conn.: Greenwood Press, 2004.

Levi, Darrell E. *Michael Manley: The Making of a Leader.* Athens: University of Georgia Press, 1989.

Lockwood, Lee. *Castro's Cuba: Cuba's Fidel—An American Journalist's Inside Look at Today's Cuba in Text and Picture.* New York: Macmillan, 1967.

Lundberg, Ferdinand. *Imperial Hearst: A Social Biography.* New York: Equinox Cooperative Press, 1936.

Manley, Edna. *Edna Manley: The Diaries.* Edited by Rachel Manley. London: A. Deutsch, 1989.

Martínez Fernández, Luis and D. H. Figueredo, eds. *Encyclopedia of Cuba.* Westport, Conn.: Greenwood Press, 2003.

Martin, Cheryl E., and Mark Wasserman. *Latin America and Its People.* New York: Pearson Education, 2004.

Masur, Gerhard. *Simón Bolívar.* Albuquerque: University of New Mexico Press, 1948.

McDonald, Scott B. *Trinidad and Tobago: Democracy and Development in the Caribbean.* New York: Praeger, 1986.

Meeks, Brian. "The Jamaican Moment: New Paths for the Caribbean?" *NACLA Report on the Americas* (New York) 39, 6 (May/June 2006). Available online. URL: www.proquest.com. Accessed on December 5, 2006.

Melendez, Miguel. *We Took the Streets: Fighting for Latino Rights with the Young Lords.* New York: St. Martin's Press, 2003.

Mellersh, H. E., ed. *Chronology of World History.* 4 vols. Santa Barbara, Calif.: ABC CLIO, 2001.

Miller, Jake C. *The Plight of Haitian Refugees.* New York: Praeger, 1984.

Mills, Therese. *Norman Manley.* Trinidad, West Indies: Giuseppi, 1976.

Montejo, Esteban. *The Autobiography of a Runaway Slave, Esteban Montejo.* Edited by Miguel Barnet. New York: Pantheon Books, 1968.

Montes-Huidobro, Matías. *El laud del desterrado.* Houston, Tex.: Arte Público Press, 1995.

Morison, Samuel Eliot, ed. and trans. *Journals and Other Documents on the Life and Voyages of Christopher Columbus.* New York: The Heritage Press, 1963.

Morris, Arthur. *Latin America: Economic Development and Regional Differentiation.* Totowa, N.J.: Barnes and Noble Books, 1981.

Moss, Joyce, and Wilson, George. *Peoples of the World: Latin Americans.* Detroit: Gale Research Inc., 1989.

Moss, Joyce, and Valestuck, Lorraine. *World Literature and Its Times.* Vol. I. Detroit and San Francisco: Gale Group, 1999.

Ojito, Mirta A. *Finding Mañana: A Memoir of a Cuban Exodus.* New York: Penguin Press, 2005.

Oppenheimer, Andrés. *Cuentos chinos. El engaño de Washington, la mentira populista y la esperanza de América Latina.* Buenos Aires: Editorial Sudamericana, 2006.

Palmer, Colin A. *Eric Williams and the Making of the Modern Caribbean.* Chapel Hill: University of North Carolina Press, 2006.

Paquet, Sandra Pouchet. *Caribbean Autobiography: Cultural Identity and Self Representation.* Madison: University of Wisconsin Press, 2002.

Paton, William Agnew. *Down the Islands: A Voyage to the Caribbees.* New York: Charles Scribner's Sons, 1887.

Patterson, Orlando. *Slavery and Social Death: A Comparative Study.* Cambridge, Mass., and London: Harvard University Press, 1982.

Pèrina, Mickaëlla. "Martinique." In *African Caribbeans,* edited by Alan West-Durán. Westport, Conn.: Greenwood, 2003.

Pina, Digenes. "Dominican Republic: President Militarizes Anti-Crime Patrols." *Global Information Network.* New York. August 29, 2006.

Plaza, Galo. *Latin America: Today and Tomorrow.* Washington, D.C.: Acropolis Books, 1971.

Postma, Johannes. *The Atlantic Slave Trade.* Westport, Conn.: Greenwood Press, 2003.

Price-Mars, Jean. *So Spoke the Uncle.* Translated by Magdaline W. Shannon. Colorado Springs, Colo.: Three Continents Press, 1994.

Rapley, John. "The New Middle Ages." *Foreign Affairs* 85, 3 (May/June 2006): 95.

Reid, Vic. *New Day.* New York: Alfred A. Knopf, 1949. Reissued by Chatham Bookseller, Chatham, N.J., 1972.

Renda, Mary A. *Taking Haiti: Military Occupation and the Culture of U.S. Imperialism 1915–1940.* Chapel Hill and London: The University of North Carolina Press, 2001.

Ribes Tovar, Federico. *Historia cronológica de Puerto Rico; desde el nacimiento de la isla hasta el año 1973.* New York: Hill and Wang, 1997.

Rivero Muniz, José. *Tabaco, su historia en Cuba.* Habana, Cuba: Instituto de Historia, Comisión Nacional de la Academia de Ciencias de la República de Cuba, 1964–65.

Rodriguez, Junius P. *Chronology of World Slavery.* Santa Barbara, Calif.: ABC-CLIO, 1999.

Rodriguez, Junius P., ed. *The Historical Encyclopedia of World Slavery,* 2 vols. Santa Barbara, Calif.: ABC-CLIO, 1997.

Rogoziński, Jan. *A Brief History of the Caribbean: From the Arawak and the Carib to the Present.* New York: A Meridian Book, Penguin, 1992.

Ros, Martin. *Night of Fire: The Black Napoleon and the Battle for Haiti.* New York: Sarpedon, 1991, 1994.

Sana, Mariano and Douglas S. Massey. "Household Composition, Family Migration, and Community Context: Migrant Remittances in Four Countries." *Social Science Quarterly* (Austin) 86, 2 (June 2005). Available online. URL: www.proquest.umi. Accessed on November 30, 2006.

Santovenia, Emeterio S., and Shelton, Raul M. *Cuba y su historia,* Tomo I. Miami: Cuba Corporation, 1966.

Saunders, Nicholas J. *The Peoples of the Caribbean: An Encyclopedia of Archaeology and Traditional Culture.* Santa Barbara, Calif.: ABC-CLIO, 2005.

Security Problems and Policies in the Post–Cold War Caribbean. Edited by Jorge Rodriguez Beruff and Humberto Garcia Muniz. New York: St. Martin's Press, 1996.

Sekou, Lasana M. *National Symbols of St. Martin.* Philipsburg, St. Martin: House of Hesehi Publishers, 1997.

Sellén, Francisco Hatuey. *Poema dramatico en cinco actos.* Nueva York: A. da Costa Gómez, 1891.

Silén, Juan Angel. *Nosotros solos: Pedro Albizu Campos y el nacionalismo irlandes.* Río Piedras, P.R.: Editorial Libreria Norberto González, 1996.

Steele, Beverly A. *Grenada: A History of Its People.* Oxford: Macmillan Caribbean, 2003.

Strong, L. A. G. *The Story of Sugar.* London: Weidenfeld & Nicolson, 1954.

Syrett, David. "The Navy Board and Transports for Cartagena, 1740." *War in History* 9, 2 (April 2002): 127–141.

Thomas, Hugh. *Cuba or the Pursuit of Freedom.* London: Eyre and Spottiswoode, 1971.

Torres-Saillant, Silvio, and Hernandez, Ramona. *The New Americans: The Dominican Americans.* Westport, Conn., and London: Greenwood Press, 1998.

Wagenheim, Kal, and Wagenheim, Olga Jimenez de, eds. *The Puerto Ricans: Documentary History.* Princeton, N.J.: Marcus Wiener Publishers, 2002. Updated edition.

Walvin, James. *An African's Life: The Life and Times of Olaudah Equiano, 1745–1797.* London and New York: Cassell, 1998.

West-Durán, Alan. *African-Caribbeans. A Reference Guide.* Wesport, Conn.: Greenwood Press, 2003.

Wilkinson, Bert. "Health-Caribbean: Meeting Plans Region's Fight against HIV-AIDS." *Global Information Network* (New York) (April 22, 2002): 1.

Williams, Byron. *Puerto Rico: Commonwealth, State, or Nation?* New York: Parents' Magazine, 1972.

Williams, Eric. *Capitalism and Slavery.* New York: Russell and Russell, 1961.

Williams, Eric. *From Columbus to Castro: The History of the Caribbean.* New York: Vintage Books, 1970, 1984.

Williams, Patrick, and Chrisman, Laura, eds. *Colonial Discourse and Post-Colonial Theory.* New York: Columbia University Press, 1994.

Williams, Stephen. *Cuba: The Land, the History, the People, the Culture.* Philadelphia: Running Press, 1994.

Wilson, Andrew, ed. *The Chinese in the Caribbean.* Princeton, N.J.: Markus Wiener Publishers, 2004.

Winn, Peter. *Americas: The Changing Face of Latin America and the Caribbean.* 3rd ed., Berkeley, Calif.: University of California Press, 2006.

Wood, Betty. *The Origins of American Slavery: Freedom and Bondage in the English Colonies.* New York: Hill and Wang, 1997.

Wood, Peter, ed. *The Seafarers: The Spain Main.* Alexandria, Va.: Time-Life Books, 1979.

Wyden, Peter. *Bay of Pigs: The Untold Story.* New York: Simon and Schuster, 1979.

Appendix 5

SUGGESTED READING

Pre-Columbian Inhabitants

Coll y Toste, Cayetano. *Selección de leyendas puertorriqueñas*. Boston and Washington, D.C.: Heath, 1932.

Theodora Web site. *Countries of the World*. Available online. URL: www.theodora.com/wfb/abc_world_fact_book.html. Accessed on May 30, 2006.

Humboldt, Alexander von. *Personal Narrative of a Journey to the Equinoctial Regions of the New Continent*. London: Longman, Hurst, Rees, Orme, and Brown, 1800.

Martinez-Cruzado, J. C., et al. "Mitochondrial DNA analysis reveals substantial Native America ancestry in Puerto Rico." *Human Biology* (Aug. 2001). Available online. URL: http://www.findarticles.com/p/articles/mi_qa3659/is_200108/ai_n8981492. Accessed on April 24, 2006.

Silva Lee, Alfonso. *Coqui y sus amigos: los animales de Puerto Rico* (Coqui and his friends: the animals of Puerto Rico). St. Paul, Minn.: Pangaea, 2000.

Two Worlds in Collision: The Spanish Conquest (1492–1552)

Bedini, Silvio, ed. *The Christopher Columbus Encyclopedia*. New York: Simon and Schuster, 1992.

de Las Casas, Bartolomé. "The Horrors of the Conquest." In *The Borzoi Anthology of Latin American Literature,* edited by Emir Rodríguez Monegal. New York: Knopf, 1977.

Díaz del Castillo, Bernal. *The Discovery and Conquest of Mexico*. Translated by A. P. Maudslay. New York: Farrar, Straus and Giroux, 1956.

Information Please® Database, 2006 Pearson Education, Inc. Available online. URL: http://www.infoplease.com/ipa/A0875904.html. Accessed on May 16, 2006.

Johnson, Sherry. *The Social Transformation of 18th Century Cuba.* Gainesville: University Press of Florida, 2001.

O'Callaghan, Joseph F. *Reconquest and Crusade in Medieval Spain.* Philadelphia: University of Pennsylvania Press, 2003.

Ortiz, Fernando. *Cuban Counterpoint, Tobacco and Sugar.* Translated by Harriet de Onis. Durham, N.C.: Duke University Press, 1995.

Picó, Fernando. *History of Puerto Rico. A Panorama of Its People.* Princeton, N.J.: Markus Wiener Publishers, 2006.

Richardson, Bonham C. *The Caribbean in the Wider World, 1492–1992: A Regional Geography.* New York: Cambridge University Press, 1992.

Rienits, Rex, and Rienits, Thea. *The Voyages of Columbus.* New York: Crescent Books, Crown Publishers, 1970.

Rouse, Irving. *The Tainos: Rise and Decline of the People Who Greeted Columbus.* New Haven, Conn.: Yale University Press, 1992.

Stannard, David. *American Holocaust: The Conquest of the New World.* New York: Oxford University Press, 1993.

Wilford, John Noble. *The Mysterious History of Columbus: An Exploration of the Man, the Myth, the Legacy.* New York: Knopf; distributed by Random House, 1991.

Williamson, Edwin. *The Penguin History of Latin America.* New York: Penguin Books, 1992.

European Challenges to Spanish Rule (1500–1850)

Esquemelin, John. *The Buccaneers of America.* Translated from Dutch by Alexis Brown. Baltimore, Md.: Penguin Books, 1969.

UNESCO. *Fortificaciones del Caribe.* 1997.

Geggus, David Patrick. *Haitian Revolutionary Studies.* Bloomington: Indiana University Press, 2002.

Marrin, Albert. *Terror of the Spanish Main: Sir Henry Morgan and His Buccaneers.* New York: Dutton's Children Books, 1999.

Martin, Colin, and Ellis, Sian. "Gun Ships and Sea Dogs." *British Heritage* 23, 4 (June/July 2002): 34–42.

Salmoral, Manuel Lucena. *Piratas, bucaneros, filibusteros y corsarios en América.* Madrid: Editorial MAPFRE, 1992.

Tennat, Anne W. "Architect of a King's Defense." *Americas* 5, 5 (Sept./Oct. 2003): 6–14.

Williams, Eric. *From Columbus to Castro: The History of the Caribbean.* New York: Vintage Books, 1970.

Industry and Slavery (1500–1850)

Brathwaite, Edward Kamau. *The Development of Creole Society in Jamaica 1770–1820.* Oxford: Clarendon Press, 1971.

———. *Folk Cultures of the Slaves in Jamaica.* London and Port of Spain: New Beacon Books, 1981.

Burnside, Madeleine, and Robotham, Rosemarie. *Spirits of the Passage: The Transatlantic Slave Trade in the Seventeenth Century.* New York: Simon and Schuster, 1997.

Curtin, Philip D. *The Rise and Fall of the Plantation Complex: Essays in Atlantic History.* 2nd ed. New York: Cambridge University Press, 1998.

Dunn, Richard S. *Sugar and Slaves: The Rise of the Planter Class in the English West Indies, 1624–1713.* Chapel Hill: University of North Carolina Press, 1972, 2000.

Thornton, John. *Africa and Africans in the Making of the Atlantic World, 1400–1680.* 2nd ed. New York: Cambridge University Press, 1998.

Revolutions in America, France, and Haiti (c. 1700–1850)

Dash, J. Michael. *Haiti and the United States: National Stereotypes and the Literary Imagination.* 2nd ed. New York: St. Martin's Press, 1997.

Geggus, David Patric. *Haitian Revolutionary Studies.* Bloomington: Indiana University Press, 2002.

Hoffman, Leon-Francois. *Haitian Fiction Revisited.* Pueblo, Colo.: Passeggiate Press, 1999.

Ireland, Bernard. *Naval Warfare in the Age of Sail.* New York and London: W. W. Norton, 2000.

Kiernan, James Patrick. "George Washington's Barbados Connection." *Americas* (Washington) 53, 3 (May/June 2001): 5.

Schutt-Ainé, Patricia, and the staff of Libraire au Service de la Culture. *Haiti: A Basic Reference Book; General Information on Haiti.* Miami and Port-au-Prince: Libraire au Service de la Culture, 1994.

Shepard, Odell. *Jenkins' Ear; a Narrative Attributed to Horace Walpole, Esq.* New York: Macmillan, 1951.

Slave Rebellions, Antislavery Movements, Wars of Independence (c. 1700–1850)

Blassingame, John, ed. *Slave Testimony: Two Centuries of Letters, Speeches, Interviews, and Autobiographies.* Baton Rouge: Louisiana State University Press, 1977.

List of Presidents of the Dominican Republic. Available online. URL: http://www.answers.com/topic/list-of-presidents-of-the-dominican-republic. Accessed on July 5, 2006.

Moya Pons, Frank. *The Dominican Republic: A National History.* Princeton, N.J.: Markus Wiener Publishers, 1998.

Prince, Mary. *The History of Mary Prince: A West Indian Slave.* London: F. Westly and A. H. Davis, 1831.

Reid, Vic. *New Day.* New York: Knopf, 1949.

Rodriguez, Junius P. *Historical Encyclopedia of World Slavery.* 2 vols. Santa Barbara, Denver, and Oxford: ABC-CLIO, 1997.

Tikasingh, Gerad. "Toward a Formulation of the Indian View of History: The Representation of Indian Opinion in Trinidad, 1900–1921." In *East Indians in the Caribbean: Colonialism and the Struggle for Identity.* New York and London: Kraus International Publications, 1982.

Welcome to Puerto Rico. Available online. URL: www.welcome.topuertorico.org/reference/flag.shtml. Accessed on June 29, 2006.

Puerto Rico, Cuba, and the Spanish-Cuban-American War (1850–1900)

Cisneros, Evangelina. *The Story of Evangelina Cisneros Told by Herself.* New York: Continental Publishing, 1897.

Fernández Cabrelli, Alfonso. *La francmasonería en la independencia de Hispanoamérica.* Montevideo, Uruguay: Ediciones America Una, 1988.

Freidel, Frank Burt. *The Splendid Little War.* New York: Little, Brown, 1958.

Helg, Aline. *Our Rightful Share: The Afro-Cuban Struggle for Equality, 1886–1912.* Chapel Hill: University of North Carolina Press, 1995.

Lopez Nieves, Luis. *Seva: historia de la primera invasion norteamericana de la Isla de Puerto Rico, ocurrida en mayo de 1898.* San Juan, P.R.: Editorial Cordillera, 1984.

Lopez Sanchez, José. *Carlos J. Finlay: His Life and His Work.* Habana, Cuba: Editorial José Martí, 1999.

Martí, José. *Our America: Writings on Latin America and the Struggle for Cuban Independence.* Edited by Philip S. Foner. New York: Monthly Review Press, 1977.

Montaner, Carlos Alberto. *Trama.* Esplugues de Llobregat, Barcelona: Plaza & Janeés, 1987.

Musicant, Ivan. *Empire by Default: The Spanish–American War and the Dawn of the American Century.* New York: Henry Holt and Co. 1998.

Perez, Louis A., Jr. *Cuba: Between Reform and Revolution*. 3rd ed. New York: Oxford University Press, 2006.

———. *Cuba and the United States: Ties of Singular Intimacy*. Athens: The University of Georgia Press, 1990.

———. *Cuba under the Platt Amendment, 1902–1934*. Pittsburgh: University of Pittsburgh Press, 1986.

Rickover, Hyman G. *How the Battleship* Maine *Was Destroyed*. Washington, D.C.: Dept. of the Navy, Naval History Division, 1976.

Scott, Rebecca J. *Slave Emancipation in Cuba: The Transition to Free Labor, 1860–1899*. Pittsburgh: University of Pittsburgh Press, 2000.

Swanberg, W. A. *Citizen Hearst: A Biography of William Randolph Hearst*. New York: Charles Scribner's Sons, 1961.

Cuba: Dictatorship and Revolution (1900–2000)

Argote-Freyre, Frank. *Fulgencio Batista: From Revolutionary to Strongman*. New Brunswick, N.J.: Rutgers University Press, 2006.

Mesa-Lago, Carmelo, ed. *Cuba after the Cold War*. Pittsburgh: University of Pittsburgh Press, 1993.

Mesa-Lago, Carmelo. *Cuba in the 1970s: Pragmatism and Institutionalization*. Rev. ed. Albuquerque: University of New Mexico Press, 1978.

DePalma, Anthony. *The Man Who Invented Fidel: Castro, Cuba, and Herbert L. Matthews of the New York Times*. New York: Public Affairs, 2006.

Encyclopedia of Cuba: People, History, Culture. Edited by Luis Martínez-Fernández and D. H. Figueredo. Westport, Conn.: Greenwood Press, 2003.

Latell, Brian. *After Fidel: The Inside Story of Castro's Regime and Cuba's Next Leader*. New York: Palgrave Macmillan, 2005.

Lewis, R. Anthony. "Language, Culture and Power: Haiti under the Duvaliers." *Caribbean Quarterly* 55, 4 (Dec. 2004): 42–53.

Machado y Morales, Gerardo. *Ocho años de lucha*. Miami: Ediciones Historicas Cubanas, 1982.

Perez, Louis A., Jr. *Cuba: Between Reform and Revolution*. 3rd ed. New York: Oxford University Press, 2006.

Perez-Stable, Marifeli. *The Cuban Revolution: Origins, Course and Legacy*. 2nd ed. New York: Oxford University Press, 1999.

Stein, Stanley J., and Stein, Barbara H. *The Colonial Heritage of Latin America; Essays on Economic Dependence in Perspective*. New York: Oxford University Press, 1970.

Whitney, Robert. *State and Revolution in Cuba: Mass Mobilization and Political Change, 1920–1940*. Chapel Hill: University of North Carolina Press, 2001.

Fragmentation and Occupation: Haiti and the Dominican Republic (1900–2000)

Crassweller, Robert D. *Trujillo: The Life and Times of a Caribbean Dictator.* New York: Macmillan, 1966.

Derby, Lauren. "The Dictator's Seduction: Gender and State Spectacle during the Trujillo Regime." *Callaloo* 23, 3 (Summer 2000): 1,112–1,146.

Dold, Gaylor. *Dominican Republic Handbook.* Chico, Calif.: Moon Publications, 1997.

Renda, Mary A. *Taking Haiti: Military Occupation and the Culture of U.S. Imperialism, 1915–1940.* Chapel Hill and London: University of North Carolina Press, 2001.

Roorda, Eric Paul. *The Dictator Next Door: Good Neighbour Policy and the Trujillo Regime in the Dominican Republic, 1930–1945.* Durham, N.C.: Duke University Press, 1998.

Ruíz Burgos, Victor Eddy. *Los gobiernos de la República Dominicana.* Santo Domingo: Biblioteca Nacional, 1993.

Sagas, Ernesto. *Race and Politics in the Dominican Republic.* Gainesville: University Press of Florida, 2000.

Schmidt, Hans. *The United States Occupation of Haiti, 1915–1934.* New Brunswick, N.J.: Rutgers University Press, 1971.

Stein, Stanley J., and Stein, Barbara. *The Colonial Heritage of Latin America: Essays on Economic Dependence in Perspective.* New York: Oxford University Press, 1970.

Commonwealth, Federation, and Autonomy: Puerto Rico, Martinique, Guadeloupe, and the Dutch Caribbean (1900–2000)

Caban, Pedro A. *Constructing a Colonial People: Puerto Rico and the United States, 1898–1932.* Boulder, Colo.: Westview Press, 1999.

Bosque-Pérez, Ramón, and Morera, José Javier Colón, eds. *Puerto Rico Under Colonial Rule: Political Persecution and the Quest for Human Rights.* Albany: State University of New York Press, 2006.

Dietz, James L. *Economic History of Puerto Rico: Institutional Change and Capitalist Development.* Princeton, N.J.: Princeton University Press, 1986.

Duany, Jorge. *The Puerto Rican Nation on the Move: Identities on the Island and in The United States.* Chapel Hill: University of North Carolina Press, 2002.

Fernandez, Ronald. *The Disenchanted Island: Puerto Rico and the United States in the Twentieth Century.* Westport, Conn.: Praeger, 1996.

Meléndez, Edwin, and Meléndez, Edgardo. *Colonial Dilemma: Critical Perspectives on Contemporary Puerto Rico.* Boston: South End Press, 1993.

Report by the President's Task Force on Puerto Rico's Status, December 2005.

Jamaica, Trinidad, and Grenada (1900–2000)

Black, Jan Knippers, et al. *Area Handbook for Trinidad and Tobago.* Washinton, D.C.: U.S. Government Printing Office, 1976.

Finkel, Steven E. "Can Democracy Be Taught." *Journal of Democracy* 1, 4 (October 2003): 137–151.

Hurwitz, Samuel J., and Hurwitz, Edith. *Jamaica: A Historical Portrait.* New York: Praeger, 1971.

Lewis, Vaughan A. "The Small State Alone: Jamaican Foreign Policy, 1977–1980." *Journal of Interamerican Studies and World Affairs* 25, 2 (May 1983): 139–169.

Libby, Ronald T. "The United States and Jamaica: Playing the American Card." *Latin American Perspectives* 17, 1, Caribbean Crisis and Global Restructuring (Winter, 1990): 86–109.

Millette, Robert E. *The Grenada Revolution: Why It Failed.* New York: Africana Research Publications, 1985.

Oxal, Ivar. *Black Intellectuals Come to Power: The Rise of Creole Nationalism in Trinidad and Tobago.* Cambridge, Mass.: Schenkman Publishing Company, 1968.

Sekou, Lasana M. *37 Poems.* Philipsburg: St. Martin: House of Nehesi Publishers, 2005.

Stephens, Evelyne Huber, and Stephens, John D. *Democratic Socialism in Jamaica: The Political Movement and Social Transformation in Dependent Capitalism.* Princeton, N.J.: Princeton University Press, 1986.

The 21st Century: Immigration and Uncertainties

Alvarez, Julia. *How the Garcia Girls Lost Their Accents.* Chapel Hill, N.C.: Algonquin Books of Chapel Hill, 1991.

de Grave, Analisa, et al., eds. *Issues.* Dubuque, Iowa: Contemporary Learning Series/McGraw-Hill, 2007.

Durbin, William. *El Lector—The Reader.* New York: Wendy Lamb Books, 2006.

Duval, David Timothy. *Tourism in the Caribbean: Trends, Development, Prospects.* New York: Routledge, 2004.

Freeman, Gary P. "Caribbean Migration to Britain and France: From Assimilation to Selection." In *The Caribbean Exodus,* edited by Barry Levine. Westport, Conn.: Praeger, 1987.

Kanellos, Nicolás. *Hispanic Literature of the United States: A Comprehensive Reference.* Westport, Conn.: Greenwood Press, 2003.

Levine, Barry B., ed. *The Caribbean Exodus.* Westport, Conn.: Praeger, 1987.

Levine, Robert M., and Asís, Moisés. *Cuban Miami.* New Brunswick, N.J.: Rutgers University Press, 2000.

Office of the Chief Economist. "Remittances: Not Manna from Heavens." Available online. URL: http://web.worldbank.org. Accessed on December 1, 2006.

Ojito, Mirta. *Finding Mañana: A Memoir of a Cuban Exodus.* New York: Penguin Press, 2005.

Pator, Robert, ed. *Migration and Development in the Caribbean: The Unexplored Connection.* Boulder, Colo., and London: Westview Press, 1985.

Ryan, Chris, and Hall, C. Michael. *Sex Tourism: Marginal People and Liminalities.* New York: Routledge, 2001.

Sagás, Ernesto, and Sintia E. Molina, eds. *Dominican Migration: Transnational Perspectives.* Gainesville: University Press of Florida, 2004.

Santiago, Esmeralda. *When I Was Puerto Rican.* New York: Vintage Books, 1994.

Whalen, Carmen Teresa. *From Puerto Rico to Philadelphia: Puerto Rican Workers and Postwar Economies.* Philadelphia: Temple University Press, 2001.

Yglesias, Jose. *A Wake in Ybor City.* Houston, Tex.: Arte Público Press, 1998.

INDEX

Page numbers in *italic* indicate illustrations. Page numbers followed by *m* indicate maps, by *t* indicate tables, and by *c* indicate the chronology.